Positioning Theory

Positioning Theory: Moral Contexts of Intentional Action

Edited by
Rom Harré and Luk van Langenhove

Copyright © Blackwell Publishers Ltd 1999

First published 1999

Transferred to digital print 2003

2 4 6 8 10 9 7 5 3 1

Blackwell Publishers Ltd
108 Cowley Road
Oxford OX4 1JF
UK

Blackwell Publishers Inc.
350 Main Street
Malden, Massachusetts 02148
USA

British Library Cataloguing in Publication Data

A CIP catalogue record for this book is available from the British Library.

Library of Congress Cataloging-in-Publication Data

Positioning theory: moral contexts of intentional action / edited by Rom Harré and Luk van Langenhove.; written by L. Berman . . . [et al.].
    p. cm.
    Includes bibliographical references (p.) and index.
    ISBN 0-631-21138-1 (hardbound: alk. paper). − ISBN 0-631-21139-X (pbk.: alk. paper)
    1. Social psychology − Moral and ethical aspects.   2. Intentionalism − Moral and ethical aspects.   I. Harré, Rom.   II. Langenhove, Luk van.   III. Berman, L.
    HM291.P676   1998
    302 − dc21   98-16534
                                                                                      CIP

Typeset in 10 on 12 pt Bembo
by Best-set Typesetter Ltd, Hong Kong

Printed and bound in Great Britain by
Marston Lindsay Ross International Ltd,
Oxfordshire

Contents

Acknowledgements

The editors are grateful for permission to reprint the following articles, in edited form:

Davies, B. and Harré, R. (1990). 'Positioning: the Discursive Production of Selves'. *Journal for the Theory of Social Behaviour*, 20 (1), 43–63.

Harré, R. and Van Langenhove, L. (1992). 'Varieties of Positioning'. *Journal for the Theory of Social Behaviour*, 20, 393–407.

Sabat, S. R. and Harré, R. (1995). 'The Construction and Deconstruction of Self in Alzheimer's Disease'. *Ageing and Society*, 12, 443–61.

Tan, S. L. and Moghaddam, F. M. (1995). 'Reflexive Positioning and Culture'. *Journal for the Theory of Social Behaviour*, 25, 387–400.

Van Langenhove, L. and Harré, R. (1995). 'Positioning and Autobiography: Telling Your Life'. In N. Coupland and J. Nussbaum (eds), *Discourse and Life-span Development*. London: Sage.

1

The Dynamics of Social Episodes

R. Harré and L. van Langenhove

Introduction

The study of everyday language use or discourse has become one of the major tenets of a new paradigm in psychology. Not only has discourse become a firmly established topic for study in its own right, it has also become a key-concept in the new theoretical developments sometimes called social constructionism. Applications of some of these ideas in practice have revealed the necessity of paying close attention to the local moral order, the local system of rights, duties and obligations, within which both public and private intentional acts are done. For example, in certifying recollections as genuine memories, not everyone involved in a discussion of the past has the same rights to confirm or deny a claim about what happened. The study of local moral orders as ever-shifting patterns of mutual and contestable rights and obligations of speaking and acting has come to be called 'positioning theory'. The word 'position' has been used in many ways in social and psychological writings. In recent years it has come to take on a quite specific meaning for developing work in the analysis of fine-grained symbolically mediated inter-actions between people, both from their own individual standpoints and as representatives or even exemplars for groups. In this technical sense a position is a complex cluster of generic personal attributes, structured in various ways, which impinges on the possibilities of interpersonal, intergroup and even intrapersonal action through some assignment of such rights, duties and obligations to an individual as are sustained by the cluster. For example, if someone is positioned as incompetent in a certain field of endeavour they will not be accorded the right to contribute to discussions in that field. If someone is positioned as powerful that person may legitimately issue orders and demand obedience in those engaged in some strip of life, in which this position is acknowledged. Generally speaking positions are relational, in that for one to be positioned as powerful others must be positioned as powerless. Even in the case of competence, among a group of pretty hopeless butterfingers, there will be relative positionings as better or worse at whatever it is that is to be done. People can and sometimes are offered the opportunity to acquiesce in such an assignment, contest it or subvert it. The internal lines of coherence in positions may take various forms. In some cases the relations are deductive, in others classificatory, so that a generic attribution sustains a specific demand on or right to be exercised by an actor. In some cases the internal structure is that of determinable to determinate, as when positioned as incompetent someone is denied the right to use the kitchen.

The present book aims to bring together a number of theoretical explorations and applications of 'positioning theory' as an explanatory scheme to understand and study discourse and its relation to different psychic and social phenomena. This chapter introduces some basic issues from social constructionism and discourse analysis in order to frame positioning theory as one possible conceptual apparatus that allows for social constructionist theorizing based on a dynamic analysis of conversations and discourses. In each study presented in this book the internal patterning of the positions that appear salient to the analysis will be likely to be somewhat different. If in one case a duty is demanded by virtue of a positioning based on social status, there are likely to be other cases in which duties derive from biologically based positionings, such as 'the strong one', and so on. The concept of 'position' is general enough to capture diversity, but we believe precise enough to help articulate the ephemeral conditions that matter so much in social life.

Social constructionism

'Social constructionism' is a rather loose term for a variety of anti-nativist positions in general psychological theory within at least one version of which positioning theory has a natural place. Common to all varieties are two basic principles.

i.   What people do, publicly and privately, is intentional, that is, directed to something beyond itself, and normatively constrained, that is, subject to such assessments as correct/incorrect, proper/improper and so on
ii. What people are, to themselves and to others, is a product of a lifetime of interpersonal interactions superimposed over a very general ethological endowment.

As a model both for the analysis of cognition and for processes of personal development, social conversational processes are held to be the most enlightening. Social constructionism stresses that social phenomena are to be considered to be generated in and through conversation and conversation-like activities. As such, discursive processes are considered to be the 'place' where many if not most of the psychological and social phenomena of interest to cognitive and social psychologists are jointly created. Social constructionism comes in many varieties. In its strongest form, it asserts that as everything is socially constructed and thus relative to local contexts, there is no possibility of coming to an objective and universal human science. It has been argued that the physical world is as much a construction as are social institutions. In its weaker forms, social constructionism asserts that it is possible to come to correct descriptions of the world but that there will usually be more than one such description and the place of the formulator of such theories has to be taken into account. Whatever form of social constructionism one adheres to, the common feature is the epistemological challenging of the traditional way of doing psychological research (Van Langenhove, 1995). This epistemological challenging has been presented by several contemporary authors as a second cognitive revolution that radically breaks with a psychology based on an uncritical and often inaccurate imitation of the methods of the physical sciences. While physics and chemistry make use of numerical measures and characteristically theorize by proposing unobservable causal processes, descriptions and explanations in the human sciences must pay regard to other standards of precision than the numerical, and make use of other explanatory modes than the reference to theoretical entities.

The behaviourist viewpoint implied that psychological phenomena should be analysed in terms of stimuli and responses (with the mind as a 'black box' irrelevant even if standing between them), and that there was no place in psychological science for mental phenomena. However, the cognitive paradigm continued to use the experimental methods that only allowed for 'passive' people as subject to psychological testing and experimenting. Taking up different aspects of Wittgenstein's work on meaning and language, many scholars started working on a different approach to psychology in which there was room for active persons, for analysis of ordinary language outside the laboratory and for the crucial insight that the only thing inside people's heads are their brains. Skills are discursive and cognitive but the mechanisms for their implementation are physiological. There are no 'central processing mechanisms' whose substance is mental states and hidden patterns of information processing. So the second cognitive revolution leads towards a cognitive study not based upon the metaphor of computational devices, but:

It will be the study of the intentional use of symbolic systems of various kinds by active and skilled human beings in public and private contexts, for the accomplishment of various tasks and projects, jointly with others. (Sabat and Harré, 1992: 146)

This new cognitive psychology can be summarized as follows (Harré and Gillett, 1994: 27):

1   Many psychological phenomena are to be interpreted as properties or features of discourse. Some are public (intentional behaviour) and some are private (thought).
2   Individual and private uses of symbolic systems are derived from interpersonal discursive processes, perhaps in the manner described by Vygotsky (1978).
3   The production of psychological phenomena in discourse depends upon the skills of the actors, their relative moral standing in the community and the storylines that unfold.

The main implication of these three principles is that discursive phenomena are not regarded as manifestations of what goes on 'inside' the mind, but that they have to be represented as the phenomena themselves!

Social constructionism, despite its different tendencies, can be regarded as an effort to link the insights of the second cognitive revolution to concrete research topics. Positioning theory focuses on understanding how psychological phenomena are produced in discourse. Its starting point is the idea that the constant flow of everyday life in which we all take part, is fragmented through discourse into distinct episodes that constitute the basic elements of both our biographies and of the social world. The skills that people have to talk are not only based on capacities to produce words and sentences but equally on capacities to follow rules that shape the episodes of social life. Not only what we do but also what we can do is restricted by the rights, duties and obligations we acquire, assume or which are imposed upon us in the concrete social contexts of everyday life.

Skills and rules for discursive processes

Discursive processes are made possible because people have certain skills and because rules allow for the accounting for the joint-actions. When a person says 'I feel OK', this involves not only the skills necessary to talk and to make a judgement about oneself, but also to know when it is appropriate to say such a thing and to have insight into what will happen when saying it. It is only because people have some knowledge of rules, and have expectations, that meaningful communication is possible. The discursive skills upon which social constructionists claim that social psychology should focus, are deployed in the joint production of the episodes of everyday life. Episodes can be defined as 'any sequence of happenings in which human beings engage which has some principle of unity' (Harré and Secord, 1972: 10). But episodes are more than just visible behaviour, they also include the thoughts, feelings, intentions, plans and so on of all those who participate. As such, episodes are defined by their participants but at the same time they also shape what participants do and say.

In formal episodes, this shaping is of such a nature that explicit rules determine the sequence of actions. A wedding ceremony is a classical example of such a formal episode: here the rules to follow are so strict that the participants have to stick even to pre-given wordings ('Do you, X, take this woman, Y, as your lawful wedded wife?' 'I do' and so on). It would be misleading to call such a verbal ceremony a 'conversation', even though several people take it in turns to speak and what they say is integrated into a well-structured social episode. Nevertheless the assumptions people make as to the character of the episode in which they are engaged can have a profound influence on what people say and do. It is clear that while being a participant in, for instance, a 'lecturing' episode, people will say different things to each other than when they taking part in an episode that is taking place in a 'pub', even if the same people are involved. In such 'informal' episodes, not only rules determine their form and content but also the biographical backgrounds of the people and the 'history' of what already has been said in that episode participate. What exactly will be said in a 'pub' episode in thus partly determined by general rules, but equally so by the stories that people have to tell in such an episode. For instance, if one of the participants recently has attended a football match then the pub episode might be the moment to bring it up. But of course the appropriateness of doing so is dependent on what has already been told. If the conversation has been about a serial killer who operates in the neighbourhood, a sudden changing of the subject to football might be almost impossible!

Episodes as the structures of social encounters are like melodies in that they come into existence sequentially. If one wants to understand how psychological phenomena are created in the sequential development of structured sequences of act–actions, one has to understand the dynamics of social episodes. This is what positioning theory aims at. Of course, there already exists a powerful and mature sociology for the analysis of episodes. It can be found in the writings of Erving Goffman (1968) and in the work of the ethnomethodologists, inspired by Harold Garfinkel (1967). But this work has focused primarily on the interactions between individuals and the social environment in which they operate. As such a lot of attention has been paid to the general aspects of interactions between people, given the situation in which they find themselves. Goffman and Garfinkel have contributed enormously to the understanding of interactions between people with different roles. A nurse–patient interaction can be analysed in a Goffmanian way, but this analysis is not focused on the idiosyncratic aspects of that interaction. Put in other words: whenever a nurse and a patient find themselves in a nursing episode, what they do will not only be understandable in terms of the roles they occupy in that episode but also of their previous conversations (the 'history' of their interactions) and also of the specific dynamics of that one single episode. Indeed, any episode has something which cannot be understood by referring to general rules and roles. Knowledge of the past and insight into the current conversation are necessary as well. And even then, there is something that stays indeterminate. It is that something that makes it impossible to predict what will happen next in an episode. But this does not mean that one is not able to understand episodes and interactions in detail. It is our belief that if one looks to three basic features of interactions, one is indeed able to understand and explain much of what is going on and how social and psychic phenomena are 'constructed'. These three basic features are:

i.   the moral positions of the participants and the rights and duties they have to say certain things,
ii.   the conversational history and the sequence of things already being said,
iii. the actual sayings with their power to shape certain aspects of the social world.

This, however, calls for an appropriate conceptual and methodological framework that allows one to take into account the specifics of a conversation and other intentional and normatively constrained patterns of interaction, together with the more general aspects of the episodes that are constituted by those conversations and conversation-like exchanges. The positioning theory to be presented in this book can be seen as such a conceptual and methodological framework based on the position/act-action/storyline triad, and drawing upon the analogy of all of social life to one of its manifestations, conversation.

We have adopted three main ways of classifying acts of positioning. On one dimension of difference what matters is whether individual persons are positioned by individuals or collectives by collectives. On another dimension what matters is whether an individual or collective reflexively positions themselves, or whether it is by some other which positions and is positioned. The third dimension is whether the positioning act is symmetrical or asymmetrical, that is, whether each positions the other or whether in positioning one the other is also positioned in the same act.

Positioning and Selfhood

From the constructionist point of view, as described by Coulter (1981), selfhood is publicly manifested in various discursive practices such as telling autobiographical stories, taking responsibility for one's actions, expressing doubt, declaring an interest in care, decrying the lack of fairness in a situation, and so on. There are kinds of identity which we attribute to people, and that we refer to by the use of the word 'self'. There is the self of personal identity, which is experienced as the continuity of one's point of view in the world of objects in space and time. This is usually coupled with one's sense of personal agency, in that one takes oneself as acting from that very same point. Then there are the selves that are publicly presented in the episodes of interpersonal interaction in the everyday world, the coherent clusters of traits we sometimes call 'personas'. These are the selves referred in the title of Goffman's famous study (1959) *The Presentation of Self in Everyday Life*. One's personal identity persists 'behind' the publicly presented repertoire of one's personae. Both have been called 'selves'. We shall call the former 'self1', and the latter we shall refer to as our repertoire of 'personas'.

One's personas are presented discursively by ensuring that one's public performances conform to the requirements of the person-types that are recognized by one's fellows. Each community has its repertoire of recognizable and acceptable person-types. However, one's personal identity (self1) can only be presented 'formally'. It has no content because it is a structural or organizational feature of one's mentality. However much the content of our thoughts and feelings may change, we are intact as persons if these are organized into one coherent whole. We each display the singularity of our selfhood, in the personal identity sense, in the use of such discursive devices as the first person-pronoun 'I', with which we each index our sayings (and indirectly our doings) as ours. 'I' is not used to name or to refer to oneself, nor to one's body. Its use expresses one's personal identity. We can see the difference between referring to oneself and expressing one's selfhood by contrasting the function in talk of indexicals like 'I' and 'you', 'this' and 'now' with that of proper names which can be used to refer to people or to places. Indexical expressions have sometimes been called 'token reflexives'. Their meaning is completed only by the knowledge one may have of who used them, when and where. It is this feature that fits them for their role as indices, with which we mark the social force of what is said as ours, the speaker's. 'Luk and Rom will take you to lunch' could be a prediction or an indirect command. 'We will take you to lunch' is an act of personal commitment. The self expressed by 'I' is singular, while 'we' creates a double singularity of public personhood. In normal circumstances each human being is the seat of just one person, but of many personas. The same individual (self1) can manifest any one of their repertoire of personas in clusters of behaviour displayed in the appropriate social context. Taken over a period of time it becomes clear that each person has many personas, any one of which can be dominant in one's mode of self-presentation in a particular context. It is important that it should actually be the 'right' one! Since the self1 is a formal unity, a mere point in 'psychological space', it does not require the cooperation of any other person in order to exist, nor does it require intact recent or remote recall memory. Indexing a speech-act with the speaker's commitment to its content and consequences is a here and now act. However, the existence of personas does hinge on the social cooperation or consent, of others. One's display of the characteristics of a certain persona enters 'social space' only in so far as it is recognized, responded to and confirmed in the actions of others. Indeed, without the cooperation of others in the social sphere, personas cannot be constructed at all. Consequently the social recognition, or lack thereof, of a given persona will have profound effects upon the ways in which the person's behaviour is viewed and the ways in which the person is then treated by others. If what one says or does cannot be fitted coherently into a locally acceptable cluster of the types of behaviour that define a persona, that person is bound to be treated with reserve or even suspicion.

Constructionists (Shotter, 1983) have argued that personhood is created primarily in the process of engaging in certain types of spoken discourse. The subjective sense of self emerges in the mastery of *sotto voce* discourse. The main persona-displaying discursive acts are declarations and narrations. Declarations consist of those speech-acts in which the speaker gives some sort of report on how things or events appear from the speaker's point of view. Point of view refers both to the speaker's locus in time and space as well as his or her reputation for reliability and other moral qualities, his or her 'character' as Goffman called it. Narrations, on the other hand, consist of those communicative productions in which there is a storyline. People present themselves, and others, as actors in a drama. Technically these presentations create what have been called 'discursive positions' (Hollway, 1984). There are instances in which a narration can also be a declaration, for example, 'If you ask me, John had no reason to . . .' And to the extent that a declaration concerns some aspect of the speaker's lived experience, the declaration is a narration of an autobiographical nature for it involves the use of 'I', which indexes the declaration as performed by a self1, and so as belonging to the history of that person.

It is not an intact memory that constitutes one's self or one's personal identity in the sense of self1: one could dispense with psychological memory in favour of a surrogate, a prosthetic memory, without ceasing to meet the criteria for personhood. What this argument shows, is that it is the indexical properties of first person discursive practices that count for personhood rather than the specific psychological conditions for their fulfilment' (Harré, 1993). Thus, the use of first-person indexicals ('I', 'me', 'myself', 'my', 'mine') confirms, on the constructionist account, the existence of the self of personal identity, the self1, since, in a sense, to be able to index one's discourse in this way *is* to have a personal identity. Thus if the sufferer from Alzheimer's condition can be shown to employ first-person indexicals coherently in his or her discourse, on the constructionist account, that person has displayed an intact self1. It must be admitted that there is the possibility that a mere verbal habit of the use of the first person may persist, which could produce the illusion of a survival of selfhood. One supposes that the illusion would soon be dispelled by study of the discourse as a whole.

Whereas on the constructionist account there is a singularity of self1, there is a multiplicity of personas that are dependent upon the social context. Thus among the personas might be the authoritative professor who has the right to determine a student's grade, another might be the respectful son or daughter who speaks in a deferential way to a parent, another might be the parent who acts from a senior position in coming to the aid of a child in the midst of a difficult homework assignment; another might be the patient who acts from a junior position when being treated by a physician. In each instance, the quality of the persona and the cluster of behaviour is different, given the different exigencies of the social situation. Thus it is in the interaction of both parties that personas are manifested. It is in the constant interplay of mutual recognition of one's own and the other's position that the particular version of public self appropriate to the occasion is constructed. Again, from the constructionist point of view, the meanings of speech-acts and other forms of behaviour derive from the behaviour itself as it occurs within the confines of a mutually agreed upon context which can called the narrative convention, or storyline, which itself derives from the mutual construction of the personas in question. In other words, the behaviour of person A can be interpreted in a multiplicity of ways by person B. The way in which the latter finally does interpret person A's behaviour will depend upon what sort of storyline has been confirmed given the way person A has displayed a coherent public self that has been created in the situation. Thus personal being, in one of its several aspects, and positioning are mutually supporting.

In general psychology a further distinction in ways of personal being is important. It is that between what an individual believes about themselves, the self-concept; and what they are able in the circumstances to display as personas. For the most part the psychological issues that arise from disparities between presented selves and self-concept will be tackled in the context of the life situation of sufferers from Alzheimer's condition, for whom the disparity can be particularly ominous.

Introduction to the Chapters

Positioning theory should not be regarded as a 'general theory' that calls for a deterministic application to several specific subject matters. It is not like gravitational theory. Rather, it is to be treated as a starting point for reflecting upon the many different aspects of social life. The reflections in this book are organized around three major themes or levels of interaction: the interpersonal level, the institutional level and the cultural level. As such the classical micro, memo and macro levels are addressed, although it should be stressed that we do not think that society can be split up into three ontologically distinct levels (each with its own discipline: psychology, social psychology and sociology). Rather, we think of the social world as consisting of one basic realm, that of conversations and analogous patterns of interaction, in which psychological and sociological phenomena are generated, including such complex interpersonal relations and belief systems as social class.

In chapter 2, the basic conceptual apparatus of positioning theory will be presented. The core of positioning theory, summed up in the notion of the 'positioning triangle', pictures a dynamic stability between actors' positions, the social force of what they say and do, and the storylines that are instantiated in the sayings and doings of each episode. Several analytical distinctions come together to lay out the possible forms in which positioning can occur as a discursive practice. The main dimension will reflect the degree to which the initiator of an exchange is capable of imposing positions upon others or refusing those which he or she has been assigned.

Chapter 3 focuses on how the rights and duties of speakers and hearers are jointly constituted through engaging in discursive practices, while at the same time those practices act as a resource that allows the people involved to negotiate new positions and so establish new storylines implemented through newly recognized social acts. An immanentist treatment of social order is advocated that leads to the idea of positioning as a dynamic process. The contemporary multiplicity of positions and storylines is examined by the analysis of some case studies.

In chapter 4 the conditions that enable a person to engage in active and positive positioning are explored. These conditions turn out to be characteristic of the Vygotskian symbiotic relationships through which all acquisition of skill occurs. Drawing on the results of two case studies it does seem as if positioning skills can be acquired, though their successful use is vulnerable to stressful situations.

In chapter 5 the autobiographical aspects of self-construction in terms of positioning are further explored. One has to sustain a sense of personal identity, self-continuity, through life at the same time as one registers and reports a multiplicity of events and positions through which one lives one's one and only life. In this chapter the subtleties of first-person grammar are used to display the nature of autobiography in both its oral and literal forms.

In the preceding chapters positioning has been studied in the contexts of public discourse. But there is also intrapersonal and private discourse. In chapter 6 analysis of soliloquy shows that cultural considerations are inescapable in analysing the way that reflexive positioning practices enter into the formation of concepts people have of themselves, in the sense of the beliefs one has about oneself. In telling stories of one's life to oneself positioning is as evident as it is in public story-telling. In this way it becomes clear how cultural assumptions are incorporated in one's sense of oneself.

When thinking about the relationships between conversations and person, self and persona, an interesting issue is the question on how the self can be understood for those persons who have for one reason or another not a full access to conversations (babies, deaf people, people with brain injuries, and so on). In chapter 7 we examine the positioning and related discursive practices by which sufferers from Alzheimer's condition are deprived of selfhood and demonstrate in some real cases how a change of discursive practices re-establishes and restores a sense of personal worth. At issue are both a person's sense of identity as a unique being, and the self – the kind of person – they display in the public realm. These studies show how a positioning in social 'space' that allows the sufferer to recover their personal dignity, so that the persona displays that person's self-concept in a worthy and reputable manner.

Not only persons but also social worlds (or 'social fields', to use Bourdieu's terminology) can be regarded as being produced discursively. As such, the concepts of positioning and rhetorical reconstruction can be used to understand the creation of different social worlds as well as of the selves that inhabit them. By a social world we mean a network of interactions framed within some relatively stable repertoire of rules and meanings. Positioning theory can thus also be used to understand many institutionalized discursive processes such as the law, science, politics, art criticism and so on. In each case, the practices of such an institutionalized field can be understood in terms of the positioning activities of the participants and of how the discursive practices typical of that field generate specific redescriptions of certain aspects of the world, thus constituting them. In this book, one such an institutionalized discursive process is further studied in terms of positioning theory: science and technology. In chapter 8 the dynamics of scientific publishing are analysed in terms of positioning theory. This chapter also presents an outline of how the differences between the social and the natural sciences can be better understood from the perspective of the texts (publications) that are produced and the related positionings in and through such texts. Chapter 9 deals with the analysis of technological assessments in terms of positionings. As such it offers a theoretical framework to understand and further develop the practice of technology assessment as a dynamic, interpersonal conversation.

A powerful aspect of the use of positioning theory as an analytical tool is that not only persons and their identities both individual and social, but also societal issues on a cultural level can be tackled with the same conceptual apparatus. Chapter 10 focuses on cultural stereotypes and offers an analytical refinement of that concept by framing it within positioning theory.

In cultures such as that of Java, there is a deeply entrenched avoidance of the taking of personal stances on any matter. Communication is personally indirect and the public media are the main vehicles of the kind of discursive positioning that constitutes a social order. In Chapter 11 the role of Javanese newspapers in the enforced positioning of people as defined by family is investigated. The existing regime is positioned as 'benevolent father' and the citizens as 'children'. Thus the familiar and the traditional storylines of Indonesian culture are continuously recreated. A subcultural group, able, at least for awhile, to publish its own newsletter, illustrates how even on the social scale group refusal of positioning is possible.

Using a substantial corpus of material culled from television, newspapers and so on, the adoption and display of positions within the available frameworks of 'American' social identities can be unravelled. On the one hand positioning defines and protects dignity, while on the other hand there are positionings that hinge on the defence of honour. In chapter 12 the dynamics of these positionings are followed in a close study of a public discourse in which protagonists display their allegiances discursively. Examples of displays of personhood are used to show how such manifestations are transitory but sometimes durable interactional accomplishments that creatively invoke cultural meaning systems. This contention is demonstrated with several instances of interactive talk. The demonstration yields some of the interactional workings of one cultural model of personhood that is prominent in contemporary America. It shows how that model is creatively played against others, drawing attention to its occasional tendency to supplant them.

Continuing on the larger scale in chapter 13, positioning theory is applied to research of intergroup relations in order to show how this can help in focusing attention on previously neglected aspects of the psychology of rivalry and conflict. By reinterpreting Sherif's famous experiment in positioning theory terms, it becomes possible to understand how the discursive frameworks offered by the experimenters constrained the positions open to the groups, through the positions that were displayed in all sorts of symbolic and ritual ways.

Together, all the chapters of this book should present the reader with an overview of how positioning theory can be used in many different contexts. Of course, this does not exhaust the possibilities of attention to the local moral order not only in social psychology but in some branches of cognitive psychology as well. In the epilogue, a few possible future directions are presented in which positioning theory can be further developed as a powerful framework for social discourse analysis. If the species-wide and history-long ongoing conversation between people can be regarded as a labyrinthine network, positioning theory offers a possibility to shift from the perspective of *maze traders*, those who are within the labyrinth, to a perspective of *maze viewers*, those who can see the labyrinth from above.

2

Introducing Positioning Theory

L. van Langenhove and R. Harré

Introduction

The concept of positioning can be seen as a dynamic alternative to the more static concept of role. Talking of positions instead of roles fits within the framework of an emerging body of new ideas about the ontology of social phenomena. Hence before embarking upon a detailed presentation of the concept of positioning, a few words have to be said about this new ontological paradigm within the social sciences.

Although there have always been many epistemological differences amongst social scientists, there does seem to be a relative consensus about what the relevant social entities are that make up the subject matters of the social sciences, the 'substances' of the social world, so to speak. In the standard ontology, three different levels of societal phenomena are usually considered: people, institutions and societies. People tend to be treated as complex, causally interacting 'things'; institutions as groupings of people (the personnel or staff); and societies as higher order aggregates of people in groups. As thing-like substances each of them can be located in the Newtonian–Euclidian space/time grid of the natural world, just like natural entities and phenomena. This seems so obvious that it hardly receives any attention. However, by locating social phenomena within the places and times of the natural world, the door is opened for the unnoticed transposing of properties of material things and their relations to the social realm. As a result, the social realm is all too often pictured as one in which causes are deterministic in a Humean sense and in which space and time are independent. The Humean aspects of the social sciences have in recent years been much criticized (e.g., Harré and Secord, 1972 and Manicas, 1987) and several attempts to formulate alternative ways of theorizing and researching have been undertaken (e.g., ethno-methodology, ethogenics, structuration theory and so on . . .) In most cases, however, the Newtonian and Euclidian space/time grid has been left unquestioned as the framework in which social phenomena have to be considered. But this is not as obvious as it seems to be at first glance. Of course, social phenomena are always located in a time/space grid but this does not necessarily have to imply that this is also the most adequate referential grid in which to study them, particularly when questions about the individuation and identity of social entities and phenomena are raised. The complex rules linking material thing, property and process to places and moments in Newtonian space/time may not be transferable to the social world. Besides, even in the natural sciences that referential grid is no longer considered to be the only possible one: both on a cosmological and quantum physical scale the time/space grid has proved to be inadequate and other grids have been constructed in which the independence of physical space from time vanishes.

It has first been argued that the time/space grid is equally inadequate for locating and understanding social phenomena. As an alternative the persons/conversations referential grid is proposed to go along with a reassessment of assumptions about the 'substance' of social and psychological realities. If social acts, including speech-acts, are taken as the 'matter' of social reality, a new grid can be constructed in which people are seen as locations for social acts. As a 'space', a set of possible and actual locations, the array of persons is not necessarily Euclidian. The grid of temporal locations, the time-aspect of human life, also changes. The distinction between past, present and future does not go over neatly into psychological time, partly because the social and psychological past is not fixed. The social future can influence the social past. The occurrences of acts are the moments of social time.

Within such a persons/acts referential grid, the social realm can be pictured as composed of three basic processes: conversations and other close-order symbolic exchanges, institutional practices and the uses of societal rhetorics; all forms of discursive practice. Symbolic exchanges in general, 'conversations', are the most basic substance of the social realm. It is within conversations that the social world is created, just as causality-linked things according to their properties constitute the natural world. Within conversations, social acts and societal icons are generated and reproduced. This is achieved by two discursive processes, one of which is 'positioning' and the other 'rhetorical redescription'. The latter can be understood as the discursive construction of stories about institutions and macrosocial events that make them intelligible as societal icons (Harré, 1975). The former is the subject of this book. It will become clear that the elements of the standard ontology (people, institutions and societies) can be understood within the new ontology in terms of both positioning and rhetorical redescription.

The idea of psychology as the study of discursive practices is the central intuition in the methodological background to the argument of this chapter.

Many, if not most, mental phenomena are produced discursively. By this we do not mean that discursive activities cause mental phenomena to come into existence. Many mental phenomena, like attitudes or emotions, are immanent in the relevant discursive activities themselves. Something of this idea can be found in the writings of Bakhtin (1986). It is explicit in the work of E. Benveniste: 'It is in and through language that man constitutes himself as a subject, because language alone establishes the concept of 'ego' in reality' (Benveniste, quoted in Silverman, 1983).

The Position/Act-action/Storyline Triad

The concepts of 'position' and 'positioning' that we want to introduce have several sources. Among their origins is the field of marketing where positioning refers to communication strategies that allow one to 'place' a certain product amongst its competitors. This usage is close to the military meaning of a 'position': in that sense a position is always taken against the position of the enemy. Within the social sciences, the concepts of 'position' and 'positioning' have been first introduced by Hollway (1984) in her analysis of the construction of subjectivity in the area of heterosexual relations. Focusing on gender differentiation in discourses, Hollway spoke of 'positioning oneself' and 'taking up positions': 'Discourses make available positions for subjects to take up. These positions are in relation to other people. Like the subject and object of a sentence . . . women and men are placed in relation to each other through the meanings which a particular discourse makes available' (Hollway, 1984: 236). Our usage of these concepts is in line with how Hollway used them.

Within the persons/conversations grid, positioning can be understood as the discursive construction of personal stories that make a person's actions intelligible and relatively determinate as social acts and within which the members of the conversation have specific locations. Just what a conversational location or 'position' is, will be explained below. While some social actions are instantly recognized and accepted as determinate acts, other actions are either not immediately intelligible or their status as acts is questionable (what did the person mean by that?), and may even be radically indeterminate (Tannen, 1990). It is important to stress that in our view everything in the human world is, in some measure, indeterminate. What this principle means, has been neatly illustrated by the following example in the field of attitudes: The attitudes one expresses are usually quite vaguely specified: 'I'm not very keen on Chinese food.' But they can be made more or less determinate as the situation and the other people involved in an episode require: 'I'll have Peking duck but not white mushrooms, thanks.' (Harré and Gillett, 1994: 35) The procedure for voting in an election is a practice by which those who take part are forced to display a determinate political attitude, since there are only a finite range of choices displayed in the ballot paper. Positioning is thus to be understood as a procedure of making determinate a psychological phenomenon for the purposes at hand. But positions can and do change. Fluid positionings, not fixed roles, are used by people to cope with the situation they usually find themselves in.

A position in a conversation, then, is a metaphorical concept through reference to which a person's 'moral' and personal attributes as a speaker are compendiously collected. One can position oneself or be positioned as e.g., powerful or powerless, confident or apologetic, dominant or submissive, definitive or tentative, authorized or unauthorized, and so on. A 'position' can be specified by reference to how a speaker's contributions are hearable with respect to these and other polarities of character, and sometimes even of role. Positioned as dependent, one's cry of pain is hearable as a plea for help. But positioned as dominant, a similar cry can be heard as a protest or even as a reprimand. It can easily be seen that the social force of an action and the position of the actor and interactors mutually determine one another. Conversations have storylines and the positions people take in a conversation will be linked to these storylines. Someone can be seen as acting like a teacher in the way his/her talk takes on a familiar form: the storyline of instruction, of the goings-on in the classroom. Living out in one's speech and actions one of the pedagogical storylines involves adopting such and such a position, for example having certain obligations to the students, and at the same time it makes one's sayings and doings relatively determinate as social acts of instruction, correction, reprimand, congratulation and so on.

Throughout the book we shall make use of Austin's (1961) distinction between the illocutionary force of an utterance, that which achieved *in* saying something, say congratulating, and its perlocutionary force. The latter is what is achieved *by* saying something, for instance in this case pleasing the recipient of the award.

The act of positioning thus refers to the assignment of fluid 'parts' or 'roles' to speakers in the discursive construction of personal stories that make a person's actions intelligible and relatively determinate as social acts. For example, in a conversation between a teacher and a pupil, rights to make certain kinds of remarks will be differentially distributed between the conversants. This is what is meant by identifying 'teacher' (P1) and 'pupil' (P2) as *positions*. The same utterance will have different social meaning when uttered by the person in position P1 from that which it has when uttered by the person in position P2. The utterances that go to make up a conversation unfold along a storyline, say in the form of a tutorial. Thus we have a mutually determining triad, as in figure 2.1.

Figure 2.1   Mutually determining triad

Positions may emerge 'naturally' out of the conversational and social context. But sometimes an initial seizure of the dominant role in a conversation will force the other speakers into speaking positions they would not have occupied voluntarily, so to say. Initial positionings can be challenged and the speakers sometimes thereby repositioned. One can position oneself as a commentator upon the positions, social acts and storylines generated in one conversation by creating a higher order conversation in which the conversation commented upon is merely a topic. Since actors may conceive their positions differently it is not unusual for the very same words and actions to be bearers of more than one conversation. This point raises questions in the philosophy of language, namely what counts as 'the same word', but we shall slink by this problem, relying on what we unreflectingly understand by it.

The structure of conversations is thus tri-polar: it consists of positions, storylines and relatively determinate speech-acts. By means of this triad conversations can be analysed to uncover their episodic structures. An episode transcribed by Deborah Tannen (1990: 82) can, by way of example, be analysed in those terms. (See figure 2.2.)

A position driven analysis runs as follows:

From (9) to (17) there is one storyline being followed, while from (18) to (28) there is another. The shift in positions takes place at (18) in the remark ascribed to Peter. The first episode displays Deborah and Peter positioned as the complementary pair 'teacher' and 'learner'. The storyline is 'instruction' and the speech-actions of the positioned interlocutors accomplish the relevant acts. But at (18) Peter repositions himself as 'martyr' and this move is confirmed by Deborah who herself takes up the complementary position of 'friend'. A new storyline unfolds in which Peter tells a strip of his life with the narrative conventions of 'hard times'. Again the speech-acts shift to create the story. There is a sequence of statements, overtly describing a way of life, which have the performative force of complaints. But these complaints are also displays of personhood, as one who continues despite difficulties, a supervenient storyline, 'hero triumphing over the odds', in which the 'hard times' storyline becomes a sustaining element. Deborah's remarks are a continuous stream of confirmations of the double line – how hard your life is and how heroically you overcome it.

(9)   DEBORAH: 'Yeah?'
(10) PETER: Before that . . . I read The French Lieutenant's Woman?
                 Have you   ⌐ read that?   ⌐
(11) DEBORAH: ∟ Oh yeah   ⌐ No. Who wrote that?
(12) PETER: John Fowles.
(13) DEBORAH: Yeah I've heard that he's good.
(14) PETER: He's a great writer. I' think he's one of the best
                 writers   ⌐
                 DEBORAH   ∟ hm
(15) DEBORAH: /?/
(16) PETER: 'He's really, good.
(17) DEBORAH: /?/
(18) PETER: But I get very busy . . ⌐ Y'know?
                                        ∟ Yeah. I- . . hardly ever read.
(19) DEBORAH: . . . . . .
(20) PETER: What I've been doing is cutting down on my sleep.
(21) DEBORAH: Oy! ⌐ (sighs)
(22) PETER: ∟ And I've been (Steve laughs) . . . . .
                     and I   ⌐ s
(23) DEBORAH: ∟ I do that too
                 but it's painful⌐
(24) PETER: ∟ Yeah. Five, six hours a night,
                 and ⌐
(25) DEBORAH: ∟ Oh God, how can you do it. You survive?
                     . . . . .
(26) PETER: Yeah late afternoon meetings are hard . . . But outside
                                            DEBORAH: ≪mmm≫
                 of that I can keep going   ⌐ pretty well
(27) DEBORAH: ∟ Not sleeping enough
                 is terrible . . I'd much rather not eat than not sleep.
                                                                    p
(Sally laughs)
(28) PETER: I probably should not eat so much, it would . . . it
                 would uh . . . save a lot of time.

Figure 2.2 The episodic structure of conversation

This is a mere sketch. Much more would be required to complete an analysis. The choice of vocabulary, pronouns and so on are crucial elements in the way the effect is achieved. We need only enough detail here to point out two significant features of the example.

Neither storylines nor positions are freely constructed. The conversation has a familiar air. It reflects narrative forms already existing in the culture, which are part of the repertoire of competent members, who, like Peter and Deborah, can jointly construct a sequence of position/ act-action/storyline triads. What psychological phenomena are these two jointly creating? At least Peter's personality – or rather, one should say, the one on show in this conversation. They are also creating a relationship, maybe a friendship, for the accomplishment of which this kind of joint work is a necessary ritual part. And so on. (Harré, 1993: 120–1).

Modes of Positioning

Several analytical distinctions can be introduced regarding positioning which together will define some of the possible forms in which positioning can occur as a discursive practice.

First and second order positioning

The most basic distinction is that between first and second order positioning. First order positioning refers to the way persons locate themselves and others within an essentially moral space by using several categories and storylines. For instance, if Jones says to Smith: 'Please, iron my shirts', then both Smith and Jones are positioned by that utterance. Jones as somebody who has the moral right (or as someone who thinks he has the moral right) to command Smith, and Smith as someone who can be commanded by Jones. When such a positioning occurs, two things can happen. Smith can indeed do Jones's ironing (in that case Smith is perhaps Jones's servant) and the storyline will evolve without any questioning of the positioning. Smith can continue the conversation by saying: 'Yes of course, which one do you need immediately?' But Smith can also object to what Jones said and answer something like 'Why should I do YOUR ironing? I'm not your maid.' We can imagine that in this case Smith is for instance Jones's wife. At this moment a second order positioning occurs in which the first order positioning is questioned and has to be negotiated. Jones will have to make a case why he – who always pays lip-service to feminism – wants his wife to do his ironing. The storyline then will shift from its original object to the story itself. In other words, second order positioning occurs when the first order positioning is not taken for granted by one of the persons involved in the discussion. Note that it is an essential feature of rituals that second order positioning is impossible. If one tries to impose a second order positioning in a ritual, then the person trying to do so will be said to 'break' the ritual.

Performative and accountive positioning

A somewhat similar though not identical distinction is between what we shall call performative and accountive positioning. In first order positioning people position themselves and others within an ongoing and lived storyline. The acts thus made determinate have immediate perlocutionary effect. The ironing might get done, or Smith might be offended and so on. As this is unlike second order or reflexive positioning when such acts are subject to challenge or revision, it can therefore also be called performative positioning. First order positionings can be questioned in two ways: either within the conversation (as in the case discussed above) or within another conversation about the first conversation. Both cases can be seen as forms of accountive positioning as they both involve talk about talk. Second order positioning thus amounts to accountive positioning within an ongoing discussion. If accountive positioning occurs outside the initial discussion, then this can be called third order positioning. Such third order positioning can, but does not necessarily, involve other persons than the ones performing in the original discussion. For instance, Jones can talk to Adams about the conversation he had with his wife Smith concerning the ironing. A story is then created in which Smith is positioned as a radical feminist because she would not even do Jones's ironing. Of course, in telling that story and replying to it, both Jones and Adams are also again involved in first order positioning of themselves. And what is more, the story about the ironing conversation will also be a rhetorical redescription of the event. Jones will not reiterate to Adams all that was said by him and his wife.

Moral and personal positioning

People can be positioned with regard to the moral orders in which they perform social actions. It is often sufficient to refer to the roles people occupy within a given moral order or to certain institutional aspects of social life to make actions intelligible and to understand the positions that people take. If Smith asks Jones to make his bed, then this first order positioning can be perfectly understood if we know that Smith is a patient and Jones a nurse. But if we consider a second order positioning in which Smith asks Jones why she has not made his bed yet, as he asked her to, then the storyline between Smith and Jones is likely to shift from moral to personal positioning. In order to answer Smith's question, Jones can no longer reply by referring to her role as a nurse. She will have to bring in a story that accounts for the 'deviance' of what was expected from her in terms of roles. Such a story is likely to contain references to individual particularities, for example: 'I am sorry I forgot to make your bed, but I am a bit confused today as I just received this letter in which . . .' Thus, people can not only be positioned morally, they can also be positioned in terms of their individual attributes and particularities. Such personal positioning can range from rather general, using very broad categories (e.g., 'Jones is a nice nurse'), to very detailed in which several elements of the person's characteristics including their life-history are brought in (e.g.: 'I once had an incredible nurse who was actually the daughter of . . .'). When people are positioned or position themselves, this will always include both a moral and a personal positioning. The more a person's actions cannot be made intelligible by references to roles, the more prominent personal positioning will be.

Self and other positioning

Positioning is a discursive practice. As already indicated above, within a conversation each of the participants always positions the other while simultaneously positioning him or herself. Whenever somebody positions him/ herself, this discursive act always implies a positioning of the one to whom it is addressed. And similarly, when somebody positions somebody else, that always implies a positioning of the person him/herself. In any discursive practice, positioning constitutes the initiator and the others in certain ways, and at the same time it is a resource through which all persons involved can negotiate new positions.

Tacit and intentional positioning

Most first order positioning will be of a tacit kind: the people involved will not position themselves or others in an intentional or even conscious way. But when a person is acting in a 'machiavellian' way, or on occasions where (s)he is lying or teasing, the first order positioning can be intentional. For example, Smith can say to Jones 'Iron my shirt', not because he really needs a clean shirt but in order to demonstrate or test his dominance of Jones. Second and third order positioning must always be intentional. But while an intentional second order positioning is going on, a tacit first order positioning will have occurred as well.

The above analytical distinctions allow us to distinguish between three typical kinds of positioning talk. First, there are the discursive practices in which people position themselves, position others and are positioned by them. This kind of talk comprises first order acts of positioning, mostly of a tacit nature. Such performative positioning talk takes place within an evolving storyline. The perlocutionary effects of such talk include constraints on and openings for kinds of illocutionary acts available to speakers as so-and-so positioned. This follows directly since a position is just a set of 'locations' on a variety of polar pairs of moral attributes. If I have made you unhappy by what I said (perlocutionary force) I may remedy this by apologizing (illocutionary force).

Secondly, there are the discursive practices in which acts of positioning of the first kind become a topic or target. Such positioning-talk occurs within, but is about, the ongoing storyline. Thus for someone to refuse a positioning laid on him by someone else's discursive practices is to act relative to that original act of positioning. The perlocutionary effect of such accountive practices is to delete, block or accept the perlocutionary effect of discursive practices of the first type. We could call the discursive practices by which these second order positioning acts are accomplished second order practices.

Thirdly, there are discursive practices in which the positioning-talk has as a topic the first or second order positioning that occurred in another discursive practice than the current one. This paper is itself the product of a discursive practice, namely that of writing about discursive positioning practices of the first and second order. It might have all sorts of perlocutionary effects, including drawing the attention of speakers to the nature of what they have said, the effect of their habitual discursive practices, etc. Such third order accountive talk is not confined to the writing practices of sociolinguists. It also occurs in everyday life, as when someone spells out what their interlocutor has said. An accusation that a certain remark was patronizing would be a case in point.

Situations for Intentional Positioning

Positioning always takes place within the context of a specific moral order of speaking. What Jones can say to Smith and about Smith is relative to Jones's rights, duties and obligations within the moral order in which the discursive process occurs. In other words, the rights for self-positioning and other-positioning are unequally distributed and not all situations allow for or call for an intentional positioning of the participants. The subtle way in which tacit positioning relates to moralities is further discussed in chapter 3. In the remaining part of this chapter, we will focus on intentional positioning. Across all possible moral order contexts, four distinct forms of intentional positioning can be identified relative to the discursive situations in which they occur: (i) situations of deliberate self-positioning; (ii) situations of forced self-positioning; (iii) situations of deliberate positioning of others; and (iv) situations of forced positioning of others. These four types of positioning can be understood as products of the performative/accountive and self/other dimensions already introduced. Each of these types of intentional positioning will be

Table 2.1 *Types of intentional positioning*

	Performative positioning	*Accountive positioning*
Self-positioning	deliberate self-positioning	forced other positioning
Other-positioning	deliberate positioning of others	forced positioning of others

discussed below. Of course it should be noted that these distinctions are merely analytic and that whenever positioning occurs, several forms of positioning are likely to be occurring simultaneously. In the discussion below, we will each time focus on one pregnant aspect of positioning talk. (See table 2.1 for a schema.)

Deliberate self-positioning

Deliberate self-positioning occurs in every conversation where one wants to express his/her personal identity. This can be done in at least three different ways: by stressing one's agency (that is, presenting one's course of action as one from among various possibilities), by referring to one's unique point of view, or by referring to events in one's biography. Expressing personal identity through a display of self-consciousness and of agency (for example, by using pronouns) is found in cultural settings. Expressing personal identity by telling autobiographical stories is discussed in chapter 4.

How is positioning achieved in displays of agency, self-consciousness and autobiography? In this paper we are focusing on the adoption of certain discursive practices as the means through which the display of identity is accomplished. Human beings must display both a personal identity (appear as singularities) and a social identity (appear as instances of types) in order to appear fully as persons. Appearance as a singularity is achieved grammatically through the use of the first person singular. The grammatical rules for the use of such constructions show that, for example, in English usage the pronoun 'I' is an indexical locating various aspects of the speech-act it labels with respect to a specific and marked location in the space-temporal manifold of embodied persons and in a variable location in a multitude of manifolds of morally responsible persons, unique in each act. Having presented oneself as a unique person through one's choice of grammatical devices appropriate to that act, one is then in a position to offer personal explanations of personal behaviour. There seem to be at least three distinct ways of explaining personal behaviour: by referring to one's powers and one's rights to exercise them, by referring to one's biography (what one did, saw, etc. and what happened to one) and by referring to personal experiences that one has had as legitimating certain claims, for example 'expertise'.

When a person is engaged in a deliberate self-positioning process this often will imply that they try to achieve specific goals with their act of self-positioning. This requires one to assume that they have a goal in mind. Paraphrasing Goffman's conception of 'strategic interaction', this could be called 'strategic positioning'. The tri-polar structure of discourse considered with respect to its effectiveness in positioning should be kept in mind. Positions, storyline and relatively determinate speech-acts mutually define one another. We are now introducing an element of deliberate intention into this structure and theoretically this can be done at any of the three poles: one could intend to adopt a certain position (and to locate someone else relative to it); one could intend to take up a certain lived narrative form or one could be intending only a certain act in what one says or does. Given this indeterminate structure we must take account of the possibility of indirect intentional acts of positioning if the actor's intention is directed to either the narrative or to the speech-act pole. The stories people tell about themselves will differ according to how they want to 'present' themselves. Jones and Pittman (1982) have distinguished five categories of self-presentation which we will locate as project-descriptions at the narrative (storyline) pole: ingratiation, intimidation, self-promotion, exemplification and supplication. It would be very interesting to study how stories differ according to the type of strategic self-positioning involved. Consider the following exchange:

SMITH: Why don't I see you at guest nights these days?
JONES: What a stupid question. It's because I am not there.

Smith opened with an act of overt positioning of both himself and Jones, which can be neatly mapped onto the three poles of position, speech-act and storyline. Strategically Smith intended to place Jones as already guilty of a failure in collegiate duty. Jones, appreciating Smith's strategy, refused the positioning, the act-force and the storyline, and repositioned himself as the sophisticated critic of Smith's naivety. His statement confirms Smith's question as merely empirical with a consequential reformulation of the storyline. We can say, without much fear of error, that both conversants were fully aware of the strategic character of their exchange and were intentionally positioning and repositioning each other. In this exchange the tone is amiable since the positioning was a kind of adult play.

A special case of intentional self-positioning is when people position themselves in a story told to themselves. Such positioning can again take many forms (from asking oneself the question 'Am I happy with my life?' to writing an autobiography). Our generally Vygotskian approach to the relations between conversation structures and patterns of thought inclines us to propose as an initial hypothesis that private acts of self-positioning conform to the tripolar structure of public acts of self and other positioning. However, whatever the details of the storyline and the determinant act-force of self-addressed discourse, one should expect a separation of pronouns or corresponding grammatical devices into two first persons that index the content of the speech-acts with the same singularity of personhood and some devices to express one's personhood as a object of contemplation and judgement. This is a special case of the narrative voice (the pseudo or anaphoric first person; cf. Urban, 1989). I say he said 'I will . . .' becomes I^1 says I^2 said 'I^1 say . . .', a narrative voice with which to support my own actions to myself or anyone else. What we call 'I^2' can be called the mediating pronoun. We think it worthwhile investigating empirically the extent to which people (and perhaps different cultures) differ on the person and number of mediating pronouns, and how the choice is related to issues of acceptance of person responsibility in the storyline coordinate with the speech-acts and self-positioning of the soliloquy. In Carlos Fuentes' novel *El Muerte de Artemio Cruz* the narrator's story shifts among various mediating pronouns, and so expresses differences in the way he sees himself as having responsibility for this or that act reported in the narrative, sometimes taking it and sometimes repudiating it.

Forced self-positioning

Forced self-positioning differs only from deliberate self-positioning in that the initiative now lies with somebody else rather than the person involved. The 'forced' aspect can be very mild, as for example the demand 'How have you been lately?', which merely asks one to make a serious or even only formal self-report. But the demand for positioning can also come from a person who represents an institution and then it may take more pressing forms. Institutions are interested in positioning persons in two cases: when the institution has the 'official' power to make moral judgements about people external to the institution, and when decisions about people inside the institution have to be made.

When an institution has the power to make moral judgements about persons and about their behaviour, it will ask people to account for what they are doing (or not doing). In being asked to account for their behaviour, people are required to position themselves as agents. This occurs in legal and quasi-legal practices. Offering an excuse by way of explanation is not just a way of resisting an accusation of guilt, but is also an act of self-positioning through which one adopts the position of one who is helpless and has a right to special treatment. Such a move fits nicely with the idea that positions be defined with respect to bipolar dimensions such as 'helpless–responsible', 'passive–active', etc.

The second case of institutional positioning occurs when an institution wants to classify persons who are expected to function within that institution, performing a certain range or tasks in coordination with the task load of others. A typical example of this can be found in selection practices and the consequent acts of appointments to posts, in the course of which applicants and appointees are acquainted with job descriptions and rosters of duties. In our view such descriptions not only prescribe what is to be done but also involve tacit and sometimes explicit acts of forced positioning. When an institution asks a person to position him or herself, this will always result in a positioning of the person asked to position him/herself. In other words, institutions ask persons to position themselves in order to have information upon which to base their own positionings of the envisaged person as well.

Deliberate positioning of others

When people deliberately position someone else, this can be done in either the presence or absence of the person being positioned. When the person is absent then this positioning can be understood as gossiping. Sabini and Silver (1982) have convincingly argued that gossiping can be understood as a medium of self-disclosure. In taking a stance about another's behaviour, people also 'dramatize' themselves: it points to behaviour which could be but is not the behaviour of the person who is gossiping. The discursive act of gossiping also positions the persons involved in the gossiping. Telling a gossip story to somebody can be a sign of 'trusting' that person ('don't tell this to anyone; but . . .'). Deliberate positioning when the person is present is creating a place in the speaker's storyline which may or may not be taken up by the person positioned (cf. chapter 3). Such positioning can take the form of a moral reproach.

Forced positioning of others

Forced positioning of others can, just as deliberate positioning of others, occur either in the absence or presence of the person being intentionally positioned. Consider three persons: Smith, his wife Jones, and their son. When the mother is blaming her son for coming home late, she can turn to her husband for support: for example, 'You tell him what kind of behaviour this is . . .' Such an instance of forced positioning of others (here Smith is forced by his wife to position his son) are particularly interesting because of the complex positioning games that can emerge. When Smith is disinclined to take up his wife's storyline and shows that he is not prepared to blame his son, then he has positioned himself towards his wife, and the storyline can then easily shift from blaming the child to blaming each other. Quite another positioning situation would have occurred had the son been absent. It can easily be understood that at that time Smith may talk very differently about his son for the sake of marital peace and position himself very differently towards his son; unless of course the mother later tells her son 'Your father and I discussed this, and we think that . . .'

The most dramatic form of forced other-positioning by an institution is no doubt the criminal trial. Trials not only allow (or force) a defendant to position him/herself, they also allow other persons to position the defendant as well. In appearing before a court a defendant is being positioned by several persons each representing specific powers (lawyers, prosecutor, witnesses for the defence and for the prosecution, psychiatrists, social workers and so on). Each of them will tell different stories about the defendant. Some of the parties involved in a trial will try to stress all possible excuses and justifications while others will try to show that the criminal acts are related to permanent characteristics of the defendant. On the basis of all that information the judge or the jury will then render a verdict that can be understood as part of yet another intentional positioning. Note that if we try to make a judge's or juror's verdict intelligible, this again implies positioning: not only of the defendant but of the judge or jurors as well. Explaining why a particular judge or jury renders a verdict requires information about the personality of the judge or jurors (Van Langenhove, 1989). Also, note that the ultimate defence in a trial is to position oneself as a person who lacks agency or self-consciousness. Once positioned as insane; then all positioning acts that would have made the person responsible for the actions (s)he committed are rendered empty.

Conclusion

In the preceding paragraphs, many different categories have been introduced as possible tools for understanding discursive practices. As such the emphasis of this chapter has been on developing a broad taxonomy. It is, however, important to grasp the inherently dynamic character of positioning. In opening a conversation a speaker generally takes up or adopts a position. This act does not and indeed could not preempt the future structure of the conversation. The fact that both storyline and illocutionary force of the speech–acts are jointly created by the conversants and so made determinate means that rejection of the original positioning by other conversants and the adopting of other positions redefines every aspect of the conversation. Indeed positions may modulate as a conversation unfolds, forever retrospectively redoing the conversation that has already occurred. The taxonomy which we have advocated here represents an abstraction from conversations which have achieved a degree of stability and a level of consensus. We would also point out, though it ought to be obvious, that the catalogue of kinds of positions that exist here and now will not necessarily be found at other places and times. In so far as the content of a position is defined in terms of rights, duties and obligations of speaking with respect to the social forces of what can be said, and these 'moral' properties are locally and momentarily specified, positions will be unstable in content as well.

If positioning is to be understood as a way in which people dynamically produce and explain the everyday behaviour of themselves and others, then the question arises how this relates to the explanations that social scientists develop about that same everyday behaviour. If such social science explanations involve the idea of individual persons, then, in accordance with the above remarks, such explanations can equally well be regarded as acts of positioning. And this requires us to ask what will be the storyline of such 'scientific positionings'?

It is important to stress that, as all conversations always involve some sort of positioning, the conversational act of interviewing or asking a person to tick an answer on an item in a questionnaire also necessarily has to be understood in terms of the triad 'position, speech-act, storyline'. This signifies that concepts such as 'attitudes' or 'traits' hardly have any claim to refer to enduring attitudes of real people. As such they would imply that there is something inside the head of persons that at any time can be 'tapped' by a social scientist. Asking a person questions about, for example, locus of control or authoritarian behaviour is a form of positioning and has to be understood as such: it tells something about how people position themselves when answering a questionnaire administered by a scientist. When that same person is talking to his girlfriend about why he failed his exams and how that relates to the behaviour of his tutor, quite other positioning will occur than those that relate to locus of control or authoritarianism. In other words the 'external validity' involves much more than just the relation between answers on a questionnaire and 'real life behaviour'. In order to assess the relation between scientific positioning and how people position themselves in other situations, not only the speech-acts (be it test items) but also the positions and storylines have to be taken into account. Referring to Shutz's (1962) concepts of first and second order accounts it can be said that scientific positioning should always start by analysing the 'first order' positionings that occurred before the scientist started to converse with people about a given topic. Rather than asking questions like 'what do you think about X?', questions should be asked that inquire if and on which occasions people think about X. and what they think of the scientist's interest in their thinking about X. Furthermore, it also makes sense to analyse research-acts themselves in terms of positioning. Rather than the sterile repetition of methodological clichés (e.g., 65 subjects whose age ranged between . . .'), a research report should include the story of that research.

The concept of positioning as defined and illustrated in this chapter, not only allows us to bring together many different aspects of social life under a single theoretical framework (including the act of doing research), it also generates many interesting questions for empirical research. Clearly, persons are constantly engaged in positioning themselves and others. The concrete forms such positioning will take differ according to the situations in which they occur. One individual can thus undertake several varieties of positioning. But, as positioning is a discursive practice undertaken by several individuals at a time, the question also arises regarding to what extent there exist variations in positioning across individuals? In answering this question one must distinguish between three aspects. First, people will differ in their capacity to position themselves and others, their mastery of the techniques so to speak. Secondly, they will differ in their willingness or intention to position and be positioned. Thirdly, they will also differ in their power to achieve positioning acts. While the first two variations are individual attributes, the latter is social: powers are derived from specific locations in social orders and networks. Within these aspects one can think of a number of dimensions of 'individual differences' in positioning. We may for instance expect to find differences in the ability people have to succeed in positioning themselves in few or many ways. This involves something like conversational dominance, conversational charisma, etc., which are independent of socially endowed powers of positioning. We also may expect positioning to vary according to whether actors are highly individualized or on the contrary relying heavily on cultural stereotypes. The relevant storyline can be taken from a cultural repertoire or can be invented. People will differ on how clever they are at narrative invention. Finally, we may also expect to find variations in the extent to which the different ways in which a person positions him/herself are closely related to each other or not. In other words, to what extent is a coherent life possible and to what extent do people feel obliged to establish such a coherence across positionings? One can also wonder to what extent private intentional self-positioning can vary between persons and if that can be related to any of the above dimensions.

A final word should be said about the positioning of research. Given the mutually determining triad 'position–speech-act–storyline', whenever there are storylines, there are positionings. Narratological studies have shown that scientific research papers themselves produced according to a discursive practice are organized by traditional storylines (cf. Knorr-Cetina, 1981), so there must be positioning present in scientific discourse as well as speaking or writing with illocutionary force. Every research paper can be understood as a form of tacit and intentional positioning of the authors which includes a rhetorical redescription of both the events that happened (e.g., a laboratory experiment) and of publications by other authors (the ones quoted and commented on). While oral conversations always imply some reciprocal positioning, the written text is a unilateral act. Consequently, once a research paper is written, authors have to wait until some colleagues position them or engage in a rhetorical redescription of their work. If what is claimed in a research paper is not taken up in any 'scientific' storyline, it is as if that theory did not exist. Taking into account the rapid growth of the number of scientific publications, the old adage 'publish or perish' might well be reformulated as 'be positioned, or do not exist'.

3

Positioning and Personhood

B. Davies and R. Harré

Introduction

There are many problems inherent in the use of the concept of role in developing a social psychology of selfhood. Here we explore the idea that the concept of 'positioning' can be used to facilitate the thinking of linguistically oriented social analysts in ways that the use of the concept of 'role' prevented. In particular the new concept helps focus attention on dynamic aspects of encounters in contrast to the way in which the use of 'role' serves to highlight static, formal and ritualistic aspects. The view of language in which positioning is best understood, we believe, is the immanentist view expounded by Harris (1980), according to which language exists only as concrete occasions of language in use. *La langue* is an intellectualizing myth – only *la parole* is psychologically and socially real. This position is developed in contrast to the linguistic tradition in which 'syntax', 'semantics' and 'pragmatics' are used in a way that implies an abstract realm of causally potent entities shaping actual speech. In our analysis and our explanation, we invoke concepts such as 'speech-act', 'indexicality' and 'context', that is, the concepts central to ethogenic or new paradigm psychology (Davies, 1982). Feminist poststructuralist theory has interesting parallels with this position. The recognition of the force of 'discursive practices', the ways in which people are 'positioned' through those practices and the way in which the individual's 'subjectivity' is generated through the learning and use of certain discursive practices are commensurate with the 'new psycho-socio-linguistics' (Davies, 1989; Henriques et al., 1984; Potter and Wetherall, 1988; Weedon, 1987).

The Immanentist Account of Orderly Human Productions

According to long-established tradition the orderliness of many human productions, for instance conversations, is a consequence in some way of rules and conventions which exist independently of the productions. In some readings of the Chomskian school of linguistics, for example, transformational grammars are taken as pre-existing their roles in actual psychological processes of language production. We shall call this kind of view 'transcendentalism'. In this book we take a contrary or 'immanentist' view. We shall assume that rules are explicit formulations of the normative order which is immanent in concrete human productions, such as actual conversations between particular people on particular occasions. These formulations are themselves a special kind of discourse having its own social purposes. According to the immanentist point of view there are only actual conversations, past and present. Similarities between various conversations are to be explained by reference only to whatever concretely has happened before, and to human memories of it, which form both the personal and the cultural resources for speakers to draw upon in constructing the present moment. Though artificial mnemonic devices such as books and manuals are often understood as evidence for pre-existing knowledge structures independent of any speaker, these only have meaning to the extent that they are taken up by any speaker-hearer as encodings to be attended to. It is the actual conversations which have already occurred that are the archetypes of current conversations. We remember what we and others have said and done, what we believe or were told that they have said and done, where it was wrong and where it was right. In this view, grammar is not a potent psychological reality shaping syntactical forms. It is an aspect of a specialist conversation in which some people talk and write to and for each other about what other people say and write. In highly literate societies instances of this kind of writing can be drawn upon as concrete exemplars of how to talk. We take an immanentist stance to all similar theories about the sources of patterned human productions, in particular towards social rule sets.

If we want to talk about 'sexism' or 'ageism' in the use of language, what we are talking about is the highlighting of certain past conversations as morally unacceptable exemplars for talking and writing now. The basis on which a cluster of past conversations can be deemed to be objectionable as exemplars for speaking now, is not whether the speakers in the past or present intended their speaking to be derogatory of women or of the aged. Rather, it is because it can be shown that, as in the past, there can be negative, even if unintended, consequences of those ways of talking. 'Position' will be offered as the immanentist replacement for a clutch of transcendentalist concepts like 'role'.

Conversation as Joint Action for the Production of Determinate Speech-acts

Since 'positioning' is largely a conversational phenomenon we must make clear at what level of analysis speaking together is to be taken as relevant to a conversation. We take conversation to be a form of social interaction the products of which are also social, such as interpersonal relations. We must therefore select analytical concepts that serve to reveal conversation as a structured set of speech-acts, that is, as sayings and doings of types defined by reference to their social (illocutionary) force. This level of analysis must be extended to include non-verbal contributions to conversation. For example, it has been said that there are phenomenologically identifiable markers by which people can distinguish telephone rings that are summoning them from those that are summoning others. 'Summoning me' is an analytical concept of the speech-act level. So our domain is broader than the range of interactions of which only the spoken or written aspects are recorded.

Are we to think of conversation as a hazardous decoding (by the hearers) of the individual social intentions of each speaker? Searle's (1979) version of Austin's (1961) speech-act theory of conversation certainly tends in that direction, since he takes the type of a speech-act to be defined by the social intention of the person who uttered it. We will argue here that, on the contrary, a conversation unfolds through the joint action of all the participants as they make (or attempt to make) their own and each other's actions socially determinate. A speech-*action* can become a determinate speech-*act* to the extent that it is taken up as such by all the participants. So what it is that has been said evolves and changes as the conversation develops. This way of thinking about speech-acts allows for there to be multiple speech-acts accomplished in any one saying and for any speech-act hearing to remain essentially defeasible (cf. Muhlhauser and Harré, 1990; Pearce, 1989). As we develop our account of positioning we will argue for a productive interrelationship between 'position' and 'illocutionary force'. The social meaning of what has been said will be shown to depend upon the positioning of interlocutors which is itself a product of the social force a conversation action is taken 'to have'. We shall use the term 'discursive practice' for all the ways in which people actively produce social and psychological realities.

In this context a discourse is to be understood as an institutionalized use of language and language-like sign systems. Institutionalization can occur at the disciplinary, the political, the cultural and the small group level. There can also be discourses that develop around a specific topic, such as gender or class. Discourses can compete with each other or they can create distinct and incompatible versions of reality. To know anything is to know in terms of one or more discourses. As Frazer (1990) says of adolescent girls she interviewed: 'actors' understanding and experience of their social identity, the social world and their place in it, is discursively constructed. By this I mean that the girls' experience of gender, race, class, their personal-social identity, can only be expressed and understood through the categories available to them in discourse.'

In this sense 'discourse' plays a similar role in our social theory to that played by 'conceptual scheme' in contemporary philosophy of science. It is that in terms of which phenomena are made relatively determinate. An important distinction, though, between the two terms, as we understand them, is that conceptual schemes are static repertories located primarily in the mind of each individual thinker or researcher almost as a personal possession, whereas discourse is a multi-faceted public process through which meanings are progressively and dynamically achieved.

A particular strength of the poststructuralist research paradigm, to which we referred above, is that it recognizes both the constitutive force of discourse, and in particular of discursive practices, and at the same time recognizes that people are capable of exercising choice in relation to those practices. We shall argue that the constitutive force of each discursive practice lies in its provision of subject positions. A subject position incorporates both a conceptual repertoire and a location for persons within the structure of rights and duties for those who use that repertoire. Once having taken up a particular position as one's own, a person inevitably sees the world from the vantage point of that position and in terms of the particular images, metaphors, storylines and concepts which are made relevant within the particular discursive practice in which they are positioned. At least a possibility of notional choice is inevitably involved because there are many and contradictory discursive practices that each person could engage in. Among the products of discursive practices are important aspects of the very persons who engage in them.

An individual emerges through the processes of social interaction, not as a relatively fixed end product but as one who is constituted and reconstituted through the various discursive practices in which they participate. Accordingly, who one is, that is, what sort of person one is, is always an open question with a shifting answer depending upon the positions made available within one's own and others' discursive practices and within those practices, the stories through which we make sense of our own and others' lives. Stories are located within a number of different discourses, and thus vary dramatically in terms of the language used, the concepts, issues and moral judgements made relevant, and the subject positions made available within them. In this way poststructuralism shades into narratology.

In this chapter we focus on the development of the notion of 'positioning' as a contribution to the understanding of personhood. The psychology of personhood has been bedevilled by the ambiguity of the concept of 'self', a concept which has played a leading role in psychological discourses of personhood. This is a deep ambiguity of the question 'Who am I?' Human beings are characterized both by continuous personal identity and by discontinuous personal diversity. It is one and the same person who is variously positioned in a conversation. Yet as variously positioned we may want to say that that very same person experiences and displays aspects of self that are involved in the continuity of a multiplicity of selves. In this chapter we take personal identity, the singularity of self, for granted. However, we believe that selfhood in this sense is as much the product of discursive practices as the multiple selfhood we wish to investigate.

Multiplicities of Reflexive Concepts: Personal Discourse about Oneself

Our acquisition or development of our own sense of how the world is to be interpreted from the perspective of who we take ourselves to be, involves, we claim, the following processes:

1   Learning the categories which partition the universe of human beings into male/female, father/daughter; grandparent/parent/child; player/referee/ spectator and so on, that is, relate to dichotomous, trichotomous and other patterns of subgroups.
2   Participating in the various discursive practices through which meanings are allocated to those categories. These include the storylines through which different subject positions are elaborated.
3   Positioning of oneself, as a person, in terms of these categories and storylines. This involves imaginatively positioning oneself as if one belongs in one category and not in the other (e.g., as girl and not boy, or good girl and not bad girl).
4   Recognition of oneself as having the characteristics that locate oneself as a member of various subclasses of dichotomous, trichotomous and other category formations and not of others, i.e. the development of a sense of oneself as belonging in the world in certain ways and thus seeing the world from the perspective of one so positioned. This recognition may entail an emotional commitment to the category membership but will certainly involve the development of a moral system organized around the belonging.
5   All four processes arise in relation to a theory of the person as a certain kind of self embodied in a pronoun grammar in which a person under-

stands themselves as historically continuous and unitary. The experiencing of contradictory positions as problematic, as something to be reconciled or remedied, stems from this general feature of the way being a person is done in our society. Within feminist poststructuralist theory the focus has been on the experience of contradictions as important sites for gaining an understanding of what it means to be a gendered person. Such contradictions do not define different people. It is the fact that one person experiences themselves as contradictory that provides the dynamic for understanding (Haug). We wish to defend the adoption of 'position' as the appropriate expression with which to talk about the discursive production of a diversity of selves the fleeting panorama of Meadian 'me's' conjured up in the course of conversational interactions. But then 'me's' are only of significance as ways of being of continuous 'I's'!

Positioning and its Dynamics

Smith (1988: xxxv) introduces the concept of positioning by distinguishing between 'a person' as an individual agent and 'the subject'. By the latter he means 'the series or conglomerate of positions, subject-positions, provisional and not necessarily indefeasible, in which a person is momentarily called by the discourses and the world he/she inhabits'. In speaking and acting from a position people are bringing to the particular situation their history as they themselves conceive it, that is, the history of one who has been in multiple positions and engaged in different forms of discourse. Self reflection should make it obvious that such a being is not inevitably caught in the subject position that the particular narrative and the related discursive practices might seem to dictate at any moment and in any episode.

Positioning, as we will use it, is the discursive process whereby people are located in conversations as observably and subjectively coherent participants in jointly produced storylines. There can be interactive positioning in which what one person says positions another. And there can be reflexive positioning in which one positions oneself. However, it would be a mistake to assume that, in either case, positioning is necessarily intentional. One lives one's life in terms of the kind of person one takes oneself to be, whoever or whatever might be responsible for its production.

Taking conversation as the starting point we proceed by assuming that every conversation is a discussion of a topic and the telling of, whether explicitly or implicitly, one or more personal stories whose force is made determinate for the participants by that aspect of the local expressive order which they presume is in use and towards which they orient themselves. The same anecdote might seem boastful according to one expressive convention, but an expression of proper pride according to another. In either reading the anecdote becomes a fragment of autobiography. People will therefore be taken to organize conversations so that they display two modes of organization: the 'logic' of the ostensible topic and the storylines which are embedded in fragments of the participants' autobiographies. Positions are identified in part by extracting the autobiographical aspects of a conversation in which it becomes possible to find out how each conversant conceives of themselves and of the other participants by seeing what position they take up and in what story, and how they are then positioned.

In telling a fragment of his or her autobiography a speaker assigns parts and characters in the episodes described, both to themselves and to others, including those taking part in the conversation. In this respect the structure of an anecdote serving as a fragment of an autobiography is no different from a fairy-tale or other work of narrative fiction. By giving people parts in a story, whether it be explicit or implicit, a speaker makes available a subject position which the other speaker in the normal course of events would take up. A person can be said thus to 'have been positioned' by another speaker. The interconnection between positioning and the making determinate of the illocutionary force of speech-acts may also involve the creation of other positionings by a second speaker. By treating a remark as, say, 'condolence', in responding to that remark a second speaker positions themselves as, say, the bereaved. The first speaker may not have so intended what they said, that is, they may not wish to be positioned as one who would offer condolences on such an occasion. But since having been so positioned they may find themselves moving into the fulfilment of that storyline.

When one speaker is said to position themselves and another in their talk, the following dimensions should be taken into account:

1   The words the speaker chooses inevitably contain images and metaphors which both assume and invoke the ways of being that the participants take themselves to be involved in.
2   Participants may not be aware of their assumptions nor the power of the images to invoke particular ways of being and may simply regard their words as 'the way one talks' on *this sort* of occasion. But the definition of the interaction being 'of this sort' and therefore one in which one speaks in this way, is to have made it into this sort of occasion.
3   The way in which 'this sort of occasion' is viewed by the participants may vary from one to another. Political and moral commitments, the sort of person one takes oneself to be, one's attitude to the other speakers, the availability of alternative discourses to the one invoked by the initial speaker (and particularly of discourses which offer a critique of the one invoked by the initial speaker) are all implicated in how the utterance of

the initial speaker will be heard. This is also the case for any subsequent utterances, though the assumption is usually made by participants in a conversation that utterances by speakers subsequent to the initial speaker will be from within the same discourse.

4   The positions created for oneself and the other are not part of a linear non-contradictory autobiography (as autobiographies usually are in their written form), but rather, the cumulative fragments of a lived autobiography.

5   The positions may be seen by one or other of the participants in terms of known 'roles' (actual or metaphorical), or in terms of known characters in shared storylines, or they may be much more ephemeral and involve shifts in power, access, or blocking of access, to certain features of claimed or desired identity, and so on.

One way of grasping the concept of positioning as we wish to use it, is to think of someone listening to or reading a story. There is the narrative, say *Anna Karenina*, which incorporates a braided development of several storylines. Each storyline is organized around various poles such as events, characters and moral dilemmas. Our interest focuses on the cast of characters (for instance, Anna, Karenin, Vronsky, Levin and Kitty). The storylines in the narrative describe fragments of lives. The cast of characters offer imagined points of view from which the events described in the narrative will display different aspects and qualities. This opens up the possibility for multiple readings. Any reader may, for one reason or another, position themselves or be positioned as outside the story looking in. Such positioning may be created by how the reader perceives the narrator and/or author to be positioning them (as reader) or it may be created by the reader's perception of the characters themselves.

Transferring this conceptual system to our context of episodes of human interaction, we arrive at the following analogue: There is a conversation in which is created a braided development of several storylines. These are organized through conversation and around various poles, such as events, characters and moral dilemmas. Cultural stereotypes such as nurse/patient, conductor/orchestra, mother/son may be called on as a resource. It is important to remember that these cultural resources may be understood differently by different people.

The illocutionary forces of each speaker's contributions on concrete occasions of conversing can be expected to have the same multiplicity as that of the culturally available stereotypes as they are individually understood by *each* speaker. A conversation will be univocal only if the speakers severally adopt complementary subject positions which are organized around a shared interpretation of the relevant conversational locations. Even then, the fact that the conversation is seen from the vantage point of the two different positions, however complementary they are, militates against any easy assumption of shared understanding.

One speaker can position others by adopting a storyline which incorporates a particular interpretation of cultural stereotypes to which they are 'invited' to conform, indeed are required to conform if they are to continue to converse with the first speaker in such a way as to contribute to that person's storyline. Of course, they may not wish to do so for all sorts of reasons. Sometimes they may not contribute because they do not understand what the storyline is meant to be, or they may pursue their own storyline, quite blind to the storyline implicit in the first speaker's utterance, or as an attempt to resist. Or they may conform because they do not define themselves as having choice, but feel angry or oppressed or affronted or some combination of these.

In our analysis of an actual conversation we will illustrate the importance of the insight that the same sentence can be used to perform several different speech-acts. Which speech-act it is will depend in part on which storyline speakers take to be in use. It follows that several conversations can be proceeding simultaneously. It also follows that one speaker may not have access to a conversation as created by another or others, even though he or she contributes some of the sentences which serve as pegs for the speech-acts the others create (Pearce and Cronen, 1981). Our analysis indicates that any version of what people take to be a determinate speech-act is always open to further negotiation as to what the actual act (if there is such a thing) is.

To illustrate the use of the concept of 'positioning' for analysing real conversations we will describe a conversational event in which each speaker positioned the other but asymmetrically. What the positioning amounted to for each conversant will be shown to depend on the point of view from which the conversation is seen. Our example will draw on a case where a single attribute, namely powerlessness, was made salient, rather than a typified role model. The main relevance of the concept of positioning for social psychology is that it serves to direct our attention to a process by which certain trains of consequences, intended or unintended, are set in motion. But these trains of consequences can be said to occur only if we give an account of how acts of positioning are made determinate for certain people. If we want to say that someone, say A, has been positioned as powerless we must be able to supply an account of how that position is 'taken up' by A, that is, from where does A's understanding or grasp of powerlessness derive? We can raise the same issue by asking what psychological assumptions cluster around the single attribute, say powerlessness, which the act of positioning has fastened on A? We shall call this an extension of the significance of the attitude.

For analytical purposes we propose two kinds of such extension.

Indexical extension. For some people in some situations a position-imposed attribute is interpreted and the consequences of such positioning taken up in terms of the indexical meanings developed through past experiences. 'Power-lessness', for example, might be grasped in terms of what was felt on past occasions when a person took themselves to be powerless. With respect to this particular attribute we have observed that women in industrial societies tend to make such extensions of the significance of the concept. The case is probably reversed for the attribute of powerfulness, in which women need to consult a typification, say mother, to know what it means. It follows that we would expect it to be the men among disadvantaged races or classes within such societies who take up the significance of being positioned as powerless indexically, that is, in light of their particular experiences of being robbed of choice or agency.

Typification extension. In other cases the extension of the significance of an initial act of single attribute positioning comes about through the association of or embeddedness of that attribute within a culturally well-established cluster of attributes, called up by the positioning. In this case we think metaphorically of a person scanning their past experience for a concrete occasion on which to build an interpretation of the position they have been assigned (whether they accept or reject it) until they encounter the record of a typified occasion such as 'nurse/patient'.

In both forms of extension the storyline in which the person takes them-selves to be embedded is a crucial element in the process of establishing the meaning of the utterance in question.

Alternative Analytic Schemes

The classical dramaturgical model has focused on 'role' as the determining basis of action. Though there have been attempts to recruit 'improvised theatre' to the models available for social psychology (Coppierters, 1981) it is the traditional drama that has served as the almost ubiquitous source model. In the dramaturgical model people are construed as actors with lines already written and their roles determined by the particular play they find themselves in. Nor do they have much choice as to how to play these roles in any particular setting. They learned how to take up a particular role through observation of others in that role. 'Positioning' and 'subject position', in contrast, permit us to think of ourselves as choosing subjects, locating ourselves in conversations according to those narrative forms with which we are familiar and bringing to those narratives our own subjective lived histories through which we have learnt metaphors, characters and plot. For example, consider the 'role' of mother. Everyone 'knows' what that is, and anyone finding themselves in that role or in relation to someone in that role, knows the multiple expectations and obligations of care for children that are entailed. There may be variations on the theme, such as 'Jewish mother', but these are simply mothers who take up their role within a further set of constraints embedded in 'Jewish culture'. But everyone does not know each of our personal understandings and sets of emotions connected to our idea of mother, developed out of experience of our own mothers in the first instance. And those who develop their particular concept of mother in anticipation that they will one day be positioned as mother will do so differently from someone who knows that they will never be so positioned. The way we have been positioned and have positioned ourselves in relation to 'mother', the narratives that we have lived out in relation to particular mothers, mean that we bring to each new encounter with someone positioned as mother a personal history with its attendant emotions and beliefs *as well as* a knowledge of social structures (including roles) with their attendant rights, obligations and expectations.

Any narrative that we collaboratively unfold with other people thus draws on a knowledge of social structures and the roles that are recognizably allocated to people within those structures. Social structures are coercive to the extent that to be recognizably and acceptably a person we must operate within their terms. But the concept of a person that we bring to any action includes not only that knowledge of external structures and expectations but also the idea that we are not only responsible for our own lines but that there are multiple choices in relation not only to the possible lines that we can produce but to the form of the play itself. We are thus agent (producer/ director) as well as author and player, and the other participants co-author and co-produce the drama. But we are also the multiple audiences that view any play and bring to it the multiple and often contradictory interpretations based on our own emotions, our own reading of the situation and our own imaginative positioning of ourselves in the situation. Each of these will be mediated by our own personal histories. Finally, lived narratives, as we will show, can change direction and meaning in ways entirely surprising to the participants to such an extent that the metaphor of a prestructured play begins to lose plausibility as a viable image to explain what it is that we do in interaction with each other. If we are to come close to understanding how it is that people actually interact in everyday life we need the metaphor of an unfolding narrative, in which we are constituted in one position or another within the course of one story, or even come to stand in multiple or contradictory positions, or to negotiate a new position by 'refusing' the position that the opening rounds of a conversation have made available to us. With such a metaphor we can begin to explain what it means to 'refuse' to accept the nature of the discourse through which particular conversation takes place.

The closest one might come conceptually to 'role' in our framework is 'subject position'. A subject position is made available within a discourse. For example, in the discourse of romantic love there are two major complementary subject positions made available – the male hero or prince who has agency and who usually has some heroic task to perform, and the female heroine or princess who is usually a victim of circumstance and is reliant on her prince to save her from whatever it is that fate has done to her (Brownstein, 1984; Zipes, 1986). In everyday life, if two people are living out some version of the romantic love narrative then they will position themselves and each other in the complementary subject positions made available within the discourse of romantic love. In other words, they will engage in the discursive practices through which romantic love is made into a lived narrative. The origins of the conceit in the court of Eleanor of Aquitaine involved a positioning very different from that above. The historical transformation from one to the other would be well worth studying in terms of positioning theory.

In Goffman's later works of 1974 and 1981 a different terminology appears as he shifts further from the dramaturgical model that animated his earlier work. An interest in the ubiquitous role of conversation in creating and maintaining social interaction led him to develop analytical concepts for understanding its properties. The earlier of his attempts was the idea of 'frame'. That this was not a well thought through concept can be seen in the following. He begins by asserting that frames and schemata are the same thing:

> Frames vary in degree of organisation. Some are neatly presentable as a system of entities, postulates and rules; others, indeed most others, appear to have no particular articulated shape. (Goffman, 1974: 21)

The aim of the analyst is to isolate basic frameworks (primary frames) 'for making sense out of events'. The task is made difficult by the fact that while one thing may appear to be going on something else is happening, e.g. an autobiographical anecdote may be intended as a joke, a wedding may be in a play, etc.

We can understand what is happening in a play, by seeing that while the primary frame is being used by the audience to make sense of what the actors are doing, it must be understood 'non-seriously', that is, not have its usual consequences (or perlocutionary effects). Goffman called the use of a primary frame in play-going a 'change of key'. The analogy with music was deliberate. Key change involves a 'systematic transformation across materials already

meaningful in accordance with a scheme of interpretation' to which participants are privy. Frames are, like roles, already given in a cultural system, and
the occasions of their use, either in this key or that, provided for socially, for
example by designating a certain arena as a playhouse. Thus the dynamic
concept of positioning oneself in a discourse is not reducible to adopting a
frame. However, a frame may well come along with a position. Nor is an act
of positioning reducible to a change of key, even though the fact that one is
positioned may be revealed in the intuition that there has been a key change.

His later idea of 'footing' is more promising as an alternative to positioning.
The metaphor is double. We gain or lose our footing in conversations, social
groups and so on, much as we gain or lose it on a muddy slope. In the second
layer of metaphor we speak from and can change our 'footings' in conversations. Goffman's own account of his new notion is rather vague, since it relies
on various other ideas which themselves are not well defined. 'Change of
footing' is concerned with occasions when alignment, or set, or stance, or
posture, or projected self of 'participants' is somehow at issue. 'A change of
footing implies a change in the alignment we take up to ourselves and to the
others present as expressed in the way we manage the production and
reception of an utterance' (Goffman, 1981: 128). So 'alignment' emerges
highlighted from these remarks. But one's hopes for clarity are dashed since in
the very next line Goffman ties footing back to his earlier and vague concept
of frame thus: 'A change in our footing is another way of talking about a
change in our frame of events.' But if we consult Goffman (1974) we find that
a frame is simply a working set of definitions of the familiar Burkean kind, in
which a scene, actor and action are specified in what is essentially a version of
role analysis.

So let us return to 'footing'. Goffman's analysis includes a conception of
the speaker as fulfilling three speaking roles, that of 'animator', the person
who speaks; that of 'author', the person who is responsible for the text; and
that of 'principal', the person 'whose position [i.e., where the speaker stands]
is established by the words that are spoken, someone whose beliefs have been
told, someone who is committed to what the words say' (Goffman, 1981:
144). This is the basis of the production format of the utterance. On many
occasions, animator, author and principal are one and the same person.

Similar complexities attend the hearers. There is always a participation
framework in place, including differentiations of 'official recipients' of a
speaker's talk from bystanders, eavesdroppers and so on.

Staying now with alignment and relating it to production formats and
participation frameworks, we still lack an account of what the key term
means. Tannen tells us (personal communication) that alignment is a relational
notion, but so far as we can judge the relata of alignments are speakers'
conceptions, linking the one adopted by the speaker with what sort of person

the speaker takes the hearer to be. Similarly and sometimes reciprocally, there will be a pair of hearer's conceptions of the personae engaged in talk. An actual conversation will then realize, probably imperfectly, these beliefs as actual relations between participants. This could not be in sharper contrast to our conception of positioning, since it takes for granted that alignments exist prior to speaking and shape it, rather than that alignments are actual relations jointly produced in the very act of conversing. It should be clear that Goffman, even in his later work, did not escape the constraints of role theory. Frames and schemata are transcendent to action and stand to it as pre-existing devices (or tools) employed by people to create conversations. For us, the whole of the 'apparatus' must be immanent, reproduced moment by moment in conversational action and carried through time, not as abstract schemata, but as current understandings of past and present conversations.

A Lived Narrative and its Analysis Using the Concept of 'Positioning'

The best way to recommend our proposal is to demonstrate its analytical power in a worked example. The story is about two characters, Sano and Enfermada, who, at the point the story begins, are at a conference. It is a winter's day in a strange city and they are looking for a chemist's shop to try to buy some medicine for Enfermada. A subzero wind blows down the long street. Enfermada suggests they ask for directions rather than conducting a random search. Sano, as befits the one in good health, and accompanied by Enfermada, darts into shops to make enquiries. After some time it becomes clear that there is no such shop in the neighbourhood and they agree to call a halt to their search. Sano then says 'I'm sorry to have dragged you all this way when you're not well'. His choice of words surprises Enfermada, who replies 'You didn't drag me, I chose to come', occasioning some surprise in turn to Sano.

Sano and Enfermada offered separate glosses on this episode, whose differences are illustrative of the use of the concept of positioning and instructive in themselves since they reveal a third level of concepts beyond illocutionary force but immanent in positioning, namely moral orders. The subsequent debate between our protagonists ran as follows:

Sano protests that he feels responsible and Enfermada protests in return that she does not wish him to feel responsible since that places her in the position of one who is not responsible, and by implication, that she is one who is incapable of making decisions about her own well-being. They then debate whether one taking responsibility deprives the other of responsibility. For Sano the network of obligations is paramount. He is at first unable to grasp the idea that anyone could suppose that the fulfilment of a taken-for-granted obligation on the healthy to take charge of the care of the ill could be construed as a threat to some freedom that he finds mythical. Enfermada is determined to refuse Sano's claim of responsibility, since in her feminist framework it is both unacceptable for another to position her as merely an accessory to their actions, rather than someone who has agency in her own right, *and* for her to accept such a positioning. Her concern is only in part for the unintended subject position that his words have apparently invited her to step into. She believes that his capacity to formulate their activity in such a way may be indicative of a general attitude towards her (and to women in general) as marginal, as other than central actors in their own life stories. She knows that he does not wish or intend to marginalize women and so she draws attention to the subject position made available in his talk and refuses to step into it. But her protest positions Sano as sexist, a positioning which he in turn finds offensive. His inclination is therefore to reject Enfermada's gloss as an incorrect reading of his words. But this of course only makes sense in his moral order of interpersonal obligations, not in the feminist moral order. Both speakers are committed to a pre-existing idea of themselves that they had prior to the interchange, Enfermada as a feminist and Sano as one who wishes to fulfil socially mandatory obligations. They are also both committed to their hearing of the interchange. Their protests are each aimed at sustaining these definitions and as such have strong emotional loading.

The episode went through a number of further cycles of reciprocal offence, too numerous to detail here. One of them involved Sano in accusing Enfermada of working off a worst-interpretation principle which he claims is characteristic of the kind of ultra-sensitive response that feminists and members of minority groups engage in when reacting to 'fancied slights'. Enfermada hears this as a claim that she is unnecessarily making life difficult for herself, alienating people (presumably including Sano) from her and her feminist views. This bothers Enfermada more than the original 'apology' because she sees herself as not only robbed of agency but as trivialized and silly, an objectionable member of a minority group who, if they behaved properly, could have equitable membership of society along with Sano. The whole point of her original protest was that his words robbed her of access to that equitable world whether he intended it or not. Until that point she had believed that his intentions were in fact good, which was why it was worth raising the issue. Now she sees that even knowing how upsetting it is to be so positioned in his narrative, his wish is to allocate all responsibility for inequitable treatment that she receives to her own personal style. And so the story went, with claims and counter claims. The complexity, if not impossibility, of 'refusing the discourse' became more and more apparent, as did the subjective commitment to implicit storylines with their implications for the moral characters of each of the participants.

Leaving aside for one moment the further cycles of offence that were generated around the original conversation, it is possible to render the episode in a symmetrical way and in terms of speech-acts and illocutionary force as follows:

Us: I'm sorry to have dragged you all this way when you are not well.
Ue: You didn't drag me, I chose to come.

Let us all call these utterances or speech-actions Us and Ue respectively. We shall use the symbols A(Us) and A(Ue) for the corresponding speech-actions which can be made determinate in the various storylines.

What speech-acts have occurred? To answer this question we have first to identify the storylines of which the utterances of S and E are moments. Only relative to those storylines can the speech-actions crystallize as relatively determinate speech-acts.

SS *S's line as perceived by S*: medical treatment with associated positions of S = nurse and E = patient. In this story A(Us) = commiseration.

SE *S's storyline as perceived by E*: Paternalism with associated positions of S = independent powerful man and E = dependent helpless woman. In this story A(Us) = condescension. Indexical offence S to E.

EE *E's storyline as perceived by E*: joint adventure with associated positions of S and E as travellers in a foreign land. In this story A(Ue) is a reminder in relation to the storyline.

ES *E's storyline as perceived by S*: feminist protest with associated positions of S = chauvinist pig and E = righteous suffragette. In this story A(Ue) = complaint. Indexical offence E to S.

The importance of positioning as a real conversational phenomenon and not just an analyst's tool is evident in this example. Here are two well-disposed people of good faith and reasonable intelligence conversing in such a way that they were entrapped into a quarrel engendered in the structural properties of the conversation and not at all in the intentions of the speakers. He was not being paternalistic and she was not being priggish, yet each was driven by the power of the storylines and their associated positions towards the possibility of such mutual accusations.

There are several further points to be made in relation to this analysis. It shows the way in which two people can be living quite different narratives without realizing that they are doing so. In the absence of any protest on Enfermada's part, Sano need never have questioned how his position as care giver would appear in the moral order of someone whose position was radically different from his. Without her particular reply he could not have realized that he could be heard as paternalistic. Her silence could only act as confirmation of his moral order.

Words as utterances do not carry determinate social meaning. Sano's use of the apology-format is ambiguous. When it is placed in the context of Enfermada's narrative it causes indexical offence. Similarly, her protest at being 'made helpless' disturbs him since, in his story, it denies what he takes to be a ubiquitous moral obligation.

We have shown the relational nature of positioning, that is, in Enfermada's moral order, one who takes themselves up as responsible for joint lines of action, may position the other as not responsible. Or if one takes up the position of being aggrieved in relation to another then the other is a perpetrator of the injustice. We have shown that what seems obvious from one position, and readily available to any other person who would only behave or interpret in the correct way, is not necessarily so for the person in the 'other' position. The relative nature of positions not only to each other but to moral orders can make the perception of one almost impossible for the other, in the relational position, to grasp.

One's beliefs about the sorts of persons, including oneself, who are engaged in a conversation are central to how one understands what has been said. Exactly what is the force of any utterance on a particular occasion will depend on that understanding.

In demonstrating the shifting nature of positions, depending on the narrative/metaphors/images through which the positioning is being constituted, we have shown how both the social act performed by the uttering of those words and the effect that action has is a function of the narratives employed by each speaker as well as the particular positions that each speaker perceives the other speaker to be taking up.

There are normative expectations at each level. Sano is surprised at Enfermada's protest because according to conventions of the nurse–patient narrative, there is a normative expectation that the poorly both need and accept care. Of course this narrative also includes the case of the difficult patient. Enfermada for her part is accustomed to being marginalized in men's talk. In hearing him as giving offence she is interpreting him as engaging in normative male behaviour. And of course within this narrative men are notoriously unable to recognize the ways in which their taking up of paternalistic positions negates the agency of the women they are interacting with.

We have shown the necessity of separating out intended meanings from hearable meanings in the process of developing discursive practices that are

not paternalistic or discriminatory *in their effect*. The (personal) political implications of attending to the discursive practices through which one positions
oneself and is positioned, are that one's speech-as-usual with its embedded
metaphors, images, forms, etc., can be recognized as inappropriate to per-
sonal/political beliefs both of one's own and of others with whom one
interacts.

Contradiction, Choice and the Possibility of Agency

Persons as speakers acquire beliefs about themselves which do not necessarily
form a unified coherent whole. They shift from one to another way of
thinking about themselves as the discourse shifts and as their positions within
varying storylines are taken up. Each of these possible selves can be internally
contradictory or contradictory with other possible selves located in different
storylines. Like the flux of past events, conceptions people have about themselves are disjointed until and unless they are located in a story. Since many
stories can be told, even of the same event, then we each have many possible
coherent selves. But to act rationally, those contradictions we are immediately
aware of must be remedied, transcended, resolved or ignored. While it is
logically impossible to act from a formally contradictory script (no one could
simultaneously go to New Orleans and go to New York), most people, most
of the time, wittingly or unwittingly accept that their beliefs about themselves
and their environment are full of unresolved contradictions which one just
lives with. This feature of being human in a Christian universe was much
more openly acknowledged in the past, with the concept of 'God's mysterious
ways'. How could a benevolent God create such an unjust world? and so on.
The possibility of choice in a situation in which there are contradictory
requirements provides people with the possibility of acting agentically.

In making choices between contradictory demands there is a complex
weaving together of the positions (and the cultural/social/political meanings
that are attached to those positions) that are available within any number of
discourses; the emotional meaning attached to each of those positions which
have developed as a result of personal experiences of being located in each
position, or of relating to someone in that position; the stories through which
those categories and emotions are being made sense of; and the moral system
that links and legitimates the choices that are being made.

Because of the social/grammatical construction of the person as a unitary
knowable identity, we tend to assume it is possible to have made a set of
consistent choices located within only one discourse. And it is true we do
struggle with the diversity of experience to produce a story of ourselves which
is unitary and consistent. If we don't, others demand of us that we do. We

also discursively produce ourselves as separate from the social world and are thus not aware of the way in which the taking up of one discursive practice or another (not originating in ourselves) shapes the knowing or telling we can do. Thus we experience these selves as if they were entirely our own production. We take on the discursive practices and storylines as if they were our own and make sense of them in terms of our own particular experiences. The sense of continuity that we have in relation to being a particular person is compounded out of continued embodiment and so of spatio-temporal continuity and shared interpretations of the subject positions and storylines available within them. How to do being a particular non-contradictory person within a consistent storyline is learned both through textual and lived narratives.

In feminist narratives the idea of the non-contradictory person inside a consistent storyline can, however, be just what is disrupted. In a study reported here pre-school children often struggled to interpret feminist narratives in terms of more familiar storylines. One such story was *The Paper Bag Princess* (Munsch, 1980). This is an amusing story about a princess called Elizabeth who goes to incredible lengths to save her prince from a fierce dragon. At the beginning of the story, Princess Elizabeth and Prince Ronald are planning to get married, but then the dragon comes along, burns Elizabeth's castle and clothes and flies off into the distance carrying Prince Ronald by the seat of his pants. Elizabeth is very angry. She finds a paper bag to wear and follows the dragon. She tricks him into displaying all of his magic powers until he falls asleep from exhaustion. She rushes into the dragon's cave to save Ronald only to find he does not want to be saved by a princess who is covered in soot and only has an old paper bag to wear. He tells her to go away and to come back when she looks like a real princess. Elizabeth is quite taken aback by this turn of events, and she says 'Ronald your clothes are really pretty and your hair is very neat. You look like a real prince, but you are a bum.' The last page shows her skipping off into the sunset alone and the story ends with the words: 'They didn't get married after all.'

The apparent intention here is to present a female hero who is not dependent on the prince in shining armour for her happiness, nor for confirmation of who she is. It also casts serious doubt on the concept of the prince who can provide eternal happiness. In this story Elizabeth must be a unitary being in order that *she* experiences the multiple and contradictory positionings we each experience in our everyday lives. She is positioned at the beginning as the uncomplicated, happy and loving princess, living out the romantic narrative of love and happiness ever after. She is then positioned as the dragon's victim, but she rejects this and becomes the active, heroic agent who is in control of the flow of events. She is then positioned as victim again by Ronald and again refuses this positioning, skipping off into the sunset, a free agent. There is personal continuity, for instance in her point of view in the material world, as other relational attributes shift and change.

When the dragon burns Elizabeth's castle and steals Prince Ronald, he also burns her clothes off and makes her very dirty. Many children see her at this point as having magically changed into a bad princess, as if the dragon had cast a spell on her. That badness, because of her nakedness, has negative sexual overtones. Some of the boys are fascinated by her naked and bereft state, but generally it is not Elizabeth who holds their interest so much as the large, powerful and destructive dragon who has devastated her castle and later goes on to devastate entire landscapes. Other boys perceive Ronald as a hero. They comment on his tennis outfit and the medallion around his neck which they perceive as a tennis gold medal. One boy even managed to see Ronald as heroic, that is, as a central agent in control of his own fate, even at the point where he was sailing through the air, held by the dragon by the seat of his pants: 'I'm glad he held onto his tennis racquet so hard. When you've done that, well you just have to hold onto your racquet tight and the dragon holds you up.'

Many of the children to whom this story was read were unable to see Elizabeth as a genuine hero, and were equally unable to see her choice to go it alone at the end as legitimate or positive. The dragon, for some, is the powerful male, whose power remains untainted by Elizabeth's trickery. In this hearing of the story, Elizabeth clearly loses her prince, not because she chooses to leave him, but because she is lacking in virtue. Many children believed Elizabeth should have cleaned herself up and then married the prince. What happens with these children who do not hear a story in which Elizabeth is the hero, is that the story is heard as if it were a variation of a known storyline in which males are heroes and females are other to those heroes. Elizabeth thus becomes a 'normal' (unitary, non-contradictory) princess who just got things a bit wrong.

If Elizabeth is read *as princess*, that is, as one in the role of princess, then the traditional reading can follow almost entirely from an understanding of *the role of princess*. In opening with the sentence 'Elizabeth was a beautiful princess' the text inadvertently invites such a reading. The only clue in the first page of the text that this is not the usual kind of princess is a reference to the castle as 'hers'. According to the traditional reading, the dragon's attack turns Elizabeth into a dirty and bad princess. (Being unitary and non-contradictory, magic is necessary to effect such a change in her.) At the end when Ronald tells her to clean herself up, he is giving her the information she needs to turn herself back into a 'real' princess, in effect breaking the magic spell. In the feminist reading the role of princess is not a dominant interpretative category. In this reading Elizabeth, like a modern woman, is caught up in a shifting set of possibilities, now positioned as one with power, now as powerless. Her adventure is one in which she makes her way among the various subject positions available to her and eventually escapes them all.

The children's responses to this story illustrate many of the points we have been making: in particular the multiple possible interpretations of any speech-action, the interactive nature of the move from words spoken (or in this case, words on the page) to the social act that is taken to have occurred, and the intimate relation between perception of the positions in which the various characters find themselves and perception of storylines. It also shows that though the story can in one reading present Elizabeth as acting rationally, in another she can be seen to behave foolishly. The many children who heard a non-feminist story illustrate the resilience of traditional discursive practices through which actions are interpreted as gender-based acts. Thus the move from role to position is both analytically and politically necessary in the study of people in their contemporary everyday worlds.

Conclusion

In moving from the use of role to position as the central organizing concept for analysing how it is that people do 'being a person of a certain sort', we have moved to another conception of the relation between people and their conversations. In role theory the person is always separable from the various roles that they take up; any particular conversation is understood in terms of someone taking on a certain role. The words that are spoken are to some extent dictated by the role and are to be interpreted in these terms. With positioning, the focus is on the way in which the discursive practices constitute the speakers and hearers in certain ways and yet at the same time they are a resource through which speakers and hearers can negotiate new positions. The motto 'unitas multiplex' captures the unity in diversity that is the characteristic quality of personal being. A subject position is a possibility in known forms of talk; position is what is created in and through talk as the speakers and hearers take themselves up as persons. This way of thinking explains discontinuities in the production of personhood with reference to the fact of multiple and contradictory discursive practices and the interpretations of those practices that can be brought into being by speakers and hearers as they engage in conversations.

4

Preparing for Positive Positioning

D. Howie

Introduction

We distinguished between three aspects on which individual differences in positioning may occur: capacity for positioning oneself and others, willingness or intention to position and be positioned, and power to achieve positioning acts. This chapter seeks to elaborate the first of these aspects, the capacity for positioning, or the skill aspect, involved in active positioning of the self and others. Work with persons suffering from Alzheimer's disease (chapter 7) has suggested that the construct of the self and positive positioning of self can be maintained in spite of significant cognitive impairment. The care giver plays an important role in adaptations made by such a sufferer in maintaining a positive selfhood and positioning of self in the current discourse.

A distinction needs to be made between what a person has the right to do in terms of positioning themselves and others, a moral capacity; and what skills or capacity the person has to utilize this right. The relationship between the two is usually 'linear' in that increasing skill is associated with expanding rights to display it. But it sometimes happens that increasing skill may not be matched by a corresponding extension of rights to exercise it. In these circumstances a person will be in much the same situation they were in prior to training. In chapter 3 the issue of rights to position and be positioned was in prime focus. This chapter presents two main discussions to elaborate the skill aspect. The first is the theoretical depiction of the symbiotic relationship in which such skills are developed. The second is the description of an example of skill development within a symbiotic relationship, utilizing the empirical approach of Feuerstein and colleagues to explore the zone of proximal development, as Vygotsky conceived it.

The Symbiotic Relationship

The early work by Vygotsky on mediated activity (1978), especially within the mother–child relationship, has been drawn on in discussions of the phenomenon of psychological symbiosis. The term 'psychological symbiosis' can be used for those cases in which a group of people complete through public symbiotic activity, particularly in talking to each other, inadequate social and psychological beings. The quality of this symbiotic relationship is elucidated by Feuerstein's theoretical and empirical writings, in which mediated learning is seen as the interaction in which 'another human being, and usually the caregiver, interprets the world to the child' (Feuerstein and Hoffman, 1985: 55). The key criteria of mediated learning seen as responsible for modification of the most important individual's learning capacity or traits are the 'intentionality' of the mediator, the 'transcendence' of the mediation from the immediate here-and-now situation, and the assignment of meaning by the mediator. A further nine criteria, including mediation for competence and mediation of the regulation of behaviour, are seen as responsible for individual difference in response to mediation (Feuerstein, personal communication).

Feuerstein and his team have developed several tools for realizing such a mediating relationship. The first is the Learning Potential Assessment Device (Feuerstein, Rand and Hoffman, 1979), an interactive and dynamic assessment procedure aimed at exploring the 'zone of proximal development'. This is the distance between the actual developmental level as determined by independent problem-solving, and the level of potential development as determined through problem-solving under adult guidance or in collaboration with more capable peers (Vygotsky, 1978). The second tool is the programme called 'instrumental enrichment' (Feuerstein, Rand, Hoffman and Miller, 1980), aimed at providing mediated learning experiences. The exercises within this programme are taught in an interactive relationship between the teacher and the learner, with outworking of the key criteria for mediation (intentionality, transcendence and assignment of meaning). In particular, the encouragement of reflexivity, whereby the learner learns to consider his or her own learning initiatives and responses, including in relation to the higher 'metacognitive' understandings of the self as learner, facilitates positive development of an autonomous and choosing self. Further, one particular instrument, 'orientation in space', focuses on the ability to orient oneself within another person's position, and understand their perspective as well as one's own.

This mediation for the enhancement of reciprocity and empathy in a symbiotic relationship is extremely valuable for skill development in positive positioning of the self and others. The thesis of social constructionism, that our self-manifestations require the mutual cooperation of individuals, can be developed by attempting to elucidate some of the particular moral qualities of the interactive relationship which may enhance positive positioning. Here, we can draw on the concept of the 'between', as the realm in which the 'I and Thou' meet, in Buber's terminology (1966).The link has already been drawn between Buber's concept of the 'between' and the mediated learning experience of Feuerstein by Freeman (1991), in her discussion of the inseparability of the individual and society. Buber (1966) himself emphasized the development of the person in a positive way through the meeting of the 'I' and 'Thou', as the following quotation indicates. 'On the far side of the subjective, on this side of the objective, on the narrow ridge, where I and Thou meet, there is the realm of the 'between' . . . Here the genuine third alternative is indicated, the knowledge which will help to bring about the genuine person again and to establish genuine community' (Buber, 1966: 55). Buber qualifies what is genuine conversation. 'Genuine conversation, and therefore every actual fulfilment of relation between men, means acceptance of otherness' (1966: 112). This acceptance, or affirmation, does not mean approval, but 'by accepting him as my partner in genuine dialogue I have affirmed him as a person' (1966: 105). Such acceptance in dialogue involves trust in the other, recognition and affirmation of the unique difference, the unique self of the other, avoidance of using meeting as a means to some end, and supplementation of experience and knowledge. In such a partnership, the initiator or the responder can become the 'loving man'. The metaphor of the 'loving man' [or woman] is an international one. We meet it simultaneously in Buber's writings and in an old Irish calendar, describing the 'festival of the loving man', celebrated on 25 September, the feast of St Fin Barre, who founded his monastic school in Cork in 606. For Buber, 'the loving man is one who grasps non-relatively each thing he grasps . . . the loving man's dream-powerful and primally-awake heart beholds the non-common. This, the unique, is the bestowing of shape, the self of the thing . . . the beloved' (1966: 99).

An Example of Skill Development within a Symbiotic Relationship

There will be different degrees of supplementation and complementation within a symbiotic relationship, depending in part on the particular individual need for such supplementation. It is important that this need is determined in a dynamic way, within an interactive relationship. Two examples are given of such an assessment of need, and attempts at supplementation from within a symbiotic relationship. They are drawn from an empirical study of the assessment and enhancement of decision-making and self-advocacy skills that have been achieved by applying techniques developed by Reuven Feuerstein and his team in Israel. They have been applied to the assessment and development of skills needed for effective positioning of the self and the communication of that position, i.e. for self-advocacy. The Vygotskian paradigm for assessment of needs, the zone of proximal development, as exemplified in Feuerstein's 'learning potential assessment device', was utilized. Two case studies have been selected to demonstrate the differing needs for supplementation and complementation, and the response to attempts to meet these needs within a symbiotic and one-to-one learning relationship.

Case Study A

This young person, in her late adolescence, is a Pakeha (white European New Zealander), with a history of special educational placement. Her actual level of problem-solving on Ravens Matrices (Raven, 1958) assessment (a measure of general cognitive functioning which is culturally reduced) was rather poor. Her actual level of real-life problem-solving and self-advocacy, as determined by a unique set of assessment tasks related to self-advocacy, and prior to dynamic mediation, was equally poor. Since all these tasks required imaginative positioning it is evident that in this aspect of social skills, Participant A was woefully inadequate. A number of one-to-one interactive sessions aimed at mediating both problem-solving on a specially selected supplementary set of Ravens Matrices tasks and real-life decision-making and self-advocacy tasks were assessed by a 'process-assessment' approach, as used by Feuerstein et al. (1979), which sought to establish the extent of mediation required for success on each type of task. The Ravens tasks were graded in difficulty. Similarly, for the self-advocacy tasks (asking for help, asking for skill training, seeking representation, requesting equal opportunity, and requesting confidentiality), the 'asking for help' task was the least difficult and the 'requesting confidentiality' the most difficult. In response to mediation of skill components, this participant was able to be more successful on the analogy-type Ravens tasks. Also, in reassessment on the Ravens Matrices following this opportunity for skill development, she did show some improvement, indicating a 'zone of proximal development' on this type of task greater than her original level of problem-solving.

However, the picture was less positive when mediation was attempted on the real-life decision-making and self-advocacy skills. She had difficulty in successfully responding to mediation on these tasks, in spite of the positive interaction between her and the mediator. 'Seeking representation' was the only task item where clear gains in association with mediation were achieved, as indicated in a lower level of mediation required. This difficulty in responding to mediation was confirmed in the assessment following mediation, in which she showed little advance on the tasks themselves, a minor improvement for planning suggestions, a slight improvement in formulating helpful thoughts regarding self-attribution, and for feeling attribution (the latter in response to the question 'What sorts of feelings are helpful?'). These latter non-outcome aspects are considered important metacognitions relating to strategy and self.

Case Study B

In contrast, this person is a Nuie Island New Zealander, an adolescent of similar age, but with a history of ordinary school placement. Little English is spoken in his home. He was in a similar segregated sheltered workshop situation to Case Study A at the beginning of the study, but disliked it and left, to be unemployed until enrolling in an open employment training scheme on the completion of the study. He obtained remarkably similar initial results to those of Case Study A on both the Ravens Matrices and the real-life problem-solving and self-advocacy skill tests.

But he was able quickly to generalize strategies taught on the Raven Matrices tasks during the mediation process. This was reflected in his showing a considerable advance on assessment with the Raven Matrices following mediation. Unlike Case Study A, he was able to benefit from mediation on the self-advocacy tasks, requiring, after initial mediation, very little mediation on the tasks 'asking for skills', 'representation', 'equal opportunity', and 'confidentiality'. Indeed, repeated exposure to opportunities to respond, with information embedded within them (a supplementation of information), seemed in itself sufficient for improvement.

These two case studies represent in a small way differing need for supplementation and complementation relating to a number of factors. One of these is past learning experience and opportunity for skill practice, related in the case of Case Study B to ethnic and language minority difference, and probable associated limitations in self-confidence within the larger culture. Another factor is specific difficulty in developing the strategic semantic and memory skills necessary to appraise the meaning of events, as was demonstrated with Case Study A. However, even for such a person, mediation in certain task areas, such as the less complex analogy tasks of the Raven Matrices, led to less need for mediation, and greater success.

These two participants, and ten others, formed an experimental group which subsequently undertook a more extensive training in decision-making and self-advocacy. This training, again largely in a symbiotic one-to-one relationship, but with one peer learner also involved for the Nuie Island subject, focused on systematic information gathering concerning the situation in which self-presentation was to occur, supplementation of the knowledge (including human, community and human service rights), orientation to other person's position and perspectives, the learning of planning, and communication skills. This training programme, especially devised to address decision-making and self-positioning (or self-advocacy skills), drew on the principles and practices of Feuerstein's 'instrumental enrichment' programme for mediating cognitive and metacognitive skills (Feuerstein, Rand, Hoffman and Miller, 1980).

When compared with 12 subjects who had not received this more extensive mediation, the experimental subjects showed a clear advantage in both outcome skill measures (p < 0.05), and in planning strategies. The findings from this study, along with a previous study of self-advocacy by persons with mental retardation, in evaluation of residential quality of care (Howie, Cuming and Raynes, 1984; and Howie and Cuming, 1986), indicated that the following will be important factors in skill development within the symbiotic relationship.

First, there is a set of factors relating to the quality of supplementation and complementation by the person mediating skill development in self-positioning or self-advocacy. This mediation will probably be most effective if the person initially responsible is seen to be removed from the powerful persons determining the self-advocate's world. This would allow for greater feeling of freedom in expression of his or her own social meanings by the self-advocate. Use of questions which are meaningful to the self-advocate, and in a response mode which is most suited to the skills of the self-advocate, are obviously of importance. Positive feedback to the self-advocate in terms of acceptance of the self-advocate's self-positioning and viewpoint (the affirmation which Buber writes about), and positive action in response to expression of preferences and needs, will encourage further positive self-positioning and self-advocacy.

Factors relating to the self-advocate include a strong sense of self as valued, having experienced the meeting of basic needs for affection and protection. Such a strong and positive sense of self is considered important in the ability to reflect on events occurring in the mediation or interactive experience, and to make an independent judgement on them. The study incorporating the two case studies reported above (Howie, 1992), indicated that self-attributions concerning capacities are intricately interwoven with the learning of self-positioning or self-advocacy strategies. Such affective or emotional beliefs, whether publicly communicated or privately held, are products of long-time practised discursive acts. There is evidence from the study that long-term and intensive training and practice is needed to modify negative self-attributions to more facilitating positive self-attributions, and hence a more dynamic attitude to positioning.

As mentioned in discussing the case studies, the strategic semantic and memory skills secured by the self-advocate are necessary for appraising the meaning of events in the past, present and future, as they impinge on the interaction experience. However, the focus should be on ensuring opportunities for developing such skills, including individually designed mediation for the development of such skills, within an expectation that with appropriate mediation such skills can be learnt. It is a challenge to match the changing attitude which has led us to believe that persons with considerable cognitive difficulties can make both rational and moral decisions, with a commitment to work in partnership with a person with special cognitive skill-learning needs, to maximize decision-making and positive self-positioning potential.

5

Reflexive Positioning: Autobiography

R. Harré and L. van Langenhove

Introduction

In this chapter, and in line with this book's priorities, we will explore how biographical studies and discourse analysis can be related to each other. The central insight we will explore is the idea that personal identity and selfhood are manifested in discursive practices, amongst which are the writing and telling of lives. It seems that people have two kinds of identity. There is the kind of identity traditionally studied by psychologists – social and cultural identity – what it is to be, and to be seen to be, a certain kind of person. It has been mainly philosophers who have been concerned with the other kind of identity – personal identity – or what it is to be one and the same individual through a life course (Williams, 1973). Generally people take their individuality for granted, little aware that this deepest aspect of selfhood may be strongly influenced by discursive practices. On the other hand people are usually quite aware of their social identity as it is produced by what they say and do – but rarely do they realize the multiplicity of social identities they deploy in their successful management of everyday life (Goffman, 1959). Somehow psychological theory of the self must encompass both stability and uniqueness, and variability and multiplicity.

The growth of a sense of personal identity is related in complex ways to the development of a person across his/her lifespan. It is within the beginnings of the lifespan that a human being acquires their personhood (cf. Shotter, 1973; 1993) and it is within his/her life that that personhood is expressed in various ways, characteristic of the local culture. Within the lifespan, while personal identity must at some level be stable, social identity generally changes. People have a strong sense of bodily continuity and identity in space and time. If these should fail the psychological consequences are serious. Amnesia and multiple personality syndrome are both, in various ways, disabling. One of the most central problems in the psychology of personhood is how continuous personal identity relates to discontinuous social diversity. If one tries to discuss this problem using only the generalized concept of 'self', confusion is almost certain to arise – as for instance one finds in the writings of some feminist authors (for instance Smith, 1988). There seems to be a tension between the multiplicity of selves as expressed in discursive practices and the fact that across those discursive practices a relatively stable selfhood exists as well. In non-pathological cases we want to say it is always the same person who has an identity, but in another sense that identity is always mutable.

We want to argue that the singularity of selfhood, that which philosophers call 'personal identity', is a product of discursive practices just as much as the multiplicity of selfhood, that which some have called 'social identity'. More-over, in order to make it possible for a person to understand him or herself as a historically continuous unity, (s)he will have to engage in very different – possibly contradictory – forms of biographical talk. One and the same person is now this and now that. One can be both Keeper of the Queen's Pictures and a KGB agent. How is that psychologically possible? Our analysis will show that since both personal and social identities are attributes of discourse, there is no ontological paradox in the evident existence of contradictions and multiplicities in the discourse. Since there is nothing to which the discourse of selfhood refers except itself, the paradoxical air of internal contradiction vanishes. However, were one's self like one's hat, a real entity existing independently of discourses, a contradictory story told about it could be a cause for concern.

In this chapter, we will try to develop the thesis of discontinuity by drawing upon the concept of positioning to show how, in the ways people position themselves in talk and writing, personal identity can be expressed through the presentation of a biography. Secondly, we will use some of the differences between 'orality' and 'literality' to differentiate biographical talk from a literary (auto)biography. Thirdly, we will briefly show how much of the present ambiguity of the concept of self and the related concepts of personhood, biography and identity emerges out of the mistaken idea that the literary biography can be a source-model for understanding biographical talk. Finally we will discuss the implications of the foregoing for lifespan research.

Positioning Oneself as Somebody with a Personal Identity

In positioning theory, the concept of positioning is introduced as a metaphor to enable an investigator to grasp how persons are 'located' within conversations as observably and subjectively coherent participants in jointly produced storylines.

One mode of positioning of particular interest to us in the context of this chapter is the intentional self-positioning in which a person expresses his/her personal identity.

The discursive practices of positioning make possible three ways of expressing and experiencing one's personal identity or unique selfhood: by stressing one's agency in claiming responsibility for some action; by indexing one's statements with the point of view one has on its relevant world; or by presenting a description/evaluation of some past event or episode as a contribution to one's biography. How personal identity can be expressed through indexing one's view of the world and one's responsibilities for action by using pronouns is discussed in Muhlhauser and Harré (1990). For example, in so seemingly simple a statement as 'I can feel a draft', the content of the utterance (the experience suffered by the speaker) is indexed with his/her spatial and temporal location, and, most importantly, as a claim about a state of affairs it is indexed with its speaker's moral standing. That is, the speaker, by using the pronoun rather than an impersonal form, takes responsibility for the reliability of the claim and thus positions themselves, in a default moral location, so to speak. The relations between the discursive practices of positioning and the telling of an autobiography can be expressed as follows. First of all, an important distinction has to be made between statements which are part of an autobiography, that is, which describe a life event from the point of view of the actor, and statements which are themselves life events. In general, the uttering of a statement descriptive of a life event is also a life event, though statements whose utterings are life events are not by any means all themselves descriptive of life events. Consider the following exchange:

A: I thought you had gone to London.
B: No, I decided to spend the afternoon in the library.

A's remark reports an event in his/her autobiography, and at the same time deletes an item from A's biography of B. B confirms the deletion. But in preparing the relevant item in his/her autobiography, namely a decision, B at the same time provides A with a substitute item for his/her biography of B. By implication, nothing being said to the contrary, B's remark also adds a further item to his/her autobiography, namely an afternoon in the library. The discursive act of positioning thus involves a reconstructive element: the biographies of the one being positioned and the positions may be subject to rhetorical redescriptions. The question is how this re-writing has to be understood with regard to the personal identity and selfhood. This requires us to pay attention to what exactly autobiographical talk is and how such talk relates to the written genre of autobiographies.

Autobiographical Talk and Written Autobiographies

A sense of self is always embedded in a particular culture. It can therefore be expected that historical and cultural differences will affect the prevailing sense of self (cf. Logan, 1987). An important aspect of any particular culture is the extent to which it is a literacy or an orality dominated culture. In most cultures today language is used in two ways: it is spoken and it is written. This distinction seems so obvious that it is often forgotten that writing is actually a rather recent invention. It developed around the year 3500 BC. Before that, all human cultures were exclusively oral cultures. The transition towards literate cultures has been a long and slow process, the technology of writing being not always applauded by everybody. Even Plato in the *Phaedrus* has Socrates say that writing is inhuman as it pretends to establish outside the mind what in reality can only be in the mind. Moreover, Plato's Socrates urges that writing destroys memory and that the written word cannot defend itself as the natural spoken word can.

All ways of using language, including writing, have structuring effects on thought since they impose structure on expression. One would expect the psychodynamics of orality to be quite different from that of the written word. In recent years, certain basic differences have been discovered between the ways of managing knowledge and its verbalization in primary oral cultures and those in cultures deeply affected by the use of writing (cf. Ong, 1982). We think that this research is of major importance in understanding how, in our literate cultures, personal identity is expressed by biographical stories. Undoubtedly such oral stories are likely to be highly influenced by literary genres, but they are still oral stories with all the properties belonging to them. Biographical talk has to be understood as stories that resemble the Greek oral narrative, the epic, more than they resemble the literary genre of autobiography in the tradition of Augustine and Rousseau. Unfortunately, within the social sciences (including lifespan development, psychobiography), it is the latter which is usually taken as a model in understanding biographical talk. In our view this choice of exemplar is a mistake. In order to show that the written autobiography is not an appropriate source model for understanding how people express their personal identity in biographical talk, we will draw attention to some major differences between orality and literacy and their relation to (auto)biographical stories (cf. Ong, 1982). Four topics will be dealt with: (a) thought and expression in oral cultures; (b) the nature of oral autobiographical stories; (c) the effect of writing on thought and expression; (d) the autobiography as a literary genre.

Thought and expression in oral cultures

In a culture with no knowledge whatsoever of writing, words have no visual presence. Nothing can ever be 'looked up': words are only sounds which may or may not be recalled. This means that in oral cultures material that has to be recalled needs to be organized in a way that facilitates recall. It has to be so organized that with help of mnemonics and phonetic formulas it can be remembered. For example, the phonetic forms of Anglo-Saxon personal names facilitated remembering family relationships. The most common way to store, organize and communicate what is known in oral cultures is through stories of human actions. Such oral stories have an important property that distinguishes them from written stories: they are changeable. Actually they need to be changeable in order to function the way they do. Not only are they subject to change because the story-teller cannot make reference back to a written standard, they are also changeable because they are told (or sung) in particular contexts. Stories are the result of an interaction between the narrator, the audience and the narrator's memory. A story-teller has to speak in accordance with the demands of his/her audience. Mbiti (1966) observed about story-telling in Kenya that 'the plot of the story and the sequence of its main part remain the same, but the narrator has to supply meat to the skeleton' (p. 26).

When words are restricted to sounds this not only determines modes of expression but also thought processes. In an oral culture it is essential to think memorable thoughts, otherwise such thoughts can never be effectively recovered. Ong (1982) has listed several characteristics of orally based thought and expression that make for memorability. Amongst others he noted the additive rather then subordinative style, the aggregative rather than the analytic style, and the redundant or 'copious' form of the stories told. All these features of oral narration should be discernible in the told autobiography

The nature of oral autobiographical stories

Autobiographical telling is a form of narration. The grammar of autobiographical discourse should, therefore, be similar to that of other forms of narration. A general scheme of pronoun grammar for expressing the narrative voice has been proposed by Urban (1989). It depends upon the common distinction between *anaphora* and *indexicality*. 'He' is an anaphor in that it forms a link in a series of expressions coreferential with an original name or definite description, and is rarely used indexically. By contrast 'I' is a pure indexical in that its reference is fixed contextually to the speaker of the moment, indexing his or her utterances with the speaker's spatio-temporal location and moral standing. 'I' is not functionally equivalent to a proper name. There are two modes of pronominal self-reference in autobiographical telling with subtly different force. Compare 'He said that I should repair the fence' with 'He said "You repair the fence".'

Urban has suggested two principles governing the grammar of the narrative voice. In such sentence frames as 'Sharon said "I shall try to do better next time" ', 'I' is coreferential with 'Sharon' and so an anaphor. Its indexical force is suspended. But in 'Sharon said to me "You cannot work here any more" ' (a1), 'You' is coindexical with 'me', the (dative) object of the main clause, and refers back to an introductory but understood 'I report that . . .' Both index the content of the whole statement with the relevant attributes of the speaker. An explicit indexical framing is not uncommon in autobiographical telling: 'I want you to know that Sharon said to me "You cannot work here anymore" ' (a2). Or in *oratio obliqua*, 'I tell you that Sharon said that I could not work there any more' (b). Is there any difference in force between the (a) forms and the (b) form?

Let us call the embedded indexical in both cases a pseudoanaphor, in that the embedded pronoun is coreferential with an indexical expression rather than with a proper name, and so distinct from the simple anaphoric first person in which I report what Sharon said about herself. Urban points out several important features of these usages in autobiographical narrations. In the (a) forms, the speaker invites the hearer to hear the utterance as if he or she were 'momentarily taking on the role of the third person referent in a kind of play-acting' (Urban, 1989: 35). It is a kind of metaphor in which only the first person (the (a) uses) provides the 'metaphorical pivot' (Urban, 1989). But in the disquotative or (b) form the speaker indexes him/herself as 'the concrete representation of a character in discourse' (1989: 37). We might put the difference thus: in the use of the (a) form I play myself while in the (b) form I am myself. According to Urban (1989: 49) the fundamental distinction is between an 'I' pointing to an everyday self (the (b) form) and an 'I' pointing to an imaginary or assumed 'self'. In the latter case, the individual speakers to whom the 'I' points are in fact anaphoric substitutes for characters in a narrative text.

We could express the distinction in forms of autobiographical telling as a difference between merely reporting what went on in a life, the (b) form, and narrating the story of a life, the (a) form. In the former the local conventions of story-telling, plot structure and so on are irrelevant. In the latter they may have a dominant role in the organization of and emphases placed on the material. We can now return to the theme of positioning. It is clear that these seemingly unimportant grammatical variations conceal functionally quite distinct positions. Positioning oneself as the subject of mere reporting is quite a different matter from positioning oneself as a character in a lively drama. In the distinction between the (b) form and the (a) form of autobiographical telling we have identified one of the major devices through which speakers adopt positions in telling their lives.

In sketching the logical grammar of first-person pronouns we emphasized the double indexicality of their use. They index content with its spatio-temporal location of the embodied speakers and the social force of an utterance with the moral standing of the speakers. Autobiographical acts of telling of the (b) form do not invoke spatio-temporal indexicality. Only in the (a) form does autobiographical telling articulate the speaker's moral commitment to the acts of narration and to the acts narrated. The (a) form is a personal story in a way that the (b) form of autobiography can never be. Thus the (a) is an act of self-positioning in a way that the (b) is not.

Restructuring of thought and expression through writing

In a literate world, words are not only events (when spoken), they also are things (signs written or inscribed on flat surfaces). The transition from orality to literacy has been a slow process but in today's Western cultures literality dominates orality. Nevertheless, even in our cultures we can find some practices that are in the mould of the old oral tradition. One of them is the oral defence of a doctoral dissertation. Another is the conventions that cover the work of some jury systems in which jurors have to 'hear' a case, without taking any notes (Van Langenhove, 1989). But script, and especially its print form, have had an enormous impact on thought and expression. Postman (1985) speaks in this respect of the 'typographic mind'. First of all, we no longer have to rely solely on our own or others' memory. When literate people say they know something about, for instance, psychology or the battle of Borodino, then this knowledge will refer to something that is eventually available to them in writing. What people experience and what needs to be recalled is often transformed into written texts.

Secondly, the possibility of producing texts has altered the form of knowledgeable things. In writing, 'backwards scanning' makes it possible to eliminate inconsistencies. There is no equivalence for this in an oral performance: a spoken word can never be erased, yet oral expressions can be retrospectively revised and redefined very easily. Knowing that texts have been scanned backwards, gives them a sense of closure: a sense that what is found in any text has been finalized. Written or printed texts are supposed to represent the words of an author in a definite or 'final' form. As recorded, the verbal past takes on an immutable and concrete form. Yet any written record can be challenged, not only with respect to its correctness as a transcription but secondly with respect to the readings to which it is subject in this or that context.

When a story is written, the reader can only try to grasp the meaning of the texts by interpreting them. He cannot, as in an oral story, intervene to change the text. In telling a story one is never really a soliloquist protected from interruptions. In writing a story one necessarily is. The writer's audience is almost always imagined, tacit. Only rarely is it present at the time of writing. In short, while oral tellings and written records are both subject to negotiation with respect to their authenticity, challenges are directed to radically different kinds of entities.

The autobiography as a literary genre

The shift from orality to literacy is registered in the many genres of the verbal arts and practices, including biography. The very idea of a biography involves the situatedness of a person in time. The first written biographies and autobiographies appeared in the Ancient Greek culture. The most famous of them are the biographies written by Theophrastus and Plutarch. But these biographies were characterized by their lack of historicity and individuality. Characters did not develop, nor were the lives recorded marked by idiosyncrasy. Probably the first 'real' autobiography was written by Augustine. Although in many ways still resembling the epic literary form, his *Confessions* have as a main innovation the creation of a narrative sequence of the biographical facts of an individual human life. It was, however, not written in order to present a chronicle of the events in an individual's life. Its purpose was to tell a story of a conversion. It chronicles person transformation, development and change.

The true originator of the autobiography as a literary genre in itself was J. J. Rousseau, whose confessions were published in 1767. Since that moment the autobiography has stood in opposition to fiction. It is supposed to represent a truth about a given and pre-existing reality, the lifecourse of an individual. As Elbaz (1988) in his study of autobiographical discourse notes: 'the myth of autobiography involves two related postulates: that the self is inside each one of us, and that it is a pregiven structure, a finished product' (p. 153). Given what has been said earlier about the restructuring of thought and expression through writing, it is evident that written biographies or autobiographies simply have to be represented in a finalized way. Given the dominance of the written word in modern literate cultures, it would not be unreasonable to expect the form of the literary genre '(auto-)biography' to serve as a social representation or template for oral 'life-telling'. Nevertheless we believe that this influence, potent in any aspect of life (such as sealing agreements and contracts), may not be so dominant in the oral tradition of autobiographical telling. This is an important and researchable question to which we do not have an answer.

The Concept of Self in Biographical Perspective

Within social psychology the self has often been regarded as an 'information processing structure' (cf. Markus and Wurf, 1987) that uses memories of past events in order to establish a sense of personal identity. This theory, proposed first in the seventeenth century by Locke, has been very much criticized by philosophers on grounds of internal incoherence. Two different approaches exist within a framework of mainly 'social cognition' research. In one, people are seen as skilful at denying personal changes and maintaining biographical consistency. In the other, people are seen as constantly 'reinventing' their past in order to fit with current circumstances. In both cases one's personal history is conceived as something 'within' the person that has to be 'recalled' and which is subject to 'cognitive biases'. Of course, all this presupposes the continuity of personal identity as a numerical singularity. The positioning of the subject as author of *the* story confirms its singularity. After all, it seems incontestable that the subject of an autobiography has a superior right to produce it over the biographer whose position is no more than vicarious.

Ross and Conway (1986) list three major problems in how people remember their own past: there is selective recall, there is reinterpretation and re-explanation of the past, and finally there is the filling of gaps in the memory by inferring what probably happened. In such a view, the self (once again hypostatized as some inner entity or core of being!) is regarded as a 'personal historian'. The use of this metaphor leads researchers to extrapolations from 'biases and errors of trained historians when they reconstruct and interpret the events of previous eras' (Ross and Conway, 1986: 122) to 'the average person's remembering of his or her personal history' (p. 122). Greenwald (1980) even pictured the self as a 'totalitarian' historian who – as occurs with recorded history in Orwell's novel *1984* – constantly 'refabricates' the story of his/her personal past. Greenwald distinguished a further three types of 'cognitive biases' which cause people to revise their history, 'thereby engaging in practices not ordinarily admired by historians' (Greenwald, 1980: 604): egocentricity (the self is perceived as more central to events than it is), benefitance (the self is perceived as selectively responsible for desired but not for undesired outcomes) and conservatism (the self is resistant to change).

Behind such views is a double conception of the self. On the one hand it is conceived as a 'thing' within people that can be 'disclosed', 'distorted', 'perceived', 'fabricated', 'be subject to inconsistencies' and so on. On the other hand it is the conscious being who perceives and experiences this 'thing' and tells the story of its life. Moreover, what people present as their selves or think about as their self is always seen as subject to comparison with the 'real' self, which is to a great extent to be equated with the 'real' biography or personal history of the person. Within such research, the self is reified as something autonomous within the person that uses personal memories to fabricate itself. But that view conflates the self as perceiver with the self as perceived. It would not be unreasonable to suggest that part of the problem with this approach is the mistaken idea that there exists one real, inner self to which all these things have happened. But there is another possibility, relating to the idea that there exists just one definite and 'real' autobiography that can be distorted. It could be that the literate conception of autobiography as a history is, in the first place, wrongly taken as a model for the story of the self.

In recent years, mainstream approaches in psychology have been much criticized. One of the new emerging specialities is 'narratology' (cf. Sarbin, 1986) in which the structures and uses of the stories that people tell are the focus of research rather than people's behaviour conceived as the lawful effects of causes. As an intentional action, often deployed in the working out of some project, story-telling, though a sequence of human actions, is not a 'behaviour' in the sense that this term has taken on in psychology. Within narratology, the self has been studied in a different way from that pictured above. In Gergen and Gergen (1988: p. xx) the idea of 'narratives of the self' is introduced. By this is meant stories that 'serve as a critical means by which we make ourselves intelligible within the social world'. Such narratives of the self are seen by Gergen and Gergen not as 'fundamentally possessions of the individual, rather they are products of social interchange'. In introducing the Gergen and Gergen chapter in the book which he edits, Berkowitz (1988) explicitly equates their conception of narratives of the self with the idea that the self is a narrative. This Delphic idea seems implicit in Gergen and Gergen (1988), since they assert that the self comes into being in a life story. But if the self is to be taken as a narrative, then the question arises what kind of a narrative it is, a literary or an oral one? And of course, also, who is telling it?

For Gergen and Gergen the answer is clearly a literary narrative. This follows from their ideas about the form of self-narratives. Referring to literary criticism, semiotics and historiography, they have synthesized what they consider to be the components 'important to the construction of intelligible narrative in contemporary western cultures' (p. 20). These components are (i) the establishment of a valued end point, (ii) the selection of events relevant to the goal state, (iii) the temporal ordering of events, (iv) the establishment of causal linkages and (v) the framing of the story by demarcation signs. Consequently, the illustrations of self-narratives they mention are all well-defined episodes such as stories about one's first love affair, the morning's class, or lunch with a companion.

In introducing the idea of written stories, their conception of the self is still a reified one. This follows from their discussion of the 'validity' of the self-narrative. While they rightly assert that such validity is determined by cultural conventions they also state that validity is not matched by the 'absolute match between word and thing'. But in that way they still emphasize that there is a 'real thing' with which socially constructed stories can be matched.

The confusion of thought in this idea of the self as narrative not only derives from privileging the literary model for their conception of an autobiography but confuses 'self' as the kind of person I think I am (disclosed in the events of my life), and 'self' as the unitary person to whom those events occur. Somehow they assume an ego while denying it. The discursive construction of storylines is just one element in the discursive triad – the positioned speaker and the social force of his/her narration are also necessary elements for any narrative to be relatively determinate.

Although it is certainly true that people can and will tell stories about themselves that are modelled upon literary biographical stories, or upon other forms of literature, these are not the only situations in which biographical talk is used. In fact, while seldom telling complete biographical stories, people are constantly engaged in all kinds of self-positioning in which self-narratives occur that are not modelled by any literate plots. Therefore, the self should not be equated with a story having a plot. Rather, selves emerge from complex bodies of knowledge that are organized like oral stories, and particularly as stories in the (a)-form in which the indexical commitments of the speakers differ throughout the discourse. The self has no plot, only persons (that is selves as expressed in social life) can have plots. The relationship between a self and a person can be understood in terms of positioning and rhetorical redescription. The self refers to the form of inner unity which all discourses of personal experiences must exemplify. While engaged in conversations, people position themselves and others. That tacit self-positioning 'reflects the self', that is, creates the necessary order, through the grammatical properties of the unfolding language games. But positioning can also be intentional and at that moment rhetorical redescriptions occur in which the self is 'transformed' into a person. The more somebody engages in rhetorical redescriptions of his/her self, the more (s)he will become a 'round' character taking responsibility for his/her life, rather than the 'flat' or formal subject of a sequence of accidental episodes. In this sense, when a person is asked or decides to write his/her autobiography, the person will begin to *change* their life and consequently their self. When a person has finished writing his/her autobiography, he/she will be a different person, and yet that only makes sense if he/she is the very same person.

Constraints on Lifespan Research

Orality and literacy, far from being mutually contradictory poles, can interact and support each other. In our culture both oral and written communication forms exist, and though it is certain that the written word has to a great extent shaped the spoken word, there still seem to be 'autonomous' oral worlds. From what has been said above, it should by now be clear that we consider the self to be a feature of a basically oral culture. When people refer to their own or others' histories, they have to rely on recollection. Only seldom is written material available. Consequently, the narrative self has to be treated as a collection of stories suspended from the identity of a person. But, as we have argued, that identity is *also* discursively produced. Whatever is needed to be recalled from a person's life will be organized in stories. But given the usual oral context of such stories, they resemble more the epic than the autobiography. As indexed with the unifying features of a person's discourse they present a self as not only embodied but responsible. They present character. Necessarily they occupy positions.

It has been argued that the self should be regarded as a theoretical entity: the sense of personal identity – how someone experiences his/her unique selfhood – is really the use that person makes of his/her 'self' theory. According to this point of view, that theoretical concept organizes knowledge and action, but has no independent referent other than the person him or herself. The distinction we have introduced between orality and literacy can be used to refine this notion of the self as a theoretical entity. From the point of view of the philosophy of science, a theory can be regarded as a set of propositions. Theories are represented in texts (scientific publications) and have as such a finalized form. But theories are also used by people or to some extent known by people. In that sense, theories also have a 'social representation' (cf. Moscovici, 1983). If we think of the self as the leading concept of a theory a person has about him/herself, it is in this latter sense: a person has several and changing representations of him/herself, centred on the theoretical concept of a personal unity. The Moscovician idea of a 'representation of knowledge across persons' can be used as a metaphor for understanding how a single person has different social or presented selves across all positioning – situations in which (s)he occurs as one and only person. Writing an autobiography, answering questionnaires like the 'who-am-I ?', can be regarded as the construction of finalized written theories. But, just as it is impossible to write a definite and complete theory on any scientific subject, it is equally impossible to write a similar theory about oneself.

If we take the distribution of knowledge in an oral culture (i.e., child-rearing knowledge amongst working-class families) as a model for how self is organized, this has important implications for research. We think that the study of lifespan development can no longer be equated with the study of (auto-)biographies. Rather it should be the study of how and for what reason people use autobiographical stories at different ages, in short the dynamics of oral positioning. In the study of a socially distributed knowledge system a key question is who has a right to use which items of knowledge under what circumstances. Up to now little research has been done on the longitudinal study of biographical presentations of single persons in relation to the positions they may occupy, from time to time. Moreover, the bulk of lifespan research and psychobiographical studies have focused on either describing the major 'stages' in the life of persons (e.g., Levinson, 1978) or on developing content-analytical tools for analysing the content of autobiographies (cf. Bromley, 1977; De Waele and Harré, 1979). However valuable these approaches, we think they have to be completed by a study of how people develop rhetorical redescriptions of their own lives. The crucial question is which actions of a person are judged by that person to be relevant as part of an autobiographical study? And this takes us back to the points made in the earlier sections of this chapter concerning the discursive triad – position–social force–storyline. A useful starting point for such a study can be found in the work of Vallacher and Wegner (1985, 1989) on action identification. According to that theory, people have a tendency to reify actions. Actions are assumed to be real (i.e. the act 'throwing a brick through a window'), while they are actually mental constructions from a multiplicity of possible interpretations of one and only one material occurrence. Any action can be identified in different ways: 'throwing a brick' can equally be identified as 'creating a nuisance' or as 'breaking glass'. Such identifications are not synonyms, they are different psychological and social identifications of what is only in its material form the same. People 'act' a whole day, a whole life course long. Most of those actions are never consciously identified while others are, for instance when a person is asked to account for his/her conduct. Whenever the identification of one's own actions is called for, this includes the use of the word 'I'. To the question 'What are you doing?', a person can answer 'I am . . .' Other questions can be asked. For instance, the question 'Who are you?'. In such cases people will make use of their own action references as well.

All this boils down to the notion that in the many different stories that people tell about themselves, reference to a limited number of past (and possibly future) actions is made in telling their own life. This has nothing to do with 'memory': the question is not what people 'forget' about their own life, but why they make use in a given situation of this and that actions as part of their personal stories. Generally speaking, this will be determined by two things. First by the stories that they already have told. Once a story is told and re-told, it begins to live a life of its own, just as with the stories told in an oral culture. The 'self' can be seen as a partly changing audience created by the stories and to which the stories about the self are told. Secondly, it should be clear that conversations with other people will give rise to new stories since different people will ask different questions. In line with positioning theory, those questions can be regarded as forcing the addressee into certain positions by adopting a position oneself.

Conclusion

Lifespan research cannot simply take for granted the widespread idea in our Western culture that we each live one 'biography'. Neither can it proceed by studying 'individual lives'. The problem, then, is that a conversational approach to the study of selves and biographies has to be developed. At present, the work of Hermans (1987, 1989) seems to be closest to such an approach. However, it should be clear that developing a suitable methodology is not enough. Along with that, the people that are 'studied' should become aware of their tendency to reify their own lives to a single biography. The above advocated idea of the self as a theory with properties of oral stories thus involves more than a scientific stance: at the end of the day the question is when and why will people think of themselves in such a way? It might well be that for those who are living in a postmodern era, such a view of oneself is more practical than the idea that one is or has a 'round' character.

6

Reflexive Positioning: Culture and Private Discourse

F. M. Moghaddam

Introduction

Within the persons/conversations referential grid, positioning can be understood as the process by which speakers discursively construct personal stories, affording positions for speakers to take up in relation to each other so that participants' actions are made intelligible and relatively determinate as social acts. In moving from the use of 'role' to 'position' as central organizing concepts of social analysis, the focus of attention shifts from the more ritualistic and formal to the more dynamic and negotiable aspects of interpersonal encounters. In this discussion, we extend the positioning concept for use in the *intrapersonal* domain, where the term 'reflexive positioning' will be taken to refer to the process by which persons position themselves privately in private discourse. At least three recent developments in the psychological literature on the self have led us to propose that the positioning concept may also be useful in the analysis of intrapersonal processes.

First, there is an increasing tendency to conceive of identity as something that is not always conferred on or ascribed to individuals, but actively negotiated and achieved by them (Erchak, 1992; Greenwood, 1994). In departing from the focus of the classical dramaturgical model (Goffman, 1959) on 'role' as the determining basis of action, the positioning concept affords us a view of ourselves 'as choosing subjects, locating ourselves in conversations according to those narrative forms with which we are familiar and bringing to those narratives our own subjective lived histories through which we have learnt metaphors, characters, and plot'.

Second, there is a growing interest in the conceptualization of such aspects of the self as 'self-esteem' and 'self-concept' not as global, generalized averages of self-images, but in terms of ongoing, dynamic and continuously changing processes. For example, such concepts as 'current ongoing self-esteem' (Wells,

1992) and 'working self-concept' (Cantor, Markus, Niedenthal and Nurius, 1986; Markus and Nurius, 1986, 1987) have been proposed to elaborate on the idea of a self-esteem and a self-concept 'of a given moment'. Clearly, there is a need for frameworks such as the positioning concept which capture the more fluid and dynamic aspects of intrapersonal processes.

Third, there is an increasing awareness that the existing views of psychology of the self tend to reflect contemporary Western, and particularly North American, ideals of personhood (Miller, in press; Moghaddam, 1987; Sampson, 1977, 1981), summarized by one researcher as analytic, monotheistic, individualistic, materialistic and rationalistic (Johnson, 1985). Accompanying this awareness of a Western ethnocentric bias in the contemporary literature on the self is an interest in modes of analysis which transcend cultural limits, such as the limits imposed by the individualistic and rationalistic conceptualization of the self which reflects a Western view of personhood (Hermans, Kempen and Van Loon, 1992; Hermans and Kempen, 1993).

Our aims in this discussion are twofold:

1   to extend the positioning concept to the intrapersonal level in an exploratory fashion, and
2   to broaden the scope of the positioning discussion by considering how positioning practices are culturally embedded.

Because reflexive positioning cannot be examined in isolation – removed from a consideration of the specific moral orders in which the speakers are operating – it is our view that a satisfying discussion of positioning (on any level) absolutely *requires* the inclusion of cultural considerations. In taking these steps, we hope to use the positioning framework to present an active and dynamic view of the self, while being mindful that fundamental aspects of intrapersonal positioning practices may vary widely with culture.

Reflexive Positioning

The concept of reflexive positioning

In the same way that autobiographical aspects of conversations are the basic matter of interpersonal positioning, reflexive positioning is a process by which one intentionally or unintentionally positions oneself in unfolding personal stories told to oneself. This process can take various forms, the most elaborate of which might be the writing of one's private diary or autobiography.

Few lives, however, are written down in diaries and autobiographies: most are offered 'locally', as fragments of unfolding personal stories of a speaker to himself or herself. One's appraisal of one's performance, one's justification for having taken a certain course of action, the attribution of one's actions to the whims of supernatural powers, one's private response to having been depicted by someone else in this way or that, one's supposing what repercussions one's actions will have on one's group, and the formulation of an anecdote about one's day that one plans to tell another (and the imagined response of the listener) are all examples of ways in which persons position themselves to themselves throughout the course of a day. Indeed, one inevitably positions oneself in ongoing internal discourse, as all utterances both position a speaker and must emanate from some position as a speaker.

Discursive positions in storylines and the 'illocutionary force' of one's speech-acts (which generally refers to the status of a communication, for instance, a promise, command, description, warning, apology or exhortation (Lyons, 1977)) mutually determine each other. More specifically, 'The social meaning of what has been said will be shown to depend upon the positioning of interlocutors which is itself a product of the social force a conversation action is taken "to have".'

In the telling of fragments of one's personal stories, various discursive positions emerge and are made available for participants to 'take up' in the storylines. For example, in the recounting of a personal story of an encounter with a con artist, one can position oneself as smart or foolish, astute or gullible, sophisticated or naive, suspicious or trusting, powerful or powerless, dominant or submissive, and so on, based on how one's utterances are hearable to oneself with respect to particular dimensions which are salient to the speaker. Claims such as 'there is nothing I could have done to prevent this; the con artist beats everybody' may reflexively position a person as helpless and ineffective, while claims such as 'I'm not a fool; I just tend to look for the best in people' may reflexively position a person as optimistic and trusting. Statements such as 'I'm a home-maker', 'I'm the youngest member of the family', or 'I'm a graduate student' have a very different social effect, and position a person in a very different manner from statements such as 'I'm *just* a home-maker', 'I'm *only* the youngest member of the family' or 'I'm *still* a graduate student'.

Conversely, the social force of the speech-act depends in part on the positions one takes up. In other words, the illocutionary force of reflexive positioning is circumscribed to some extent by the way a person positions himself or herself. Positioned as ineffective, one's utterance 'I guess I've learned something from being conned once' is hearable as a question or conjecture, but positioned as effective the same utterance is hearable as a declaration or assertion. A person who positions the self as ineffective may be unlikely to say convincingly in the next instant 'I am going to motivate myself to change my life', whereas a person who positions him/herself as effective is not likely to say convincingly, 'there is nothing I can do to change my life'. If, however, a person who was reflexively positioned as ineffective convinces himself or herself that he or she is effective, this would involve a changing and shifting in reflexive positions. We shall expand on the dynamic character of positioning, an important feature of this concept, in the next section.

A reflexive position in private discourse, then, is a figurative concept through reference to which one's moral and personal attributes as a speaker are compendiously collected by oneself so that one's speech-acts can be made intelligible and relatively determinate to oneself. The term 'private discourse' will be taken here to cover the multiplicity of speech phenomena not aimed at others, but which is similar to and perhaps stems from public conversations (Luria, 1976; Vygotsky, 1962).

Although our focus in this discussion is on intrapersonal positioning, we do not mean to isolate it from positioning practices on other levels, such as the interpersonal and intergroup levels. Clearly, persons can and often do simultaneously position themselves on more than one level at a time, a process which we call 'parallel positioning'. We can expect the three levels of positioning to mutually influence each other, so that, for example, the ways in which a person positions herself to another person both affects and is affected by her reflexive positioning. A job applicant who is privately unsure she is qualified for a job may engage in interpersonal positioning in 'congruent' or 'incongruent' ways. She may, for instance, tell the interviewer 'I feel quite anxious'. Or, she may position herself as particularly confident and experienced.

The dynamic nature of reflexive positioning

Reflexive positions are always emerging, changing and shifting based in part on how a person's utterances are hearable to oneself as speaker. One's life story and fragments of it are never fixed or sealed but are in ceaseless movement, continually retold as new experiences are integrated. So it is that the convert pays tribute to Divine intervention throughout his life from the first, even though he has lived half of it as an atheist. The objective events in his history have not changed but he recasts his story with the resources (characters, metaphors, images, etc.) afforded by the vantage points of a new repertoire of positions. By this account, Jane Bloggs' autobiography must more accurately be referred to as *one* of Jane Bloggs' autobiographies – it is only one combination of positioning steps out of an endless array of dances.

Because discursive positions and the vantage points they afford are dynamic and constantly in flux, changing and shifting in relation to an evolving storyline, meanings of what one has said to oneself can also modulate and change with the evolving narrative and one's shifting discursive positions. This is apparent when one rereads a journal, each time from new vantage points in relation to what has since transpired, and as an episode that makes sense with reference to one's presently unfolding narrative. Just as the illocutionary force of speech-acts and behaviours in interpersonal positioning is determined by a mutually created storyline, one's own thoughts and behaviours are interpreted within the framework of the particular autobiographical storyline which is unfolding at that time.

Certain storylines and particular reflexive positions, however, may become more salient to a person than others. The respective narratives of the 'former alcoholic', 'orphan', 'underdog', 'struggling artist', or 'future lawyer', and the accompanying range of positions these themes make available, may tempt the speaker into compelling narratives that fit so comfortably that they may even conceal possibilities of choice. In view of this, the goal of therapy might be better articulated as an effort to free clients from relatively 'frozen' narratives enabling them to construct new personal stories (Spence, 1981).

Reflexive positioning and the dialogical self

How is it possible for a person to be the positioner and the one positioned? For James (1890), an important and inherent characteristic of the self is its reflexivity. This is apparent in the classic Jamesian distinction between self-as-knower (self as subject, or the I) and self-as-known (self as object, the Me). The Jamesian I (characterized by continuity, distinctness, and volition), metaphorically observes and reports on the actions of the Me (comprised of material and spiritual and social constituents). In this way, the I positions the Me in the way that it reports on and interprets the movements of the Me within the particular storyline. The inherently dynamic character of the self is apparent in the problem of the 'fleeting I': as the I positions the Me the I of the previous moment becomes the Me which can then be repositioned by the I.

Is the I limited to observing the Me from one vantage point, speaking with a singular voice of an omniscient narrator – the voice, presumably, of the self? We rather follow a multivocal conceptualization of the self which resists an 'authorial self' (Wolf, 1990). Instead, one often seems to be eavesdropping on a murmur of voices in an internal dialogue (Bakhtin, 1981; Todorov, 1981) so that one has access to many vantage points, allowing multiple – and often oppositional – readings of the same thoughts, behaviours and events. Multivocal private discourse (e.g., in solitary play) has been documented in children as young as two years old, the ability to adopt multiple stances towards the same objects or events developing into 'voices' marked by distinctive patterns of performance, content and linguistic features (Wolf, 1990).

Hermans and his associates (Hermans, Kempen and Van Loon 1992; Hermans and Kempen, 1993) have elaborated on this notion of a 'dialogical self', proposing that the I can take up a multiplicity of '*I* positions' in which it not only takes up different vantage points, but 'speaks' with 'voices' emanating from these various positions. A useful link has been drawn between the notion of a dialogical view of self and Dostoevsky's polyphonic novel, in which the independent voices and stories of several heroes are braided into a common storyline (Bakhtin, 1973). So it is that a person's private narrative comprises not one, but a polyphony of 'voices'. Each voice 'speaks' from a different position, from which each can confer with and oppose the other in a dialogical relation to mutually negotiate a storyline. Thus, a person who has just been promoted to a desirable position overhears a myriad of voices as she anticipates how she will relate the news to her co-workers, imagines their individual responses, recalls what her deceased uncle used to say as he belittled her achievements, replays the conversation that just took place at the board meeting, and wonders what her supervisors might have told the board behind closed doors.

Further resisting an individualistic and rationalistic conception of the self, Hermans and his associates incorporate Caughey's (1984) and Watkins' (1986) views, rejecting the notion that social relationships should be taken to refer only to relationships with actual beings. More specifically, Caughey (1984) observed that cultural studies of social organization have neglected a fundamental aspect of subjective experience which he proposes to be characteristic of every society: pervasive involvement in imaginary social relationships with various imaginary beings. He provides a typology of three classes of such 'beings' with whom people often 'interact': media figures (such as film stars, world-class athletes, charismatic leaders, and so on, through whom people often vicariously experience a fantasy world), imaginary figures produced by an individual's own consciousness (for example, ghosts, dream figures, guardian angels, and one's conscience), and imaginary replicas of people whom we interact with or once interacted with in our daily lives (such as spouses, parents, friends, mentors, leaders). Watkins (1986) contends that imaginal others influence our encounters with 'actual' others just as our encounters with others affect imaginal interactions.

Imaginal dialogues are thought to play a pervasive and central role in daily life in both Western and non-Western cultures (Hermans et al., 1992; Hermans and Kempen, 1993). Thus, another way the self is positioned intrapersonally is through the storylines which evolve in imaginal dialogues and conversations in which the 'I' takes up a multiplicity of positions in relation to multiple 'Me's' based on the vantage points of oneself as well as a host of imaginary others.

Cultural Variations in Reflexive Positioning

Positioning always takes place within the context of a specific moral order of speaking, such as a bridge club, church choir, group of artisans, assembly of worshippers, gender group, ethnic group, tribe and society. Moral orders are maintained by certain linguistic practices through which social relations between people (such as friendship), between persons and things (such as property) and between groups of people are regulated (such as team games and social hierarchies), and by which social norms or standards for personality, character and physical appearances are promulgated.

Clearly, then, reflexive positioning cannot be considered in isolation, removed from a consideration of the specific moral orders in which the speakers are operating. Our view is that a satisfying discussion of positioning on any level absolutely *requires* the inclusion of cultural considerations. Here, we explore only three examples of how cultural factors may fundamentally affect positioning practices. Positioning practices vary with:

1 the particular cultural ideals persons desire to move toward through positioning;
2 the particular dimensions which persons find relevant in positioning themselves and others in discourse;
3 the preferred forms of autobiographic telling, which may influence the types of stories people tell themselves about themselves in the process of positioning.

Positioning and cultural ideals

Reflexive positioning is integrally associated with local normative systems through cultural ideals, which act as guides for persons in given cultures as they position themselves. Consider, as examples, American transcendentalists and Islamic Sufis, which both enjoy a rich tradition of focused discussion on reflexive positioning. Although these movements have emerged in different parts of the world and during different historical periods, they seem to have key characteristics in common, at least on the surface. Both movements emphasize intuition as a guide to universal truth. More important for the present discussion, both movements seek a 'freeing' of the self, in order to allow the self to have what they regard as a 'higher' form of experience. Thus, in the writings of American transcendentalists and Islamic Sufis, we discover a persistent and focused concern with the ideal self. This ideal is then used to position the self and others: 'That is how we all should be!' 'Shame on me that I am so far removed from the ideal!'

The case of American transcendentalism

> I went to the woods because I wished to live deliberately, to front only
> the essential facts of life, and see if I could not learn what it had to
> teach, and not, when I came to die, discover that I had not lived. I did
> not wish to live what was not life, living is so dear; nor did I wish to
> practice resignation, unless it was quite necessary. I wanted to live deep
> and suck out all the marrow of life, to live so sturdily and Spartan-like
> as to put to rout all that was not life . . . (Henry Thoreau, *Walden*)

> Whoso would be a man, must be a nonconformist . . . Nothing is at last
> sacred but the integrity of your own mind. Absolve you to your self,
> and you shall have the suffrage of the world. (Emerson, *Self-Reliance*)

From a cultural standpoint, the reflexive positioning that takes place in
American transcendentalism can be best understood in the context of a larger
and more far-reaching characteristic of American life: individualism. When
Emerson states that, 'Society everywhere is in conspiracy against the manhood
of every one of its members' (*Self-Reliance*), he is reflecting the strong biases
of the larger society, rather than a sentiment unique to transcendentalists. But
there is a peculiarity in the solution adopted by the transcendentalists to
'finding' and enriching the self, in the face of dangers represented by society.
In its most clear and symbolically powerful form, this solution is represented
by the life of Henry Thoreau, or at least that part of his life during which he
retreated to Walden Pond.

We interpret Thoreau's retreat to the woods (1845–7) as an attempt to
achieve reflexive positioning through the use of a selected ideal state. His
journals reveal a strategic use of an ideal for self-to-self positioning. Thoreau's
strategy was to 'simplify, simplify, and simplify' so that he would come to live
life in the woods in what he saw to be its raw essence. Through eliminating
what he assumed to be 'unessential' in life, he would touch the raw nerve,
the marrow of life. This did not just involve discarding material 'garbage',
but also abandoning the social rules and the baggages of 'civility' that
society loads onto individuals. By isolating himself, and by getting rid of all
non-essentials, he would come to know life in its pure and unadulterated
form.

A careful scrutiny of *Walden* reveals that a first part of the ideal form of life
Thoreau is seeking is a self unencumbered by the material and social 'baggages' of society. He seeks to 'confront himself' as he really is, on the
assumption that a person 'in' society is prevented from identifying the 'essential' self by material and social obstacles. A second aspect of this ideal is the
achievement of a relationship between an 'essential' self and nature, as represented by, for example, the woods, the pond and the sky.

Thoreau's goal, then, is to find the essential self by stripping away all that society has loaded onto his person. This essential self is 'superior', in that it allows life to be lived in its essence. The essential self is positioned as morally superior to an 'unessential' and socially imposed self, the 'baggage' that impeded the discovery of the essential self. According to our analysis that 'essential self' is none other than a position from which Thoreau, as author of his words and actions, speaks and acts.

The case of Islamic Sufism

Sufism is a mystical sect of Islam. Sufi literature and ceremonies focus to a considerable degree on the self. For example, consider the following poem by Abdollah Ansari (our translation from Farsi):

> What should he want with life, he who comes to know you?
> What should he want with children, family, and possessions, he who
>   comes to know you?
> He will be possessed when you bless him with both worlds.
> What should he want with both worlds, he who is possessed by you?

A major theme in such poetry is the finding of a 'true' self, through stripping away all that is 'worldly'. We are reminded of American transcendentalism and in particular of Thoreau's strivings to arrive at an essential self. However, while American transcendentalism starts this process at a point of departure outside the body and strives to first strip away and simplify the external world, Sufism takes a point of departure within the body and attempts to strip away all that is inside. Some aspect of this Sufi thinking is captured by Ansari, who plays on the Farsi word *khod*, which can refer to both 'me' and 'you' or 'thou'.

> In thy (*khod*) path, at first make me (*khod*) without myself (*khod*),
> Then lead me (*khod*) toward you (*khod*), without myself (*khod*).

The use of the pronoun *khod* allows for a rather special kind of reflexive positioning in Farsi, one that stands in contrast to what is possible in reflexive positioning through Western languages. This positioning is special because it assumes a much less rigid boundary for the self than is typically conceptualized in the West, so that the *khod* can at the same time be 'me', 'I' and 'you'. The movement implied in the phrase 'lead me (*khod*) toward you (*khod*) without myself (*khod*)' is only possible because of an interdependent conception of the self, where the boundaries of people are more fluid than generally assumed in the West. 'More fluid boundaries' means that individuals often do not make sharp distinctions between themselves and the ingroup when, for example, assigning and taking responsibility, defining honour, and acting on interests. In the language of traditional psychology Farsi allows an attributional style whereby causes are both 'inside' the person and 'inside' the context or the ingroup, because the line between the person and the context and/or the ingroup is blurred.

Dimensions used in positioning

One of the basic assumptions inherent in positioning theory is that a person's moral and personal attributes are the most salient dimensions by which speakers locate themselves and others in discursive positions. However, we can expect that the particular attributes or other dimensions that are taken to be most salient and relevant in positioning oneself and others will also vary widely with culture and cultural ideals (see, for example, Triandis, 1989, on cultural variations in facets of self-understanding that are prominent in self-awareness).

To cite one example, Geertz (1984) reports that one of two sets of fundamental dichotomies of the Javanese sense of personhood (the first being the 'outside'/'inside' distinction which may be more familiar to us) is grounded in an *alus/kasar* ('refined'/'vulgar') contrast. The Javanese seek to be *alus* through the use of proper etiquette (in the outer realm) and meditation (in the inner realm), to be 'pure', 'refined', 'subtle' and 'ethereal', as opposed to 'coarse', 'rough', 'impolite' and 'insensitive' (see the analysis in chapter 11, below). Of course, we can find certain equivalents to the outside/inside and *alus/kasar* contrasts in American society – for example, Americans also consider themselves and others in terms of being more 'unmannered' or more 'sophisticated'. By Geertz's account, however, the 'inner/outer realms' and *alus/kasar* contrasts represent more salient dimensions by which persons assess themselves and others in Java, compared with American society. We might also assume that the *alus* ideal in both inner and outer realms is a more important cultural ideal for Javanese than Americans to strive toward in positioning practices.

A more fundamental question is whether or not persons universally locate themselves and others in positioning practices primarily in terms of enduring individual moral attributes such as 'shy', 'helpful' or 'honest'. Some data suggest, for example, that persons in some groups tend to describe themselves in terms of their roles and social categories (e.g., see Triandis, Leung, Villareal and Clack, 1985). Personality descriptions are extremely rare in other societies: for example, among the Ilongots of the Philippines who view environmental, social, political and spiritual forces as direct influences, so that behaviour need not be mediated by self-reflection (Rosaldo, 1984). Indeed, the Wintu, a Native American people, do not even have a word equivalent to the Western meaning of 'self', nor do the Spaniards (Gergen, 1977).

The individualism–collectivism dimension (Triandis, Leung, Villareal and Clack, 1985; Triandis, 1989) refers to cultural variations in the boundaries between the self and other. More specifically, culture defines the boundaries of the self, or the distinction between that which is and that which is not to be considered to be an intrinsic part of the self. This dividing line between the self and the social and/or natural environment is not definite and may be drawn at different places, varying with contexts and cultures. This is the 'self', not as the personal singularity of being, but as the total set of attributes ascribed to a person. In an individualistic society such as the United States, social relations tend to be voluntary and temporary in nature, involving the interaction of mobile and independent individuals so that the unit of concern is the individual person and a sharp boundary is drawn between the characteristic attributes of that person and others. However, several researchers such as Markus and Kitayama (1991) argue that this notion of an independent and unbounded self is rare among the world's cultures (Geertz, 1979) and distinctly Western in its cultural orientation, and that non-Western cultures tend to embrace a more collectivistic orientation. In collectivistic societies, the group – kinship system, tribe, class and so on – is the primary unit of concern, and no sharp boundary is drawn between the self in this sense and others. Rather than striving for the Western ideal of the distinct and autonomous self, various forms of interdependence and connectedness are seen as desirable.

Tajfel and Turner (1986) use the term 'social identity' to refer to the part of a person's self-concept which derives from knowledge of his or her membership in a social group, taking into account the value (both positive and negative) and emotional significance attached to that membership. We can expect that social identity is more salient to persons in collectivistic than individualistic societies, so that *group* (as opposed to individual) attributes, identities and histories may be more important in locating speakers reflexively in positioning and other discursive practices. For example, in more collective societies one's utterances may be given and/or taken as a group declaration rather than a personal undertaking. Among his observations of Maori culture, for instance, Best wrote that 'it is well to ever bear in mind that a native so thoroughly identifies with his tribe that he is ever employing the first personal pronoun [when referring to his tribe]' (1922: 397).

The symbolic meanings assigned to attributes (or other dimensions) will also vary from culture to culture. For example, the Maori traditionally consider 'hospitality' to be one of the 'eight sources of the heart' (e warunga pu *manawa*) or qualities deemed necessary for leadership (Smith, 1981). Thus, a person's capacity to be hospitable, usually considered to be an attribute of a warm host or hostess in Western culture, appears to be associated with the 'chiefly nature' of a leader among the Maori.

In the metaphorical terms of the positioning concept, then, before one is able to evaluate whether the basic coordinates might be the same, one must first examine the different 'axes' which persons may be using to locate themselves and others in the positioning 'grid'. Even so, it would be well to remember Sapir's (1929) remark that 'the worlds in which different societies live are distinct worlds, not merely the same world with different labels attached' (p. 209).

Preferred Forms of Autobiographical Telling

Canonical forms of autobiographical telling (or what are to be considered coherent arrangements of events into satisfying personal storylines) and the poles around which the stories revolve (e.g., characters, plot) also vary with cultural ideals. Published autobiographies cannot be taken to be true examples of reflexive positioning, as an autobiographer always tells his or her story to a group of listeners (Elbaz, 1988) and releases the story to the public. Nevertheless, we can assume that written autobiographies reflect something about the writer and his or her immediate audience, and their favoured forms of public autobiographical telling. American autobiographers, for example, favour a chronological arrangement that is oriented around emblematic events and stages of life, marked by 'life crises' (explicated in the work of Erikson (1950)), and focus on the movement between private and public realms (e.g., home to school) (Bruner, 1990, 1993). Bruner (1993) contrasts this style with Crapanzano's (1988) report of a Moroccan sample which does not order events chronologically, and portrays the central character as one who is subject to external forces rather than as an active agent who negotiates life's crises.

Conclusion

In conclusion, this analysis contributes to the ongoing discussion on positioning in two ways. First, the positioning concept is extended to the intrapersonal level. Second, the scope of the discussion is broadened with the consideration of how cultural differences may fundamentally influence positioning practices. We have argued that a satisfying discussion of positioning must necessarily take into account the particular ideals, dimensions and storylines that people in different societies are likely to find relevant in positioning themselves and others, and the meanings they attach to these constructs. This would be fundamental to studying the local or 'emic' and the universal or 'etic' features of positioning styles across cultures (Moghaddam, Taylor and Wright, 1993).

7

Positioning and the Recovery of Social Identity

S. Sabat and R. Harré

Introduction

The work reported in this chapter was inspired by two events. The first was the puzzlement created by the title of a recent book, *Alzheimer's Disease: The Loss of Self* (Cohen and Eisdorfer, 1986). How could a 'self' be lost? The second event was a dialogue in which an Alzheimer's disease (AD) sufferer, Henry, was being introduced by one person to another. In that dialogue the introduction went as follows: 'This is Henry. Henry was a lawyer.' Henry interrupted the proceedings by saying, 'I AM a lawyer.' And so he was – before and at that moment, and could, in a sense, continue to be in all future moments. What was the force of that apparently simple statement? We will try to show that its analysis, in accord with the methods of constructionist psychology, can resolve the puzzlement created by the book title we have cited above. Henry had not been disbarred, nor had his degree or years of practice and achievements been nullified by his developing Alzheimer's. He was not, at that moment, practising law, and it is customary to refer to a person who has retired from some vocation as 'having been' a lawyer or a salesperson, etc. However, this moment presented a special case: Henry not only considered himself to be a lawyer, perhaps by inclination, mentality, achievement, but he also insisted that others view him as such even though he was not in practice. And, if one listened to Henry carry on a conversation one could not mistake the careful, probing, questioning approach that he took. Perhaps he would agree that he was not, in fact, a practising attorney, but he was still an attorney and would not allow another person to deny him that status. So if there is, in fact, a loss of self as a result of AD, what exactly is it that is lost, and what is it that brings about the loss? Can such a loss be prevented, and if so how? What would it mean to the AD sufferer if such a loss could be prevented?

It is the purpose of the present paper to explore these issues by making use of the constructionist theory of the nature of the self. Recently considerable attention has been drawn to discursive production of many of the phenomena of ageing (Wood and Ryan, 1991). In this paper we bring 'positioning theory' to bear on the social constructionist aspects of AD. The constructionist point of view is a new approach to some of the long-standing problems of psychology. It has developed out of recent advances in psycholinguistics, partly inspired by the writings of Wittgenstein (1953) and partly by the rediscovery of the developmental psychology of Vygotsky (1962). From the former we have learned of the central importance of language in the creation of social reality, and from the latter, the role of the acquisition of linguistic and manipulative skills in the organization of thought and experience. Using the analytical techniques of the new approach we will show that 1) there is a self, a personal singularity, that remains intact despite the debilitating effects of the disorder, and (2) there are other aspects of the person, the selves that are socially and publicly presented, that can be lost, but only indirectly as a result of the disease. In the second case, the loss of self is directly related to nothing more than the ways in which others view and treat the AD sufferer. An example of one such mode of treatment is encapsulated in the statement, 'Henry was a lawyer.' We were delighted to discover that a very similar point of view has been developed independently by Kitwood, drawing on similar ideas about personhood and coming to similar conclusions about care (Kitwood and Bredin, 1992).

Alzheimer's Disease and the Self

Although Alzheimer's disease can result in a variety of cognitive and behavioural problems ranging from disruptions in recall memory, information-processing and word-finding to the impairment of the ability to carry out sequences of skilled motor acts of linguistic and non-linguistic types, we shall show that on the constructionist account, the condition does not result in the loss of self1, the sense of personal identity, and only contributes indirectly to possible losses in selves2, coherent personae as presented in public interactions. Furthermore, given the storylines that are created, usually by care givers and others, the behaviour of the AD sufferer may be subject to radical problems of social misunderstanding wherein successful adaptations employed by the sufferer to maintain both kinds of selfhood can be interpreted as symptoms. In addition, the sufferer may also engage in adaptive practices to sustain his or her presented selves so as to conform to, or satisfy, the needs of the care giver. We will attempt to substantiate these claims from analyses of clinical material. This material is drawn from records of conversations that occurred (a) in an adult daycare centre which provides a supportive social environment for individuals who suffer from a variety of brain injuries, or (b) in interviews with care givers, or in interviews conducted by a social worker with the AD sufferer and care giver together.

In analysing discursive events, one needs very detailed empirical material which, in the nature of these cases, does not lend itself to statistical analysis. Technically speaking what follows is an instance of the intentional design. In extensional studies a population is identified and the investigation is directed to finding a central tendency and the distribution of deviations from it. The wider the extension the less information survives the analytical process. In the intentional design an individual is designated as a typical member of a class whose extension is still to be created. It will consist of all and only those entities which are taken to be sufficiently similar to the entity chosen as typical. This design is information rich but may yield only very narrow classes of similar members. In the following section we will refer to specific cases of AD sufferers which we will take to be representative of some as yet undetermined population. It remains to be seen how widely the patterns we have identified are actually exemplified.

The Discursive Maintenance of Self

Studied from the point of view of questions about discursive abilities, the cases of JB and of IR both reveal ample evidence for the existence of self1 despite the severe problems that resulted from the disease. JB was able, though with difficulty at times, to communicate effectively via spoken language, whereas IK was able to communicate effectively mainly through the medium of gestures. At the time of these studies, each subject had been diagnosed four years earlier, with the first appearance of difficulties occurring approximately two years in advance of the diagnosis. The interviews with JB were conducted over a period of eight months, twice weekly, with each interview lasting for approximately one hour. At the time of the final interview, JB was hospitalized, was only a few months away from his death and was able to speak only sparingly compared to his speech for most of the eight-month period. In the following, we will present dialogue from tape-recorded interviews with JB that occurred towards the beginning of the association, and from the last interviews, so that it will be clear that, given the discursive properties of his speech, self1 was intact both at the beginning and end of our association. In other words, self1 was intact at a time when he was still able to function in social situations, and feed and dress himself, as well as at a time when he was incapable of doing so and was hospitalized and in a state of great turmoil and pain.

Discursive Skills as Displayed in the Early Interviews

The use of first order or simple indexicals

JB: I am going back and picking up information that is useless. What is
      it that you're looking for? I get information in static things. My wife
      will talk to me and I will get information but in just a little while I
      realize that it is useless information.

SRS: Useless in what senses?

JB: Ah, well, mostly in the fact that I think about Alzheimer's. Things
      get jumbled and Alzheimer's just gives me fragments.

SRS: So when you think about Alzheimer's disease what's the first thing
      you think?

JB: I'm mad as hell . . . constantly on my mind . . . which may or may
      not screw up your project.

SRS: I don't think so.

JB: I don't want to cause problems for my wife, family.

In the above, it should be noted that JB frequently uses the indexicals 'I', 'me'
and 'my', which, from the constructionist point of view, displays an intact
self1 through the autobiographical indexing of reports of experiences as his.
Attention to the content shows a firm grasp of the elements of at least two
possible selves2, the 'scientific collaborator' and the 'family burden'.

The use of embedded or iterated indexicals

The indexical structure of English and many other languages permits the
expression of complex acts of self-monitoring. An experience, already indexed
as the speaker's, is embedded in another indexical utterance, through which
the speaker displays a grasp of his or her own personhood. This aspect of
selfhood, in which self1 manifestations become retrospectively elements in a
coherent self2, was a central feature of G. H. Mead's (1934) account of
selfhood. The capacity to manage iterated and embedded indexicals is clearly
manifested in the excerpt which follows:

SRS: You don't think that you've lost your sense of self?

JB: In what respect?

SRS: You know who you are, you know that you are.

JB: Yeah, definitely. I know who I am. And sometimes I have to fake,
      um, as to people that I deal with back and forth.

SRS: What do you have to fake?

JB: Uh, I have to fake for, uh, course I feel I could, could have done more. Can I do better now? I don't know.

Notice that it is self1 manifestations rather than factual, autobiographical 'snippets' that appear most salient here. JB's last remark is indicative of the high level of his control of some aspects of the 'mechanisms' of self-presentation.

Discursive Skills as Displayed in the Last Interviews

In the last two interviews that were conducted with JB, his emotional turmoil had deepened greatly. He was unable to carry on a conversation with as much give and take as he had evidenced in the previous months. He had severe difficulty in walking unaided, dressing, finding his way around, and gave every indication that he was in great pain. In the penultimate interview he offered the following:

JB: I'm so pissed off.

SRS: About what ?

JB: The son of a bitch.

SRS: Who's a son of a bitch ?

JB: Let's take [the social worker]. Could you and I, just the two of us, get, get, on. on someplace to the idea of what you and I do?

SRS: That's why we're here.

JB: So now I want to establish – this is ugly – oh, they're going to try to get me . . .

SRS: How so?

JB: How, so, [the social worker].

SRS: What happened?

JB: She says I don't think you should be working anymore. And then I don't think you should be de doing this.

This passage, quoted in full, displays the same discursive abilities with indexicals as the passages from the early interviews. JB's first remark is indicative of an intact grasp of the use of the first person to index the force of a performative utterance with the speaker's commitment to it. But above all it shows a reflexive grasp of the conditions for maintaining a specific self2, the persona or character of 'scientific collaborator'. In the very last remark the highest order of indexical skill is displayed in a technique Urban (1989) refers to as the story-telling voice. 'She', an anaphoric pronoun, standing for 'social worker', is used as the springboard for another kind of embedded indexical, which, within a story, indexes the social worker's utterance with her responsibility. Finally we note that JB's last turn is just what is needed to legitimate his opening remark.

In the final interview, briefly excerpted below, despite JB's evident deterioration and cognitive turmoil, his ability to index his performative utterances as his remains unimpaired. He has complete command of the discursive conventions for the making of self-indexed physiognomic avowals.

JB: I don't know what to do, what to do, what to do . . .
SRS: What's got you so sad?
JB: It's sad.
SRS: What is sad?
JB: It's so sad because, because I sit in the corner and I come I come over. I don't even known where I am, I don't even know where I am . . . It's too much, too much anxiety, too many anxiety. What are you going to do to me?
SRS: I'm not going to do anything to you.
JB: I hurt. [five times]

In another case, the case of IK, the use of indexicals was not apparent in her verbal productions, for her ability to use spoken language was severely hampered by the disorder and she spoke only rarely. On most occasions, she used gestures to communicate with others. Most notably, often she would let another person know that the other was sitting in her chair by tapping the chair and then pointing to herself as in 'that's my chair'. Often others would understand and respond in kind, and IK would then sit down. Thus, IK would communicate the indexical 'I', or 'my', or 'mine', or 'me' via gesture, not unlike the formal indexicals of ASL. On occasion, when she was in a heightened emotional state, she would speak coherently. An instance is the occasion on which when looking through a magazine she saw a·picture of former President Reagan. Upon seeing the photo, she said, 'Oh, I hate that man, I just hate that man!'

Although in the above two cases of AD sufferers the disorder affected each person in a different way, the use of the indexicals by which a self1 is publicly displayed remained throughout the course of the disease, even though certain behavioural and cognitive functions showed great declines. Thus, on the constructionist account, in Alzheimer's disease, self1, or personal identity, remains intact far beyond the disintegration of many cognitive and motor functions.

The Expression of Social Identity: the Discursive Construction of a Persona

The persistence of the sense of professional worth as 'scientist'

According to the constructionist account, personas do not exist as singularities, nor do they exist at every moment in the same way. They are coherent clusters of displays that serve to create the public impression of a type, a persona or a character, from a local repertoire. Selves2 depend for their existence upon the cooperation of others in the social context. Personas are joint productions. It is possible for the AD sufferer to attempt to construct a particular persona with another person, but if the latter refuses to cooperate in the constructive process, that persona will not come into existence. This has a profound effect upon the AD sufferer's 'position' in the social situation. Technically a 'position' is defined by a certain set of rights, duties and obligations as a speaker. Each episode of everyday life can be seen as the development of a 'storyline'. In positioning theory, as we have outlined in Chapters 2 and 3, positions and storylines are taken mutually to determine one another. So if the AD sufferer's position as a persona cannot be brought into being, a storyline may be followed out antithetical to the intentions of the sufferer when his or her actions are interpreted by the other person without reference to the presentational cues indicative of a certain persona presented by the sufferer. And in these different interpretations there is considerable possibility for social misunderstanding of the meaning of the AD sufferer's behaviour. The cases of JB and IK each offer examples of such a predicament. The personas emerged in the social interactions in which they were positioned in ways which, to them, did not reflect their views as to the sorts of persons they were. In order to provide enough detail, it will be necessary to present some background information about each person before citing the relevant examples.

JB spent his working life as an academic. He had contributed as a teacher, an administrator, and an author. His manner and tone of voice exemplified thoughtful curiosity and quiet dignity. He was also a devoted husband and father whose family occupied a central position in his life. He became deeply involved in our work together, which he came to call 'The Project', for he was an integral part in it, rather than a mere subject. He correctly felt that, in a sense, he was directly involved in research. Simultaneously, at the adult daycare centre where we met each week, there was a programme of activities each day, activities that involved games, discussions, etc. JB did not involve himself with the other participants in any of the available activities, which he called 'filler'. As a result, he would generally take walks, spend time with staff members, read, but would absent himself from the usual activities.

Without the background information it would be possible to construct a storyline for the episodes in which JB detached himself from the group, built on a simple interpretation of his behaviour. In this storyline JB would have been positioned as reclusive, antisocial, stuck-up, an alien to the group, a person who wanders aimlessly. However, if one were to cooperate in the construction of JB as an academic person, then the meaning of his avoiding the games he saw as mindless, and the ways in which he occupied his time instead, would lead to a very different perspective and storyline.

> JB: Yes, well my wife and I are very strong academic people and, uh, so we start talking to each other, we talk at a very high level right away. Uh, and uh, I mean, uh, most of these people here, most of them here are good. But when I get closer, uh, I, uh, get, information that's much, uh, that Trivial Pursuit I wish I could find out how to make it break.

In this excerpt we see the presentation of a social being, a persona, of a very different kind. Instead of the reclusive, aimless wanderer, we have an intellectual person who would rather take a walk and enjoy the outdoors, or talk with people he viewed as equals, than engage in games that he saw as a waste of his time and energy.

One problem that confronts our understanding of the effects of Alzheimer's disease is that once an AD sufferer has been positioned as helpless and confused, it is rare for his or her behaviour to be seen in a way different from that which conforms to the original positioning. Thus, having failed initially to take part in a joint construction of himself as an academic person, JB will be seen by others in some other, probably far less enriching or enhancing way. The point that must be emphasized is that such an interpretation is more a function of the willingness or ability of others to cooperate in the construction of a particular self2 presented incipiently by an Alzheimer's sufferer than it is a function of the actual symptoms of the disease. Thus, because one of us cooperated in the joint construction of JB as an intellectual, and sought to understand him with that in mind, his behaviour was found to be perfectly reasonable given his position as an academic. Of course, if JB were positioned as a misanthropic recluse, the same behaviour of avoiding the games would be explained in a different storyline. One would be inclined to blame the disease rather than the way in which others failed to participate in the construction of the aspects of JB's preferred self2 to which he laid claim. In some respects 'positioning theory' covers the same range of phenomena as 'labelling', though with a closer attention to the fine grain of the linguistic devices by which people are fatefully fitted into types. The early diagnosis of Alzheimer's disease may place a person in a certain amount of jeopardy, unless attention is paid to the sorts of considerations which we discuss in this paper.

As Goffman emphasized on many occasions, honour and reputation, the stuff of moral careers, are precious in the eyes of most of us. The presentation of selves2 and the maintenance of one's standing in the local moral order – that is, one's 'position' – are intimately interrelated. As the following excerpt shows, JB understood this relation very well. He continued to keep his moral career as a scientist in mind. He was involved in a research project and did not have any tangible thing to show regarding his contribution either to the project or to the students with whom he consented to talk, and, thus, to teach about Alzheimer's disease.

JB: I have the feeling, some feeling that I don't necessarily have status, um, because it's not really something that I'm piddling with. And you know I feel a way is that, I feel that this is a real good, big project and I'm sure you do too. This project is a sort of scientific thing.

SRS: Indeed.

JB: Because I've has this, people talk to me and then I'm blum, blum, blum. What do I do? Well, blum, blum, blum. So it may not mean very much. Maybe it's nothing. Because others go with stature and what I feel, I think my God this is real stature to do! This is maybe picky, picky, picky stuff.

SRS: I don't think so.

JB: That is stature and who can be attached to somebody, uh, in an agreeable thing. Somewhere, where we can do status. If somebody calls me and says what are you doing and then I write this thing, what is it? Now it could be a long, long thing in the project from your university or something else. Do you think I'm silly?

SRS: No. No, not at all.

JB: Some sort of status.

Once the nature of JB's wish to link this last spurt of academic effort with the final stage of his moral career became clear it was arranged for him to have a letter of commendation from the Dean of the College of Arts and Sciences. In that letter, JB was commended for giving of himself unstintingly to help with the investigation of the abilities that remain intact in spite of AD. It was a letter in which he was praised for the service he provided to us all. Upon receiving the letter, his wife made copies and he, then, brought a copy to the daycare centre where it was read aloud to the entire group of participants. In addition, when his adult children visited, he showed them the letter with great pride, for it signalled that he was, indeed, doing something important. Thus, given his vocation of a lifetime, the academic self 2 was jointly constructed once again. By virtue of the social force of the letter of commendation JB was positioned, not as a helpless and confused AD sufferer, but as one who had a contribution to make to science even in the throes of AD.

The paradoxical collusion of an AD sufferer in the deletion of her own skills

According to her family, IR had always been a service-oriented person who had travelled extensively as a result of her spouse's vocation. Whenever they lived abroad for extended periods of time, IR would always find some sort of volunteer work to do in hospitals or with abandoned children. At the daycare centre, she was observed to be extremely helpful in spite of the linguistic production problems caused by AD. As a result of such problems, she communicated via gestures which were consistent and understandable to some of the staff members. She helped to set tables before meals, aided participants who used wheel chairs, helped others to find and use the bathroom, helped to move chairs in the setting up of various activities, and pointed out to staff members those participants in need of help that she herself could not provide. She was able to feed herself and took great pride in her appearance. At the daycare centre, a self 2 as helper and provider of nurturance was constructed with the cooperation of staff members and other participants.

The persona manifested at the daycare centre was not constructed at home, where her spouse described her as no longer able to do housework and having problems with 'keeping busy' – she either watched television or did nothing. He had taken on most of the details of housekeeping, cut her food at meals especially in restaurants, picked out her clothes each day, and applied her make-up for her. As a result of her linguistic problems, he thought she was unable to follow directions and thus no longer asked for her help. But at the daycare centre, she was found to be able to follow directions when shown what to do gesturally along with the spoken word.

In this case, IR was positioned by her spouse as incapable of doing many of the things that she did routinely at the daycare centre. The grounds for this positioning were mainly her verbal problems, along with some housekeeping errors such as her putting soiled clothes in the bathroom rubbish bin instead of the hamper, and refusing at times to change into sleepwear before going to sleep. Thus her life was presented according to a familiar storyline, that of the confused, helpless AD sufferer. However, at the daycare centre, although she was positioned as an AD sufferer, given her clear gestural ability and her ability and desire to be of help to others, she was positioned as someone who could be counted upon to be of service in a variety of ways. But what is interesting about this is that her storyline, built around the position of the nurturant one, was also the foundation of a paradoxical adaptation to the needs of her spouse.

As we indicated earlier, IR allowed her husband to apply her make-up for her even though his performance of the task did not adequately cover the facial blemishes and irritations that disturbed her greatly. On one occasion, she applied some more make-up while at the daycare centre and her spouse described her work as being better at hiding her blemishes than his own, although he did offer his opinion that, despite her success, she used 'too much'. In a sense, the care giver helped to define her inadequacy in a way that would make him needed, and in accordance with her storyline IR allowed the situation to continue, thus partly adapting to his needs. Ironically, this kind of interaction helped further, but covertly, to construct her self2 as a nurturer, only in this case, she nurtured her spouse's need to be needed by allowing him to position her as incapable of being of help in a variety of ways. This sort of interaction has been discussed in terms of 'psychological symbiosis' by Shotter and Newson (1974), and as a species of undifferentiation by Bowen (1990) in which two persons function, for certain purposes, as one.

Just as in the case of JB we find IR taking action to protect her honour and dignity, though, given the circumstances, at the risk of being positioned as one of the confused. While at the daycare centre, IR was observed from time to time walking about in the corridor rather than participating in some activity. Often, the storyline that accompanies this behaviour of AD sufferers is that of 'aimless or irrational wandering' which derives from the prior positioning of the AD sufferer as one of the confused. Further investigation into the events that preceded IR taking walks in the corridor revealed that on a majority of those occasions the activity in which she could have been involved instead was a small group discussion. In such a setting, each member of the group is asked to participate in talking about a particular issue. IR, however, had severe problems with verbal production and was not able to produce the behaviour that was central to the group's activity. If there was no other activity in which she could be involved (even helping someone else on her own) she chose to go for a walk in the corridor rather than risk the humiliation of losing her standing as the persona displayed in her cooperative, nurturant activities.

Had she chosen, on those occasions, to read a magazine instead of taking a walk, would her behaviour have been described as 'irrational reading'? In the above circumstance, IR's behaviour, if typified as that expected of the 'confused, helpless' AD sufferer, would be seen as a symptom of the disorder. Given the second storyline, which is in our opinion more in keeping with her capabilities, IR's behaviour is seen as a reflection of her grasp of the social situation and her rational decision not to embarrass herself, and her desire to take a walk instead. The first storyline leads to a radical social misunderstanding wherein her rational and successful adaptation to the situation is interpreted as anything but that, and simply serves to perpetuate the original stultifying position.

Psychological symbiosis: the discursive creation of the mind of another

The interview took place on a home visit by the social worker. The social worker directed a majority of her questions to MK, the Alzheimer's sufferer, but MK's spouse, JK, always answered the questions. He did so even when it was clear from MK's behaviour that she knew the answers and simply needed more time to formulate the correct words. On one occasion as JK answered a question for her, MK said, 'I was just about to say that.' On another occasion, when asked the name of one of her daughters, her husband answered and MK then proceeded to spell the name as if to show the social worker that she did indeed know it. In this interaction, the spouse, through his inexorable efforts at psychological symbiosis, was actively preventing MK from discursively producing either a self1 on her own account or any persona jointly with the social worker. The social worker asked MK what she did during the day and MK said that she watched television. When asked if she liked soap operas MK said 'No, I don't' and shook her head in the negative. MK's comments manifest, through the use of the indexical 'I', the existence of self1, since they constitute it! But MK was not able to construct a persona, a coherent and valued persona, with the social worker. She was about to say something else when her husband cut her off: 'She can't follow the storyline. She watches the news but can't retain it for more than five minutes. She can't remember much after five minutes.' It is unclear as to the basis for JK's allegation, but a subsequent interchange revealed that MK could, indeed, retain information for more than five minutes. For example, when the social worker asked MK if her husband had told her that there would be a home visit that afternoon, she said that he had told her at seven o'clock that morning, and, indeed, he had done. When her husband left the table to answer the phone, MK was able to answer questions coherently although she was slow to respond. When asked what she liked to do, she replied 'I like to walk, but not in this cold.'

Why did JK foster the impression that MK could not even think for herself? There are several possible answers to this question, all of which may be true. Probably his positioning of her as helpless (and hopeless) stemmed, in the first instance, from her problems with recall memory and her slowness to answer questions. However, we must also take into account his embarrassment for her, and his inability to deal in a wholly satisfactory way with her condition. In any of these situations his response is likely to be the establishment of MK's selves in psychological symbiosis with his own activities. In this case as in the other cases we have described, there is overt manifestation of self1 and, but for the aggressive psychological symbiosis practised by the spouse, it would have been clear that there was a substantial surviving skill in taking part in the construction and manifestation of an appropriate persona, adequate as a public presentation of the person she knew herself to be. For instance, when the social worker began to read something, MK began to get up from her chair and said, 'You should turn that light on', referring to a lamp which was next to the social worker, and JK turned it on. Here, for a rare moment, MK had positioned herself as in command.

Conclusion

Though something similar to these ideas has been proposed before, for example by Bleathman and Morton (1988), it is clear from the foregoing that positioning theory can provide new insights into the effects of Alzheimer's disease, and the reactions of others to the diagnosis, on the personhood of the sufferer. In addition, such insights provide not only answers to the questions posed at the outset of this paper, but recommendations that can, perhaps, lead to improvements in the lives of sufferers and care givers alike even in the face of the progress of the disease.

It is clear that the thesis that the self1 of personal identity remains intact even in the face of quite severe deterioration in other cognitive and motor functions is well supported, though we would welcome the contribution of other studies, perhaps using different ways of accessing mental organization. If there is a loss of self as a result of AD, that loss is not in the management of the organizing powers of the indexical creation of self1, until the time when virtually no behaviour of any consequence occurs. It is also clear that the repertoire of selves2, the personae that are socially and publicly presented and which require the cooperation of others in the social sphere in order to come into being, can indeed be manifested even in the later stages of the disease. In the cases we have described, the threatened disappearance of any self2 is not directly linked to the progress of the disease. Rather, it is related to the behaviour of those who are regularly involved in the social life of the sufferer, though to react positively to such fragile clues requires persistence and dedication.

If such behaviour is founded on storylines that paint the sufferer as inadequate, confused, helpless, etc., then that person will be so positioned and will have his or her behaviour interpreted by others in such a way as to confirm the initial storyline and positioning. The ultimate result of such a situation is the fencing off of the sufferer so that no adequate self2 can be constructed.

Perhaps it is not stretching the point too far to refer to such a situation as a species of self-fulfilling prophecy. Thus, if there is a loss of the capacity to present an appropriate self2, in many cases the fundamental cause is to be found not in the neurofibrillary tangles and senile plaques in the brains of the sufferers, but in the character of the social interactions and their interpretation that follow in the wake of the symptoms.

Can the loss of self in AD be prevented? The sense of self as a unitary and unique being is not lost even in much of the end stage of the disease. Thus, this discussion must focus on what we have called the personas, the organized social presentations of self through which one interacts with one's fellows. It is clear that the behaviour of AD sufferers involves frequent attempts to invite others to join in the construction of a public persona. It is also clear that all too often those invitations go unheeded. We suggest that the loss of personas can, in many cases, be prevented if, and only if, the care givers and other significant individuals in the sufferer's social world can refrain from the *ad hoc* positioning of the sufferer as helpless, confused, etc., and can refrain from interpreting the speech acts and other non-verbal forms of communication as being indicative of confusion on the part of the AD sufferer. Just because person A who is listening is confused about what the AD sufferer B is trying to say it does not mean that person B is confused. It can often mean that A is confused and needs to persist in the effort to understand what person B is trying to say. JB remarked to one of the students who assisted in this study, 'Your mentor when he doesn't see what I say, he says so, and I appreciate that.' The initial assumption on the part of the listener must be that the AD sufferer is trying to say something, that there must be some coherent reason for the behaviour in question. Our cases show that it is up to the listener-observer to find the thread of reason with the help of the AD sufferer.

Only under such circumstances can personas adequate to what the person knows him or herself to be continue to be projected and recognized. What would it mean to the AD sufferer if the loss of presented selves, or personas, could be prevented? A few words come to mind: dignity, some measure of enhanced independence, the possibility of purposes fulfilled, the gratification of being understood while fighting with the tenacity of the damned, as Luria called it, to break through the difficulties posed by word-finding problems, recall memory problems, and so on. It would mean a lessening of social isolation, the continuation of personal relationships and the respect that a lifetime of living demands. It would mean that the only prison in which the sufferer would have to dwell would be that created by the boundaries of brain injury and not, in addition, the confinement that is brought about by the innocently misguided positioning and storylines created by others. It should be noted that such benefits as would be reaped by the AD sufferer would also be shared by the care giver, whose burdens and stress would be eased to a significant degree. It is the thesis of social constructionism that our personas, as manifestations of our selves, require the mutual cooperation of individuals. Such mutual cooperation allows a human being to flourish as many different selves, often in the most unpromising situations.

8

Positioning and the Writing of Science

L. van Langenhove and R. Harré

Introduction

We turn now to the positioning practised in the discourses of well-defined and differentiated social orders and institutions: in this case science. Science and the process of research are today studied in different scientific disciplines and from different viewpoints (cf. Giere, 1989 and Woolgar, 1989 for short accounts of the history of the science studies). The scientific study of science has its origins in philosophical theories of science in which first scientific statements and theories (for example Whewell, 1967) and later scientific research traditions (cf. Lakatos, 1978; Kuhn, 1962) were the subject of analysis. Across different approaches there have been two key issues. Is it the world or is it our experience of the world that is scientifically represented? Secondly, how are true and false representations to be distinguished from one another? Logical analysis of cognition played an important role in the first attempts at a science of science. The production of scientific knowledge was reckoned not to involve any social factors. With Merton's sociology of science and, more importantly, Fleck's analysis of the social processes involved in the production of 'facts', attention shifted from the cognitive functioning of individual scientists towards science as a normatively regulated product achieved by structured social groups. Neither Merton nor Fleck were reductionists. Cognitive aspects of science were preserved in their accounts. Neither fell into the genetic fallacy. The Mertonian structural-functional analysis in the study of science and the sociology of science became a relatively flourishing field. Gradually, sociology of science moved towards a more anthropological stance, challenging the Mertonian ideal of scientific norms. Both the Edinburgh school (cf. the 'strong programme' of Bloor, 1976) and the 'Paris' school (Bourdieu, Latour, Woolgar, Knorr-Cetina) emphasized the role of social factors in the scientific production of representations. The social constructionist approach associated with the works of Latour and Woolgar (1979) and Knorr-Cetina (1981) even at least appeared to advocate the view that representations create the world rather than reflect it. In these seminal studies an anthropological method is used to study how scientists work in their labs. One of their most salient conclusions was that in the process from experiment to published text, a scientific truth is constructed. As shown by Knorr-Cetina, scientific papers can also be conceived as 'an exercise in depersonalization'. All the social interactions that were an essential part of a scientific experiment are abstracted until a text remains that represents a 'clean story'. Relatively independent from the social constructionist approach a renewed interest emerged in the cognitive aspects of science (cf. De Mey, 1982). As noted by Woolgar (1989) the main question for the field of science studies today is to what extent the social and the cognitive approaches can be integrated with each other.

In this chapter we want to present the basic tenets of a theory that attempts to integrate cognitive and social approaches to the study of science, and then elaborate on two issues from that theoretical viewpoint. The focus will be on scientific discourse – particularly scientific texts. First, we will deal with the relation between the rhetorical aspects of scientific publications and the method by which scientific 'facts' are produced. Secondly, the differences between natural and social sciences will be explored in terms of rhetorical features of how and what is being published. In both cases the phenomenon of positioning will be shown to play an important part.

Positioning Theory and the Study of Science

In this chapter we will focus on the discursive practices of the scientific community, especially on scientific publishing. This we shall show can also be understood in terms of positioning and rhetorical redescriptions. The goal of such an analysis is to understand how such narratives as scientific papers are generated and reproduced. Positions involve not only speaking and writing rights, duties and obligations, but also expectations as to how someone in a certain position will exercise their rights (Rip, 1991).

If positioning is to be understood as a way in which people dynamically produce and explain the everyday behaviour of themselves and others, then the question arises how this relates to the explanations that social scientists develop about that same everyday behaviour. If such social science explanations involve the idea of individual persons, then, in accordance with the above remarks, such explanations can equally well be regarded as acts of positioning. And this requires us to ask what will be the storyline of such 'scientific positionings'?

The study of science as a social institution can be said to involve four areas of analysis: (i) the *research* process as such (what happens in the lab), (ii) the *pre-research* conditions (what happens in order to get money and people to the lab for a specific project), (iii) the *post-research* process (what happens when texts and patents of phases (i) and (ii) are written up and published) and (iv) the *assimilation* process (what befalls such texts in the public domain). Within recent sociology of science, the emphasis has to a great extent been on understanding the research as it occurs in the laboratory. Only recently, pre-research has became a topic of study as well. Before being able to embark upon a research project, scientists have to find the money and the means for it. If they work in a big team, then they will have to try to persuade the head of department to allocate time and money to their ideas. In other words, scientists need to be entrepreneurs and 'intra-preneurs' who are able to push their own ideas within the institution in which they work. If they are in charge of a scientific department their main job will be to 'attract' research funds. The many aspects of pre-research processes have been studied by Latour. It is clear that it is also increasingly becoming professionalized. Scientists are today regarded as managers and books are written and courses set up in which they are trained in the management of research and development (cf. Katz, 1988). In some universities doctoral programmes even include courses in the preparation of grant proposals. There are some excellent studies of the production of scientific texts (Knorr-Cetina, 1981), but far less attention has been paid to the assimilation processes (what happens to them, once published), except for so-called 'scientometric' studies in which citations of publications are being studied. The above-mentioned constituents of research, namely (a) achieving the ability or obtaining permission to do research, (b) the actual performing of scientific activities, (c) the writing (or lecturing) process and (d) the dissemination of research products (patents and publications) can each be studied in terms of positioning and reconstruction. In the following paragraphs, the concepts of positioning and reconstruction will be applied to two issues of post-research: (i) the relation between the facts of scientific publications and their discursive properties and (ii) the differences between natural and social sciences with respect to these issues.

Scientific Publications and Positioning

The official rhetoric of science implies that researchers should publish. According to that rhetoric they have a method for finding truth and a moral duty to disclose the findings. Such publications can take the form of books, articles in learned journals, or patents. Using the terminology of positioning theory, any scientific publication can be understood as a text with the following characteristics:

(i)   it contains a rhetorical redescription of parts of the social and material world (e.g., when concepts like 'quarks', 'attitudes' are used in order to explain events);

(ii)   it is a rhetorical redescription of the process of cognition and material manipulation that led to the publication;

(iii)   it involves acts of positionings of the authors and other writers on the same topic by means of citation and covert self-reference;

(iv)   it contains rhetorical redescriptions of parts of the work of quoted or cited authors;

(v)   it is subject to positioning and rhetorical redescription whenever the text itself is quoted or cited;

(vi)   it is a complex of speech–acts that has such illocutionary force as can be created in the act of reading between author(s) and readers. This force is maintained through into subsequent citations of the original writing, as its authority, and the subsequent positioning of authors and readers as to their authority, that is, their right to 'have the last word'.

Each of these characteristics can be used as a starting point of an analysis of scientific texts. A full understanding of the dynamics of science involves, in our view, an elaboration of all six characteristics. In this paper only a few general observations and remarks will be made on each of these topics. At this stage our aim is programmatic, rather than the achievement of a definite account of scientific activity.

It is the pretension of every scientific text to say something about either the social or the natural world. Only philosophers have seriously proposed anti-realist readings of such texts. Moreover, at least some of the statements about the world are presented as explanations of problematic aspects of the world. If we agree that there exists a world independent of the knower and that it is possible to have knowledge of that world, then scientific texts can be regarded as descriptions and redescriptions of the world. But there are many descriptive vocabularies available for the formulation of a text about some object of interest. (We shall leave aside for the purpose of this paper the question of whether an entity can become an object of human interest independently of some textual characterization, however minimal.) Such redescriptions always involve a positioning of the scientists towards a certain audience. A coin, for example, can be redescribed in terms of its chemical substance, its economic value, its historical origins and so on. In each case a different claim is being made about the same object. Traditionally the variety of possible factual claims has been referred to a corresponding variety of conceptual schemes, lately dignified as 'paradigms'. We want to refer this variety not just to paradigms but to audiences, the communities who each share a vocabulary and a conceptual scheme. This implies that the idea of scientific truth can only be dealt with from a conversational viewpoint. Every scientific statement is a statement by somebody to somebody else. Furthermore every conversation is structured according to the positions adopted by the conversants – for instance, in scientists' writing the author(s) position themselves as having authority – as having the right to speak and reciprocally demanding the trust of their readers – who, as members of the same community, are usually prepared to give it. In identifying conversational positions the main question is who has the moral right to make certain statements to certain persons. It is in terms of the answer to this question that the illocutionary force of published statements is made determinate.

A scientific publication is never supposed to be the first text in which a particular aspect of the world is dealt with. It is presupposed that other scientists have been engaged in attempting to resolve more or less the same type of research issues; this is shown by the existence of a part of any scientific text which involves references to other scientific texts. There are quotations, in oratio obliqua and recta, and comments on such quotations. The insertion of a quotation into a conversation is in itself a speech-act. What is its range of illocutionary force? It can range from deference to ridicule. The work of other scientists is never quoted in its totality. Only certain aspects are abstracted from it or it is summarized. The process of abstracting and summarizing existing publications can be understood in terms of rhetorical redescriptions. It would be an interesting study to analyse how the work of a single author is represented in the work of others. One could for instance focus on the corpus written by let's say Habermas or Prigogine and then study which parts of their work are mentioned and how it is mentioned. However complex a theory developed or however wide the span of an author's attention, in the end it is always boiled down to relative simple statements such as 'According to Habermas . . .' or 'As shown by Prigogine . . .' Needless to say any scientific text can be subject to many different rhetorical redescriptions. Since each such rhetorical redescription is a speech-action we can ask with respect to what positionings are these actions made determinate as speech-acts.

There seem to be two kinds of 'external' references to be found in scientific texts – to material things, processes and states of affairs, and to other texts. The fact that material things etc. are describable only as conceived within a conceptual system has led some philosophers to assimilate them to the realm of texts – so only one kind of 'external' reference occurs. We could call this the 'thesis of universal intertextuality'. There are any number of objections to this assimilation. If the assimilation of 'umwelt' to 'text' is made through the notion of 'reading' then we claim that the universal intertextuality thesis confuses a literal with a metaphorical sense of that word. Furthermore if everything is 'text' then nothing is 'text'. The essential contrast between *umwelt* and symbolic representation of *umwelt* could easily be reconstructed as radically disjoint kinds of 'text'.

In scientific writing the most important act of self-positioning is to claim authority – a positioning attempted in the very act of publishing. Whether the claim successfully constitutes a position will depend on the acceptance of that claim by others. And this is facilitated not only by the content of the text but by the reputation of the author as claimant. Reputation is generated in the conversational world of publication. In recent years attention has been drawn to the 'social construction' of scientific reputations. Especially Latour has emphasized how life within the laboratory (Latour and Woolgar, 1979) and the alliances between science and money (Latour, 1987) shape the whole enterprise of science. What counts as a contribution to knowledge, and hence enhances someone's scientific reputation, is not independent of the social structure of the scientific community.

There are two positioning devices common in spoken scientific discourse. Both involve the use of 'we'. According to Wales (1980) 'the surface meaning of joint activity' ((+ego) + (+voc)) (of uses of 'we') frequently disguises only thinly the true agentive 'I' or 'you' . . .' But there are cases where this gloss seems implausible. For example 'As WE will see . . .' is clearly 'inclusive' we. Should it be taken as an authoritative positioning of the speaker, though as one of too modest a character overtly to claim authority with 'I'? Wales thinks not. In some contexts it is neither the 'exclusive' nor the editorial 'we'. She proposes that we should recognize another positioning possibility, a critical or academic WE. For instance, in 'We shall note later the Fourier series methods are being applied . . .' the 'I' reference is muted and the utterance is not 'tinged with the authority of the "editorial" voice, neither does [it] invoke the suggestion of the "exclusive" WE of team-work'. From the point of view of positioning theory the speaker is not locating him or herself as the only authority, but positioning the audience both as following the talk and as working together 'by demonstration or ratiocination' (Wales, 1980: 29). Wales also notes that 'Let us . . .' may also be an overt marker of a pseudo-joint-activity conjured up by this usage, allowing (notionally) for such a response as 'No, let's not!'

The limitations of the publication 'market'

The rapid growth of scientific activity since the Second World War has had a profound influence on the epistemological aspects of science and hence on the relationship between contribution and personal reputation. Science is still presented as a collective endeavour in which individual scientists or scientific teams 'build' upon what others have done before them. Every production of scientific theories could be regarded as (a) drawing upon existing paradigms, theories and methodologies (securing the continuity of scientific thought) and as (b) bringing some novelty and creativity into the existing 'body of knowledge' (making progress possible). The balance between the continuous and discontinuous aspects that scientists bring into their work makes them both followers and challengers of existing paradigms in different degrees. The implicit voluntaristic thesis in such a view is that all scientists can contribute to the 'advancement' of science by means of their creativity, something that exists independently of their humanity. Another characteristic of this voluntaristic thesis is that science is often regarded as a system of markets (cf. Caplow and McGee, 1961 and Ziman, 1990). Contemporary scientists are faced with two enormous problems in establishing positions of authority. One is the growing impossibility of overviewing what is done by others. The other problem is the growing difficulty of communicating with others. Both problems are firmly linked to each other. Published scientific results can be compared with products offered on a 'market'. Journals and books constitute a market and researchers can tap that market in preparing their own research. Citations and quotations are the equivalent of buying and investing: what is published can be used to back one's own scientific ideas or it can be refuted by one's own results. When a scientific theory or idea has been refuted, it's 'market value' drops radically. And its dividend (the number of times cited) will be drastically lowered too.

In the classic view of science the metaphor of the market rests upon the idea of an 'invisible hand'. One just has to bring one's ideas into the market and if they are good (displayed as true), they will be 'bought', that is, they will be used by others, that is, they will be mentioned in their texts. Another assumption of this model is the transparency of the market. All scientists are assumed to have total knowledge about what is available on the market. While it probably always has been very difficult to have an overview of all that has been published on a certain topic, it is by now just impossible even by placing severe restrictions on the breadth of the subject matter. The explosion of the number of books and journals ensures that all scientists, no matter how specialized their interests may be, only have a very fragmented view of what is available. Thus the 'invisible hand' hypotheses will not work in explaining how a scientific reputation and hence an authoritative conversational position is achieved. Other 'visible' forces' operate.

One force that has rapidly gained importance is that of the 'marketing' of scientific ideas. It is not sufficient for a scientist to bring his work into the market, it also needs to be promoted. In other words, part of the post-research role of scientists is the 'public relations' and 'marketing' of results and ideas.

Stengers (1990) has hinted at this phenomenon when saying that the most vital interest for scientists in promoting their work is that it should attract interest. According to Stengers this has alarming epistemological consequences: 'l'intérét est condition de vérité; une proposition qui n'a pas intéressé n'est ni vrai ni fausse, mais bruit' (1990: 6). It would be worthwhile studying how scientists develop 'marketing strategies' in order to cope with this growing problem and how that is reflected in the form and content of their writings. Basically, such studies would have to investigate how scientists try to build up reputations. Positioning and reconstruction could be used as the main analytical concepts allowing us to use the same conceptual framework for talking about the content of scientific texts and about what happens to those texts when published. It should also be noted that the act of scientific writing is becoming more and more professionalized itself – books are beginning to appear in which academic discourse is not only analysed (Nash, 1990) but scrutinized in order to allow academics to write 'better'. Richardson's book *Writing Strategies: Reaching Diverse Audiences* (1990) was marketed by Sage as follows: 'it prepares the (academic) writer for approaching and successfully addressing diverse audiences'.

The non-publication aspects of scientific reputations

In the informal shop talk of a scientific community, its 'gossip', the phenomenon of positioning is very prominent. The art of scientific gossip is to position one's rivals as scientifically unreliable or self-deceiving by reason of their faults of character, typically either cowardice or impulsiveness or both. These positionings are framed within two standard but antithetical positions in the philosophy of science, both of which are used to complete the story. One's own data are presented as reliable – a consequence of one's impeccable moral character. The logical schema implicitly invoked is inductive support. The 'data' of one's rivals is presented as unreliable – a consequence or their shady or weak moral characters. The logical schema implicitly invoked is the theory ladenness of observations, often thought to cast doubt on the propriety of inductive generalization. One's competitors are so wedded to their theory that they are simply unable to read their results as anything other than favourable to their hypothesis. They impulsively read the hypothesis into the data. In gossip of this sort, widely reported by sociologists of science, the acts of positioning are overt. For example Latour and Woolgar (1979: 165) quote the following: 'According to my four hours in the laboratory . . . I was not impressed . . . judging by the published work it is even more embarrassing . . . Xala [Green's chemist] is Green's Achilles' heel.' The results do not speak for themselves, or at any rate are not permitted to do so. Rather it is he or she who obtained them that becomes the focus of epistemological concern. In terms of our analysis of this fragment of discourse the speaker, Green and Xala are all mutually positioned. Green appears as the victim of Xala's incompetence or bad character, while the speaker presents himself as both superior to Green and as a spectator of his pitiable condition.

Gilbert and Mulkay (1982) have also demonstrated an asymmetry between ways of accounting for true beliefs, or rather those beliefs which are thereby presented as true, and those which are presented as false. For true beliefs the scientific worker positions him or herself as rational, and the genesis of such belief to have been cognitive. Given the superior moral status given to those who ally themselves with rationality in the scientific community (Harré, 1990), this is a positioning act, with respect to a community of unknown others. On the other hand the holding of false beliefs, usually but not always ascribed to one's rivals, is attributed to social and psychological factors, such as the social standing in the community of an authority of character. For instance, Gilbert and Mulkay (1982: 399) report the following remark: 'N's numbers always agree with what S should want. I mean, it's bizarre. . . . I am sure I could do an experiment and produce any number I wanted – one needs to forget that kind of research.' N's character is neatly assassinated and his support of S undercut by virtue of that assassination.

Positioning and Reconstruction in the Natural and the Social Sciences

If we want to look into some detail at how the world is 'represented' in scientific texts, a theory about the constituents of the natural and social world has to be introduced. For the natural sciences, such a theory has been presented in Harré (1987). The tenets of this theory can be summarized as follows. From the standpoint of the epistemological possibilities for human beings, the 'world' can be pictured as consisting of three kinds of phenomena: (i) objects of actual experience which make up realm 1, (ii) objects of possible experience which make up realm 2, and (iii) objects beyond all possible experience which make up realm 3. Things like rocks, houses, people and the moon belong in realm 1. With help of instruments like telescopes, microscopes and other devices phenomena like micro-organisms or X-ray stars can be experienced. So the boundary between realm 1 and 2 is historically and technically unstable. Realm 3 is a domain of phenomena which will never be experienced because inexperienceable in principle – for instance, ensembles of quantum states prior to acts of measurement. Correlative to this triadic view of the world, one can also make a triadic classification of scientific theories according to their cognitive status:

Type 1 theories: these are cognitive objects with pragmatic properties. Theories of this type enable the constitution, classification and prediction of observable phenomena.

Type 2 theories: these are cognitive objects with iconic properties. Theories of this type enable the presentation (including sometimes the simple picturing) of certain classes of unobservable things, properties and processes.

Type 3 theories: these are cognitive objects with mathematical properties. Theories of this type enable the representation of non-picturable systems of beings and of their behaviour, interrelations and so on.

A typical type 1 theory is Newtonian kinematics, a typical type 2 theory is the bacterial theory of disease at the moment of its formulation (bacteria were at that moment still unobservable, but they were postulated by Bordet as beings which would be observable provided that certain technical advances had been made). Electromagnetic field theory and the theories of quantum field theory are typical type 3 theories. The referents of type 1 theories belong in realm 1, the referents of type 2 theories in realms 1 and 2, and the referents of type 3 theories in realms 1, 2 and 3. Harré's permutation of 'possible' and 'actual' with 'experience' thus creates epistemic categories that classify phenomena by reference to a human scientist's capacities to become acquainted with them. Scientists do not study the 'welt' but the 'umwelt'. It should be stressed that the human factor is indeed crucial: things may be beyond all possible experience because human beings lack the senses to observe them. Magnetic fields are unobservable for us, only consequences of magnetic fields can be observed. As a matter of fact our senses are only suited for the experience of realm 1 phenomena within a strict Newtonian time/space grid. If we look for instance to the sky at night the phenomenon we observe (a collection of white dots with some regularities in it) does not exist. The stars are located at different distances from the earth, and as the light from the stars needs time to reach us, some stars are 'seen' as they were 1000 years ago, others as they were 2000 years ago, and so on. In fact, some stars we still see may already have ceased to exist. In other words: the picture of a bright night sky full of stars has no referent in realm 1! Consequently, a fourth realm should be introduced: the realm 4 of apparent objects of actual experience which are nevertheless not possible. For centuries, mankind has tried to explain star constellations (cf. astrology) without knowing that they were trying to explain something that did not exist. Of course there can be no theories of this realm.

Social realms

It is tempting to extend the above scheme to the social world and the social sciences. It should however be noted that taken on the world scale, the phenomena of the natural world, realm 1, occur in a Newtonian and Euclidean space/time grid: causes are deterministic and space and time are independent and flat. But this is not the only possible space/time grid. Both on a cosmological and quantum physical scale other grids of locations are used where the independence of physical space from time vanishes. The same holds for the social world where it is not the time/space grid which has to be taken as a starting point for analysis, but as argued in Harré (1983), the persons/ conversations grid. Persons in conversation constitute the primary human reality. The people appearing in this primary structure can be thought of as locations for speech-acts. However, being real human beings, they are not merely locations: they are internally complex. This internal complexity can be called the secondary structure. This secondary structure has a formal unity (expressed in consciousness), a practical unity (expressed in agency) and an empirical unity (expressed in autobiography). Ontologically it is a partially privatized part of the general conversation.

The basic particulars of the social world can thus be pictured as speech acts created in the joint action of conversants. Speech acts can have perlocutionary effects on people. The question now arises what kind of social realms can be distinguished in the social world. We propose to distinguish between the four social realms which follow.

i) Within the persons/conversations grid the realm 1 of the social order (hereafter called the social realm 1) is the everyday behaviour and talk of persons within moral orders. During the everyday behaviour and talk of this primary structure people develop and make use of iconic representations of that primary structure, the secondary structure and the natural order. These icons serve to make social life intelligible and to account for a person's own and others' behaviour and talk. While people are 'developing' such iconical redescriptions of the world by talking about it, they are necessarily simultaneously involved in a complex process of positioning themselves and other persons (cf. chapter 1, above).

ii) Analogous to the natural world realms 3 and 4, some social objects can be beyond all possible experience. The iconic representations about the social order that emerge out of realm 1 can belong to realm 3 when they are beyond all possible experience. In that case one can speak of social realm 3 entities like mental states, personalities, social relations, public opinions and so on.

iii) Even more, such icons may belong to the social realm 4 when they are not representations of existing phenomena but constructions of non-factual things. Realm 4 consists of non-existing phenomena but with possible real consequences ('If man defines a situation as real . . .').

iv) Within the social order we would reserve the concept of social realm 2 for the behaviour and talk which is 'triggered' by social scientists in their research praxis (cf. Schutz's 'second order' knowledge), that is, in interviews, questionnaires, observational tests or experiments. Like in social realm 1, iconical representations can emerge of the primary and secondary structure out of the social scientists' practice. Such icons can again belong to social realm 3 or social realm 4.

The above structuring of the social realm can be used in order to explore the differences between positivist and realist conceptions of the social sciences. In the positivist mainstream conception of the social sciences, realm 2 practice is aimed at understanding realm 1, but in doing so it uncritically introduces social realm 3 or 4 concepts as if they belong to a natural realm 1. Within that conception the referential grid for social realm 1 is the time/space grid and not the persons/places grid. Furthermore, the positivist social realm 2 praxis does not attempt to generate new iconical representations of social realm 1. A realist conception of the social science praxis would give rise to three kinds of theories:

Type 1 social theories: descriptions of the primary and secondary structures in several moral orders.

Type 2 social theories: making explicit of common–sense explanations of the social order based on iconical representations.

Type 3 social theories: refinement of common–sense explanations by making use of (i) novel iconical representations or (ii) novel descriptive devices.

If we now return to the issue of scientific publications, it becomes clear that the natural and social sciences differ from each other in several ways if looked at from a rhetorical point of view. First, the social scientists' reconstructions of the social world are always 'second order' reconstructions. Whatever rhetorical reconstructions a social scientist develops, (s)he should bear in mind that the actors engaged in the social world being studied already have developed rhetorical reconstructions themselves. What is more, within the social world many rhetorical images occur which cannot be conceived as reconstructions of a certain social reality. As argued in Harré (1975), institutions, for example, are not to be seen as independent existents of which images ('icons') are conceived. Rather, they are icons which are used in explanations of certain problematic situations. Societal icons and rhetorical redescriptions of social events are always used in the context of a positioning. As such, a social scientist is only creating a new positioning context.

It is important to stress that, as all conversations always involve some sort of positioning, the conversational act of interviewing or asking a person to tick an answer on an item in a questionnaire also necessarily has to be understood in terms of the triad 'position, speech–act, storyline'. This signifies that concepts such as 'attitudes' or 'traits' hardly make any sense because they imply that there is something inside the head of persons that at any time can be 'tapped' by a social scientist. Asking a person questions about, for instance, locus of control or authoritarian behaviour is a form of positioning and has to be understood as such: it tells something about how people position themselves when answering a questionnaire administered by a scientist. When that same person is talking to his girlfriend about why he failed his exams and how that relates to the behaviour of his tutor, quite other positioning will occur that relates to locus of control or authoritarianism. In other words the 'external validity' involves much more than just the relation between answers on a questionnaire and 'real-life behaviour'. In order to assess the relation between scientific positioning and how people position themselves in other situations, not only the speech-acts (be it test items) but also the positions and storylines have to be taken into account. With reference to Schutz's (1966) concepts of first and second order accounts, it can be said that scientific positioning should always start by analysing the 'first order' positionings that occurred before the scientist started to converse with people about a given topic. Rather than asking questions like 'what do you think about X?', questions should be asked that enquire if and on which occasions people think about X, and what they think of the scientist's interest in their thinking about X. Furthermore, it also makes sense to analyse research-acts themselves in terms of positioning. Rather than the sterile recalcitrance of methods (e.g. '65 subjects whose age ranged between . . .'), a research report should include the story of that research.

This then brings us to a second issue: whatever a social scientist studies, it involves a positioning of him/herself towards the social actors studied. In other words, doing social science always involves a dialogue between researchers and those or that being researched. In positivist approaches to social sciences this positioning is bracketed away. In doing so the social world is mistakenly treated as a natural world. This has implications for the status of publications. Within a natural science publication, the objects under study are treated as passive agents that undergo the experimenters' manipulations. Such manipulations can have effects on the objects or substances manipulated, but the publication of an account of those manipulations cannot possibly have any direct effects. In many mainstream or positivist social sciences studies, the same is implicitly postulated. Persons are treated as 'objects' and their advice on what they think about the publications is seldom asked. Actually, most subjects in, for example, a psychological experiment, will never read any of the publications that resulted from that experiment. But there are many subtle ways in which publications indexed with the authoritative position of allegedly 'scientific' authors can ultimately influence and even transform societal reality, that is, transform the discourse practices by which that reality is created.

Conclusions

Applying positioning theory to the understanding of science as a social process allows one to combine insights from an anthropological approach with insights from a linguistic approach. Moreover, it allows one to study the scientific production process without bracketing the content.

9

Positioning and Assessment of Technology

L. van Langenhove and R. Bertolink

Introduction

It is a well-documented fact that the emergence of the concept of 'technology assessment' (TA) in scientific and political literature and the historical development of TA practices can be regarded as attempts to give form to a growing need for societal embedded decision-making processes concerning technologies (Smits and Leyten, 1991). The first TA wave that started in the 1960s has been described as an 'early-warning system' aimed at predicting future technological developments. It was expected by policy-makers as well as by scientists that such TA-generated information and forecasts could be used in technological policy-making. Gradually it became clear, however, that making predictions about technologies was a very difficult, if not impossible, job. It became equally clear that even if good TA-based information or forecasts were available there was no guarantee that policy-makers would actually use such information.

From the early 1980s onwards a new TA concept has emerged in which attention shifted from the prediction issue to the issue of how and when information about technology can or will be used by policy-makers or by any other parties involved in the technology development process. Smits and Leyten (1991) have defined this new TA paradigm as a process consisting of both (i) *analyses* of technological developments and their consequences, and (ii) *discussions* emerging out of those analyses. The goal of such analysing or discussion processes is the generation of information that can help those involved in technological developments in determining their strategic policies. Such a TA can be directed towards strengthening of the relationships between research and development (R&D) and product development on the one hand, and the application environment on the other hand.

Smits and Leyten (1991) have coined the term 'Constructive Technology

Assessment' (CTA) for such TA. It is called 'constructive' TA because it is TA directed towards the construction of technologies (Ouwens et al., 1987). CTA tries to incorporate public interest, public demands and/or aspirations in the development of technologies. Candaele (1992) has recently noted that this shift from the 'early warning' TA towards the CTA has been paralleled by a paradigm shift in the social studies of technologies: from a study of the influences of technologies on a society towards a study of the influences of society on the development of technologies.

As a practice, TA has become institutionalized in different forms. First there is the parliamentary TA with specific 'institutions' aimed at advising members of parliament. The US Office of Technology Assessment (OTA) was the first parliamentary TA office to be created in 1973. It was conceived to be the analytical branch of the US Congress. In recent years a number of European countries have created similar offices (Coenen et al., 1991). A second institutional form of TA is national or supranational efforts to promote or support the idea and practice of TA. Several governments include TA in their national science and technology programmes. In Europe, the efforts of the European Commission with regard to TA are gradually increasing. The FAST programme (Forecasting and Assessment in Science and Technology) is well known, and more recently, the EC programme VALUE II is also promoting TA initiatives. Thirdly, TA is gradually becoming institutionalized within universities as a separate department or as part of departments directed towards the study of the relationships between science, technology and society. Fourthly, an 'invisible college' of persons involved in promoting or carrying out TA is slowly institutionalizing as well. The European Congresses on Technology Assessment, for instance, attract people from all the above-mentioned institutions. Finally, the existence of an industrial form of TA should also be mentioned. A lot of TA-like work is currently done within private firms where TA is used as a tool to assist strategic planning. Often such practices are not called TA but 'entrepreneurial planning' or 'applied TA' (Maloney, 1982: 61).

Notwithstanding, the growing institutionalizing of TA, there seems to be little consensus on what exactly TA is, how it should be performed, and who are to be the commissioners and clients of TA. There is still much debate on the usefulness of TA and on how it should be organized. That debate seems blurred because TA is alternatively regarded as a political and as a (social) scientific activity, which means that some people regard TA as part of the regulatory branch of public policy, while others consider it to be an academic discipline. The TA debate is also blurred because all too often the concept of TA is treated as a 'black box'. The arguments *pro* and *con* are not addressing the basic question: how should technology be assessed? This 'basic' methodological question can only be answered if one regards TA as a social practice pivoting on scientific and political issues. Arguing for or against TA or reflecting on how TA can be organized can thus not be done independently of ongoing debates on the nature of scientific practices and political systems. In this chapter attempts will be made to partly open the TA black box by focusing on the relations between TA and the social sciences.

'Evaluation' is a practice that has it origins in the field of education. Nowadays a lot of human actions are evaluated in a scientific manner: business, therapies, research programmes and so on. Within the field of evaluation studies the same paradigm battles are fought as elsewhere in the social sciences. From the 1980s on, qualitative forms of evaluation are gaining field. The most elaborated form of qualitative evaluation was developed by Guba and Lincoln (1989). They have coined the term 'fourth generation evaluation' for an evaluation practice that is inspired by social constructionism.

The Social Constructionist Current in the Social Sciences and its Relevance for TA

As argued in the preceding section, TA has to be considered as a social practice. It refers to both a political and a scientific way of looking at reality. As such, TA is linked in two ways to the social sciences: (i) as a social practice, TA can and has to be studied itself from a social sciences perspective, and (ii) as a partly scientific practice, it is also part of the social sciences. The latter implies that conceptions of TA are necessarily influenced by ongoing debates within the social sciences. Not only is TA not value-free (something about which most scholars now agree), it is also not free from theoretical and methodological choices. Understanding TA and aiming towards more and better TA can thus not be done without placing TA in a social sciences context.

Whatever kind of TA one is speaking about, the following issues always play a major role in its success or failure as a scientific practice:

1   TA project management
2   Information gathering techniques
3   The methodological framework
4   The theoretical framework

Any project or practice entails some management issues. Especially in the case of CTA the management is extremely important, as both a scientific project and a discussion project have to be set up and linked to each other. TA cannot be undertaken without gathering some sort of information. For this process of information gathering, techniques from the social sciences are usually being 'borrowed'. The problem so far has been that the choice of techniques has been largely regarded as unproblematic. Such a choice is, however, dependent upon the methodological and theoretical framework that one works in. As will be argued below, the dominant methodological paradigm for TA has long been, and still is to a large extent, positivism. As will be argued also, there are many reasons to abandon that paradigm in the social sciences and replace it by a paradigm better adapted to the social world as studied in the social sciences. Although the positivist conception of technological developments has indeed disappeared from recent TA thinking, the TA community has not yet realized sufficiently clearly that positivism should also be abandoned on the methodological and technical level. Our claim is that TA can only be organized successfully when drawing upon the non-positivist conceptions of the social sciences. This implies making use of non-positivist research methods and techniques in the process of information gathering, and paying sufficient attention to the theoretical aspects as well. An important feature of positivism is indeed the theory-free use of techniques and methods. It is striking that TA is to a large extent organized without much theoretical underpinning. One of the few exceptions is the field of technology dynamics studies which, according to Van Boxel (1992), can act as a theory for CTA.

The social sciences, especially sociology and psychology, have long been dominated by positivism. The positivist conception of science when applied to the social world results in a mechanistic world view in which simple causal relations between social entities are assumed to exist. In the positivist practice of social sciences, social phenomena are pictured as waiting to be 'discovered' by social scientists. Greenwood (1991) has called this the 'sleeping beauty' model: the prince–investigator comes by and 'awakes' the phenomena. Such a view of the social world and social science coincides well with the old TA conception of early warning. As the first TA concepts adopted the then dominant positivist way of thinking, it is not surprising that TA was then regarded as an instrument to measure and control 'effects' of technologies. The technology assessor was a kind of 'prince–investigator' able to discover the hidden effects of technologies.

For at least three decades now, the positivist 'mainstream' paradigm within the social sciences has been subjected to heavy criticism (Harré and Secord, 1972). Non-positivist conceptions are as a result of those criticisms gaining importance. One of the most flourishing new paradigms within the social sciences today is social constructionism. The origins of social constructionism can be found in the work of Berger and Luckman (1971) who argued that an adequate understanding of 'reality *sui generis*' requires an inquiry into the manner in which that reality is constructed. Today different versions of social constructionism exist. According to Harré (1992), the one shared thesis amongst them is that all psychological phenomena and the beings in which they are realized are produced discursively. To this statement it can be added that also the social phenomena, and the practices and institutions in which they are realized, can be thought of as produced discursively as well. One of the most central points of this paradigm is that people are the constructors of their own (social) reality. Opinions differ on questions like how and to what extent social reality is constructed. A useful way of representing the varieties of social constructionism is the distinction between 'weak' and 'strong' forms. In its strong form, social constructionism will assert that it is not possible to come to 'objective' descriptions of the world as we can only speak about the world. Gergen (1985: 266) states that social constructionists see theories about the world 'as an artefact of communal interchange'. In its weak form, social constructionism will on the contrary assert that it is possible to come to descriptions of the real world, but that the place of the formulator of such theories always has to be taken into account. In the weak versions, the emphasis is on the multiplicity and relativity of the human interpretations of reality. In the strong versions, the consequences of social constructs on human thinking and doing are emphasized.

The social constructionist movement in the social sciences has up to now not been related directly to TA. However, there are some instigations to make the connection. The most important one is the convergence between CTA and the social constructionist movement in the field of technology dynamics research (Pinch and Bijker, 1984). Social constructionist studies of science and technology have in recent years been prominent in the domains of sociology of science, the studies of science–technology relationships and the studies of the dynamics of technological developments (Knorr-Cetina, 1981; Latour, 1987; Bijker, Hughes and Pinch, 1987; Doerkes and Hoffman, 1992). Studies of technological dynamics are relatively young compared to studies of scientific dynamics, and although science and technology cannot be regarded as synonymous, technology studies are, to some extent, coloured by the results and debates coming from the science studies.

The scientific study of science has its origins in philosophical theories of science in which first scientific statements and theories and later scientific research traditions were the subject of analysis. Across different approaches there have been two key issues. Is it the world or is it our experience of the world that is scientifically represented? Secondly, how are true and false representations to be distinguished from one another? Cognition played an important role in the first attempts at science-of-science studies, and the production of scientific knowledge was reckoned not to involve any social factors. With Merton's sociology of science and, more importantly, Flecks' analysis of the social processes involved in the production of 'facts', attention shifted from the cognitive functioning of individual scientists towards science as a normatively regulated product achieved by structured social groups. The Mertonian structural-functional analysis in the study of science and the sociology of science became a relatively flourishing field. Gradually, sociology of science moved towards a more anthropological stance, challenging the Mertonian ideal of scientific norms. Both the Edinburgh school (cf. the 'strong' programme of Bloor (1976)), and the 'Paris' school (Latour and Woolgar (1979) emphasized the role of social factors in the scientific production of representations. The social constructionist approach associated with the works of Latour and Woolgar (1979) and Knorr-Cetina (1981) even advocated the view that representations create the world rather than reflect it.

In these seminal studies an anthropological method is used to study how scientists work in their laboratories. One of their most salient conclusions was that in the process from experiment to published text, a scientific truth is constructed. As such, the Paris school took a stance against the Popperian view of falsification as the dynamic motor of scientific developments: Popper treats the scientific process itself as a 'black box' and sees progress as a 'battle' between falsifiable ideas. For Latour and Knorr-Cetina, the falsification process should largely be understood as an *a posteriori* account of 'constructed' facts. As shown by Knorr-Cetina, scientific papers can also be conceived as 'an exercise in depersonalization'. All the social interactions that were an essential part of a scientific experiment are abstracted until a text remains that represents a 'clean story'. Relatively independent from the social constructionist approach a renewed interest emerged in the cognitive aspects of science (De Mey, 1982). As noted by Woolgar (1989) the main question for the field of science studies today is to what extent the social and the cognitive approaches can be integrated with each other. It should be noted that in recent years a lot of effort has been made to study technological dynamics from a social constructionist perspective (Dierkes and Hoffmann, 1992). Those studies address the same questions as the social constructionist studies of scientific developments, albeit within the framework of a more economical approach.

In our view, the social constructionist movement in the social sciences can have a threefold relevance for TA. First, it provides a theoretical framework for thinking about the subject of TA, namely technological research and developments. Secondly, it provides epistemological alternatives for the positivist conceptions of TA. Thirdly, it allows one to think of TA itself as a social construction. While the first aspect is widely acknowledged in TA, the two other possible relevances are hardly explored. In the next two sections a social constructionist approach to TA that does take these issues into account will be advocated and partly developed.

A Positioning Theory Approach of TA

The social constructionist approach of technology dynamics asserts that technology is a socially constructed process. We would like to emphasize not only technology but also technology assessment as socially constructed phenomena. If one agrees that in order to understand the development of a technology, one must understand the multiple social reality in which that technology emerges, then one can conceive TA as a specific social action in which actors are actively engaged in socially constructing a technology. We are thus claiming that TA should be considered as a specific form of social construction of a technology. However, even though all technologies can be said to be socially constructed, not all technologies give rise to TA. The specificity of a TA social construction of a technology could be that the actors involved in the process are aware of the social constructionist aspects of their action.

A social constructionist approach to TA starts from the assertion that TA is a specific kind of discourse between people in which both a technology and its 'assessments' are socially constructed. This analysis involves at least the following issues: (i) identification of the persons involved *in* TA discourse and (ii) analysis of the TA discourse. Social constructionism is mainly concerned with how the actors produce discourses and with how the discourses affect the actors. In the following sections we will present and apply the basic tenets of positioning theory as an attempt to develop such a social constructionist approach towards TA. First of all the basic elements of positioning theory will be assumed; secondly, the concepts 'TA storylines' and 'TA positions' will be explored.

TA storylines

Within our society, several discourses about technology occur. Whenever a new technology is developed or an existing technology newly implemented, specific *storylines* about that technology take place. Such storylines have to be understood as conversations between actors who are in one way or another involved in a certain technology development of implementation process. The act of a 'conversation' has to be broadly defined. Written storylines, such as letters and administrative forms (e.g., research proposals, written communications, draft articles, etc.), are also to be regarded as conversations.

Consider the following exchange as an example of how technological developments can be discussed:

A: 'The development of this sensor is of great scientific importance and can be of use to industrial applications.'

B: 'Yes, I agree. In order to persuade our Board to invest more in this research we need data that support our case. Therefore, we urgently need to commission a market study.'

Another example of a conversation about technology could be the following:

The scientist X: 'This genetically modified tobacco plant is finally made immune to most of the diseases that can be found in this area. I am afraid public resistance to this may involve problems. Therefore, I think that we need more research on the risks of releasing it in its natural environment.'

The customer Y: 'I am sorry, but that was not an option. We do not want to hang about waiting for the results. We will deal later with the public's distrust.'

These two short examples illustrate that in simple conversations on techno-logical developments, much more is happening than just 'talking'. These conversations reflect that around any technological issue a complex web of discourses arises that involves several storylines. A feature of such storylines is that they lead toward a certain 'plot' (e.g., a decision being made). Within such storylines, technologies are always in one way or another being 'assessed', although that assessment is not necessarily called a TA. Such assessments are multiple: several people will on different occasions and at different times assess a given technology. All these assessments can only be understood if placed in their context of storylines and plots. If we acknowledge that any technological development or implementation is always embedded in storylines between people and between institutions and people, two things can be asserted. First it can be said that through the conversations about technologies, the technolo-gies are 'socially constructed'. Secondly, within the storylines, questions about technologies are inevitably being asked. As such, technologies are always being assessed. The question is when, by whom and as part of what kind of storylines?

If we look in some detail into question storylines, it can be said that there exist two broad categories: 1) regression questions and 2) progression ques-tions. The two basic forms of regression questions are the 'why' and the 'how' questions. For example 'Why did the machine fail?' And 'How did the accident occur?' The two basic forms of progression questions are 'What will happen?' And 'What will be the effect of the thing happening?'

Question storylines about technologies not only involve questions, they also give rise to answers. The answers on regression questions can be called *accounts* or justifications, excuses). The answers on progression questions are *prospects.* Technology assessment always involves a question–answer storyline giving rise to accountive and prospective speech-acts about technology. Such speech-acts can have a certain 'power'. For instance, when an evaluator of an R&D proposal says 'no', that speech-act has the power to stop the funding of a certain line of technological development. Speech-acts also have other powers. They determine the continuation of the storylines they are part of and they have an effect on the people involved in that storyline.

Thinking of TA in terms of storylines allows us to bring some order into the blurred discussions mentioned above. The debate on whether TA is needed or not can be answered simply by stating that it is a wrong question. TA storylines always occur, whether one calls it TA or not. More relevant questions are then about who, when, and why TA storylines are occurring. This will be considered later. It can be stated that for any given technology, several storylines exist at the same time. There is thus no single TA possible; there are as many technology assessments as there are discourses going on. This implies that there might be differences between different types of technology with regard to their assessments. Some technologies can be the subject of many diverse storylines in society, while others might hardly ever be being taken up in societal discourses. Acceptance of a new technology should not be equated with a low number of ongoing storylines. It is difficult to pinpoint the beginning and ending of a certain TA storyline. This has as a consequence that one can hardly speak of TA as 'something' to be done and of which the 'effects' after its completion are finished. At best, an actor can start a new storyline and call it 'officially' a 'TA'. It is very important to acknowledge that such an 'official' TA storyline never comes first. Other TA storylines always exist before any 'official' TA storyline is started. We could call the pre-official TA storyline the 'first order TA' (that is, assessments in ongoing discussions without them being labelled as 'TA'). In a positivist conception of TA such first order storylines have been neglected. In a social constructionist perspective, 'first order' TA storylines have to be incorporated in the 'official' TA storylines which then can be regarded as 'second order' TA storylines: specific storylines partly about other prior and ongoing ones. To give an example: whenever a factory adopts a new technology in the production process, this new technology will be assessed at the shop floor, at the management level, etc. All these are 'first order' storylines which can and should be incorporated in any 'official' TA. Seen as such, the so-called official TA can perhaps best be regarded as an attempt to bring together the different ongoing discourses. Even an 'official' TA storyline can be taken up in other higher order storylines. The storyline labelled 'technology assessment' can be assessed itself. An important difference in all those storylines is the degree to which some of their speech-acts have certain powers.

TA positions

Up to now we have focused on TA storylines as a special kind of discourse in which technologies are socially created. Such TA storylines are performed by actors who in some way or another are involved in developing or implementing technologies. All such actors can say they are in certain positions and they are also being positioned by other actors. The possible positions concerning technologies reflect the dual relation that exists between people and technologies: people are 'stakeholders' who can gain or lose by implementing technologies, and they also have a discretionary space to make decisions about technologies. Inspired by Guba and Lincoln (1989), who identified three broad evaluative classes of stakeholders, we can speak of the following groups of stakeholders involved in the development and usage of new technologies:

i.   The *agents*: those people involved in producing, developing and implementing the technologies, namely (a) the scientists and engineers, and (b) the decision-makers involved.
ii.   The *beneficiaries*: those people who profit in some way or another from the technology implemented or developed. Amongst the possible beneficiaries, one can list: (a) the direct beneficiaries, the users; (b) the indirect beneficiaries, people whose relationship with the direct beneficiaries is mediated, eased, enhanced or otherwise positively influenced; and (c) the people who gain by the fact that the technology is being produced.
iii. The *victims*: those people who are negatively affected by the technology, including: (a)groups systematically excluded from using the technology; (b) groups that suffer negative side effects, and (c) persons who suffer opportunity costs for forgone opportunities.

The above list of stakeholders is neither exhaustive, nor is it a typology. This means that a single person can have several stakeholder roles successively or at the same time. Moreover stakeholders can often be identified as groups. Each stakeholder group holds its own claims and concerns in issues related to technologies. A 'claim' is any assertion that a stakeholder may introduce that is favourable for the technology. A 'concern' is any assertion that a stakeholder may introduce that is unfavourable for the technology. An 'issue' is any state of affairs about which reasonable persons may disagree. The interplay between the different stakeholders gives rise to the TA storylines described above. This does not necessarily entail that any of those stakeholders positions themselves or are being positioned as 'technology assessors'. To state that one is performing a technology assessment or that a technology assessment is necessary is to deliberately position oneself in a very specific way. Such a position can be called the TA advocate. Taking up such a position implies, according to positioning theory, necessarily the positioning of other stakeholders. By advocating TA, some stakeholders are positioned as having to allow or perform the assessment. Because of the simple fact that in the TA advocate position one is claiming the necessity of TA, a non-TA position is opened. Such a position can easily be given a negative connotation. The positions taken up and created together make certain storylines and certain actions possible.

Conclusion

As advocated in the previous sections, TA can be regarded as a confrontation of different constructions of a technology by different groups of stakeholders. The fact that different groups of stakeholders hold different TA conceptions, does not mean that each group has a single TA concept once and for all. On the contrary, TA concepts are created in discourses (within the group and with the outside world). Hence it is partly the kind of conversations in which a group of stakeholders is involved that determine the TA concepts. In other words, TA concepts are created and re-created in discourses. A useful way to look at this process in some analytical detail is by making use of positioning theory. When a TA is regarded as the bringing together of different constructions in order to enhance a negotiation process, it should be clear that there cannot be a single TA 'truth' about a technology. Each group of stakeholders has its own TA discourse; a systematic TA differs only from those TA discourses in that (a) it tries to follow a rigorous method, (b) it attempts to put together different TA discourses, and (c) it tries to be critical about its own TA discourse. Such a social constructionist approach to TA emphasizes not the direct assessment of consequences or futures of technologies, but rather the conceptualization of such consequences and the mutual negotiating of those consequences among individuals. The role of a 'technology assessor' in such an approach is that of an organizer and facilitator who brings in (scientific) information and makes the confrontations possible. It is important to stress that a technology assessor stands not 'above' or 'beyond' the stakeholders, but is indeed a stakeholder himself!

Technology assessment has to be further developed as a tool for 'managing' technological developments. In order to achieve this, the development of the instrumental and methodological aspects of TA have to be stimulated and TA should become a topic of 'assessment' itself. It is our belief that empirical studies of TA as a practice and a discourse and the theoretical grounding of TA in discourse analysis (such as positioning theory) are necessary steps in any effort to strengthen the effectiveness and efficiency of TA.

10

Positioning as the Production and Use of Stereotypes

L. van Langenhove and R. Harré

Introduction

This chapter addresses the application of positioning theory to the issue of cultural stereotyping. A critical conceptual analysis of the words 'cultural stereotype' is presented. It will be demonstrated how the framework of positioning theory can be used to refine the concept of cultural stereotype. The main upshot of the chapter is the conclusion that within social psychology, the concept of cultural stereotype is used in a conceptually vague and blurred way and that, with the necessary conceptual refinements, other research agendas on stereotypes will have to be tackled if social psychologists want to contribute anything to the societal efforts of changing stereotypes.

Cultural Stereotypes

In this section several issues concerning the concept 'cultural stereotype' will be briefly dealt with. First, definitions of the concept will be reviewed and discussed. Secondly, the differences between so-called self-stereotypes and a cultural stereotype will be dealt with. Finally, the theoretical affinities of the concept with some social psychological theories will be addressed. Together these investigations will allow us to draw several conclusions about the vagueness of the concept and about the superficiality of most contemporary socio-psychological research on stereotypes.

The concept of stereotyping was introduced in psychology by Walter Lippman, a journalist, in 1922. As with so many concepts in psychology, an exact definition of the concept seems hardly available, as 'few if any researchers have attempted to formulate a rigorous concept' (Stewart et al., 1979: 1). Notwithstanding their conceptual vagueness, 'stereotypes' have been widely used in social psychological research, especially in research on person perception. Today, a theoretical corpus conceding stereotypes has emerged and the concept is also widely used by the general public. Stereotypes are regarded as something negative and as something that has to be 'corrected'.

Within social psychology, 'stereotypes' either refer to so-called self- or personal stereotypes, or to social or cultural stereotypes. Secord and Backman (1964: 40) have distinguished personal and social stereotypes as follows:

> we may speak of a personal stereotype as characterising a single individual's opinions and a social stereotype as representing the consensus of the majority of a given population of judges.

In Stewart et al. (1979: 12), self-stereotypes are said to arise

> when subjects ascribe traits to others in the same manner as they would ascribe to themselves, making the implicit assumption that others are to a large degree similar to themselves.

These same authors define social or cultural stereotypes as generalized expectations about how others are motivated, behave, feel, etc. Such expectations are said to be applied when called upon to judge others (Stewart et al., 1979: 13).

While self-stereotypes are seen as generalizations from one's own behaviour to the behaviour of others, cultural stereotypes are thus defined not by a person's own experiences but by 'generalized expectations'. The question is where such expectations come from, if not from one's own direct experiences. According to Schutz (1966: 232) they are

> formed in the main by others, his predecessors or contemporaries, as appropriate tools for coming to deal with things and men, as accepted as such by the group into which he was born.

Both personal and cultural stereotypes are nowadays seen as a fundamental part of the human condition. As Secord and Backman (1964: 20) put it: 'stereotyping people is almost inevitable, because of its functional usefulness'. Stewart et al. (1979: 1) speak of stereotyping as 'one of the main avenues for the expression of social and cultural attitudes'.

Theories of stereotypes can be broadly classified into two groups: those explaining stereotyping in terms of sociocultural causes and those explaining stereotyping in terms of intrapersonal processes. Amongst the sociocultural theories of stereotyping can be counted Tajfel's *Social Identity Theory* (Tajfel, 1981), which assumes individual motives to achieve or maintain positive social identities. Such motives may lead to positive differentiation of the ingroup from other groups, though this, by itself, would not entail the existence of stereotypes. Intrapersonal theories of stereotyping follow a cognitive stance in which stereotypes are conceived as categories used to cope with information overload. Lalonde and Gardner (1989) have advocated an approach that combines both the sociocultural and the cognitive elements, and analyse stereotypes as 'social cognitive structures operating in an intergroup context' (p. 290). However, it is not clear whether they mean this discursively, that is, as an interpersonal process of speech-acts within the contexts of rules and storylines (see Harré and Gillett, 1994).

Cultural Stereotypes and Positioning Theory

Whatever the theoretical approaches followed, stereotypes are in general defined as a set of consensual beliefs of one group about the attributes shared by members of another group. Stereotypes have also been seen as a 'bias' in person perception. From Lippman onwards, stereotypes have been thought of as distortions of reality. They are generally viewed as 'categories' which wrongly represent the reality to which they refer. Hence, phenomena such as 'bias', 'prejudice' or 'discrimination' are seen by social psychologists as arising out of the normal human process of categorization. It is implied that the real world is being distorted and simplified when stimuli are categorized. Billig (1987: 126) has questioned such an approach in which 'it becomes a short step to conclude that stereotypes are a necessary cognitive process'. Potter and Wetherell (1987) have pointed out three problematic basic assumptions about the phenomenon of categorization:

1   the assumption of the inevitability of biased categorization;
2   the assumption that categories have a fixed structure;
3   the assumption that categories are preformed and enduring.

On the basis of these assumptions people are viewed as carrying around a mentally encoded set of preformed, enduring and fixed prototypes. Also, stereotyping is seen as a consequence of purportedly basic and adaptive cognitive processes. In sum, people are seen as passive agents that 'undergo' their own stereotyping. Note that this viewpoint has consequences for the issue of changing stereotypes: people themselves cannot change 'their' stereotypes, but people exposed to the 'right' stimuli might be less given to stereotyping. This equally holds for cognitive theories related to connectionist analysis and neural network theories (Anderson and Rosenfeld, 1988): while it is true that such theories do emphasize the dynamically evolving nature of cognitive categories, the locus of change seems not to be at the level of autonomous, intentional people, but within 'neural networks' that impose their changes upon people.

Out of this brief discussion emerge a number of issues. First, social psychologists tend to see people as stereotypers: human beings always use stereotypes as an inevitable consequence of human cognitive functioning. Secondly, stereotyping is seen as a cognitive process which takes place inside the individual mind. Whatever is said or whatever is done, it *is* regarded as the 'expression' of the stereotypes. Discursive aspects of stereotypes are to a large extent neglected. Thirdly, there seems to be a problem with the explanation of change. If stereotyping is a 'built in' function of our cognitive functioning, how can it then ever be changed?

Stereotypes and Positions

In this section stereotypes will be analysed in terms of 'positions' and 'reconstructions'. It will be argued that stereotypes can only be understood when placed in their conversational context. The bulk of the available social psychological research on (cultural) stereotypes has focused on the 'reconstruction' aspect of stereotypes while neglecting its 'positioning' aspect. It will also be argued that introducing the positioning aspect allows one to talk about changing stereotypes in a different way from that which takes its start within the framework of cognitive models of stereotype change.

Locating stereotypes

As mentioned before, there seems to be a widely shared consensus that a 'stereotype' refers to something that is located 'inside' people (e.g., an element in a cognitive process like a premise in a formal argument). This 'thing' can become tangible when people speak or act. Within the social constructionist paradigm a new and more complex view on where to locate psychological phenomena is emerging (Harré and Gillett, 1994). Based on Vygotsky, Harré (1983) has proposed the following two-dimensional conceptual space. The two axes of this scheme are (i) a public–private axis representing the degree to which the display of one's psychological attributes is private or public, and (ii) an individual–collective dimension representing the degree to which some apparently psychological attributes can be realized as the property of the discursive interactions of one or many persons. Combining these two dimensions gives a two-dimensional space of four quadrants representing the relations between a person and his/her discursive 'environment' (see figure 10.1).

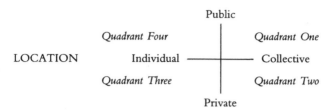

Figure 10.1   The Vygotskian space of locations of psychological phenomena

In Quadrant One can be placed all the social and psychological phenomena which are collective and public. These include the so-called 'moral orders'. The appropriation of knowledge of the discursive conventions and the moral orders of one's social environments can be represented as a transition from Quadrant One to Quadrant Two. A child can be taught that before crossing the street it first has to look left, then right and so on. At some point such a practice can cease to be rule-controlled and becomes habitual: one does not have to think about the situation any more. At the same time the cognitive processes in which a child engages with the prime caretaker, usually the mother, as the senior member of the symbiotic dyad, so to speak, become privatized. Such a combination of privatization and habituation-shift corresponds to a transition from Quadrant Two to Quadrant Three. Appropriated and privatized psychological and social knowledge can then in turn be 'publicized' (transition from Quadrant Three to Quadrant Four) and even 'conventionalized' (transition from Quadrant Four to Quadrant One). Whatever one has appropriated from a moral order can thus be brought into the public arena again by speaking about it, discursively displaying it, or behaving in an appropriate way. Such publicising can of course contain idiosyncratic transformations of the original moral order. One can for instance misunderstand the meaning of a particular traffic signal and act incorrectly. No one will follow this innovation as a new social custom! It is also possible that a personal innovation is taken up into the conventions of the moral order in which it has been publicised, for instance, the traffic moral order in Spain had originally no reference to lorry drivers letting cars behind them know if it was safe to pass them by operating the right-hand indication. Some lorry drivers must have started that useful practice and nowadays it is part of the moral order: car drivers will not be happy when a lorry driver is not helping them.

This Vygotskian conception about the location of psychological phenomena has the great advantage that it goes beyond the classical Cartesian opposition between 'inside' and 'outside' the mind. Applying this conceptual scheme to stereotypes allows one to make a clear distinction between the social representation of a stereotype (a cultural stereotype) and its expression within a speech-act (a personal stereotype). In the traditional viewpoint the difference between personal and cultural stereotypes lies mainly in the number of people who adhere to them. From the viewpoint we want to advocate, cultural stereotypes are best seen as belonging to the public/collective domain as positions in everyday discourse from which individuals can appropriate them (transition from Quadrant One to Quadrant Two). In these circumstances one person can 'use' them on certain occasions for certain purposes of his or her own. Appropriated stereotypes can be uttered while the person doing so is fully aware that it is 'only' a stereotype. But the stereotype can also be privatized (transition from Quadrant Two to Quadrant Three). It is the individually/privately 'used' cultural or public/collective stereotype that can be regarded as a personal stereotype. Instead of the entity-like 'stereotype' of the traditional theory of social judgement we propose the process-like act of stereotyping of a dynamic, discursive conception of the conventions for making social judgements. This also implies that appropriated and/or privatized social judgements can become conventionalized (transition from Quadrant Four to Quadrant One).

Using stereotypes in conversations

At this point we can now introduce positioning theory in order to understand how cultural stereotypes can become personal stereotypes by virtue of the use to which individuals put them. 'Using' a stereotype refers to 'publicising' a stereotype within a conversation. So we have to take the discursive aspects of stereotyping into account. Following positioning theory, an act of personal stereotyping can be defined as a speech-act that is (a) part of a specific storyline, (b) used in order to position both speaker and the object of the stereotyping and (c) draws upon social representations of the stereotyped objects (the cultural stereotypes) which are available in certain moral orders. The process of appropriating and using stereotypes by 'publishing' them can now be described as follows. Let's take for example the idea 'philosophers are confused and tangled persons'. This idea can be found in the collective–public realm of our Western societies: in novels, pictures, cartoons, songs, etc., philosophers are often pictured as such. Persons can appropriate that idea and actually believe that 'in general' philosophers are tangled. But what does this actually mean, that they 'believe' it? It certainly does not mean that they are forever thinking of philosophers as confused people. No, they will on certain occasions say what they think about philosopher so and so. In the classic view this means that they are 'expressing' their beliefs. The alternative model that we suggest goes as follows: people will use the appropriate idea in all situations where they have good reasons for doing so. People may use what they know to be a public image of a philosopher and they will use it according to certain conversational conventions. Probably, in many cases the reason can be very simple: people know that a certain public image is often used and that it makes rather a good impression when one simply conforms to the 'general' idea. So without too much reflection they will call upon that image. In terms of positioning this means first and above all that the speaker is positioning him/herself towards the other speaker as somebody who acts in conformity with the 'general ideas' that live in what (s)he believes to be their common moral order. If the addressee sees him(her)self as part of a moral order in which the cartoon stereotypes of philosophers are not much appreciated, (s)he will possibly object and say something like 'wait a minute, that's unfair, not all philosophers are etc.'. Whether or not the other speaker will object depends to some extent on his/her beliefs about philosophers, but equally so on how (s)he wants the conversation to proceed. If these persons are in the middle of a business transaction, person B will probably not take up this point in order not to upset the other party. Positioning as one colluding in the storyline can be resisted and even overthrown.

Stereotypes as social constructs

By locating cultural stereotypes within a certain moral order and by acknowledging that our society can be conceived as a complex collection of moral orders (some independent of each other, some partially overlapping) that can be specific for a subgroup or general for almost the whole society, it becomes clear that there always exist different social representations of the same objects. One cultural stereotype of philosophers may be that of the muddled person, another stereotype is that of the philosopher as a wise man, or as somebody who does totally useless things, and so on. On the one hand we thus have the community of philosophers, on the other hand are a number of different social representations of philosophers. It is clear that there is no single 'correct' or true representation. The problem is not to distinguish between correct and false representations, but to study how and why certain representations emerge in the conversations of members of various conversational collectives.

Another question to be studied is how these representations are distributed in a society. Some cultural stereotypes are part of the general moral order of a society (that is to say that most people of a society have access to it), other cultural stereotypes may only be part of a specific moral order. The ideas about philosophers as tangled or as wise men seem for instance to be part of the general moral order of our society. Beside those general ideas, a number of other stereotypes about philosophers also exist that are only available for specific moral orders. For instance, in the moral order of the community of psychologists live some other ideas about philosophers. Each positions the other as intellectually and methodologically defective in some way. These defects subvert the claims of each side to hegemony in the understanding of human life. And in so far as the claims of each group are seen by the others as false, the failure to realize this begins to seem to be wilful and to be explained by a kind of moral slackness. Thus 'mainstream' psychologists see philosophers as 'mere theorists', lacking the discipline of the need to obtain 'experimental results', while philosophers see mainstreamers as intellectually sloppy in their failure to discipline their use of concepts, and see the mainstreamers' 'experiments' as merely generating artefacts. By positioning each other as methodologically defective the group claim hegemony for themselves.

If there exist many different cultural stereotypes about all kinds of people, the question is how these representations relate to the people they actually represent. In our view it is a misconception to speak of one 'right' representation and of stereotypes as 'false' representations. To take up the example of the philosophers again: there is no 'right' picture of that category of people which are named 'philosophers'. The type of conversation and the people involved in the conversation will determine the stereotypes used. So we have a multitude of representations that are partly determined by the moral order. From the point of view of individuals there are two ways of 'contact' with a certain reality: one is by appropriating a representation of that reality, the other by encountering the 'real thing'. Of course one can never encounter a category of people as such: only one or some specific philosophers can be met. Thus categories of people can be represented in two ways: by a social representation (as a cultural stereotype) or by a physical representation (one specific instance of that category of people). The physical representation of, for example, a philosopher, can be thought of as a particularization of the category of philosophers, not as a particularization of the social representation of philosophers! It is again a matter of positioning and moral orders that will determine how physical and social representations relate to each other.

The stereotypes appear as positions and as characters in storylines in all sorts of discourses. In that way the third element in the positioning triangle, the storyline, can be interpreted as a vehicle for stereotypes. A storyline or narrative style incorporates not only a conventional flow of events – such as 'hero undertakes quest'; 'hero is tricked by villain'; 'hero receives magic help'; 'hero triumphs' – but also characters. In the world of everyday life there are Cinderella's ugly sisters, foolish fathers, handsome princes and fairy godmothers. Narratological analyses of the presentation of scientific work reveal

positionings of rivals and supporters in terms which fit nicely into Propp's
functions (Propp, 1968). These are, of course, stereotypes. A very extensive
opportunity for research opens up here, to identify and classify the character
types that figure in such discursive presentations of rivalry stories as scientific
controversies, environmental discourse and so on.

Changing stereotypes by changing the rules

Asking the question about changing stereotypes is asking a question about
how a social evolution can occur. If one thinks of stereotyping as a cognitive
process, that is as something that inevitably occurs then it can hardly be
regarded as changeable. Most people will, however, agree that some kind of
change is possible. If we think of evolutionary theories as a metaphor for social
evolution, then one can distinguish between two kinds of social change: (i)
evolution triggered by a mutation and (ii) evolution triggered by conditions of
selection (environment changes).

In adopting an evolutionary style of explanation for any kind of change one
must take account of the variety of ways that the basic mutation/selection
scheme can be realized. One dimension of variety emerges from what has
been called the 'degree of coupling' between mutations and selection conditions (Toulmin, 1972). In the Darwinian variety of evolutionary theory the
origins of mutations are causally independent of the conditions under which
they will be selected. Mutations and selection conditions are uncoupled. In
the Lamarckian variety the selection conditions influence the coming into
being of mutations, and in this case mutations and selection conditions are
coupled. In social evolution we have cases in which mutations affect their
own selection conditions. The originator of a new product will try to
influence the market to favour the innovation, by advertising, for example. In
setting up an analogy between organic and social evolution we need to specify
what is to be the analogue of the genotype and what is to represent the
phenotype. By building the model on the basis of gene selection theory we
can make use of the replicator/interactor distinction by which Dawkins made
the ideas of genotype and phenotype more precise. We shall adopt the
following scheme (Dawkins, 1989):

Replicator: 'rule' is analogous to 'gene'
Interactor: 'practice' is analogous to 'organism'

Thus it is rules that are copied generation by generation and it is the practices
which they normatively control that succeed or fail in the local social-
economic geographical-historical environment. There are various ways in
which new rules come to be thought of. For example, they might be a

response to a dialectical tension between the way people perceive their situations in the various practical and expressive orders in which they find themselves located. Thus if economic advances are not matched by advances in status, expressive advances, the people so located may try to set in place new rules for the expressive order. One can see this very clearly in the double-sidedness of the contemporary women's movement, which is as much a movement for a new set of rules for the recognition of personhood as it is a programme for economic or professional advancement. A rule system can sometimes simply be invented, as for instance the rules for government that were thought up as a consequence of the declaration of independence by the American colonies, which brought the United States into being.

There are also some disanalogies with organic evolutionary mechanisms which must be kept in mind. In the organic model, inheritance of genes must be from the immediately preceding generation. But we can look far back into history for sources of new rules of conduct, and indeed people do. In the organic model the fate of a gene is determined by the fate of the interactors, organisms, in the local environment. But in cultural evolution new systems of rules are often abandoned before ever they are tested as practices, in what we might call 'cultural thought experiments', discussions about the possible consequences of adopting them. But, despite the disanalogies, the parallel between the rule/practice pair and the replicator/interactor pair is close enough for the analogy to be a fruitful way of looking at the human world, and identifying the underlying sources of changes in the discursive practices that bring our psychological and social worlds into being.

If we now again turn attention to stereotypes, it becomes clear that the classical contact hypothesis is not supported by our conceptual schemes: when person A meets person B who belongs to a category of persons of which he 'has' a stereotyped presentation, then person B cannot be seen as a particularization of the stereotype. Hence, changing the stereotype will not necessarily occur when people meet each other. In our model, change can be evoked at two levels: one is at the level of cultural stereotypes that are available. One can try to create a new representation in Quadrant One by, for example, a media campaign. But as long as these new representations are not taken up in particular discourses, such a way of inducing change will be fruitless. The other level of change is then that of the conversation: by changing the rules of a conversation one can change a person. Maybe one possible way of generating change is as follows: campaigns not aimed at bringing new representations, but at pointing out to people how they position themselves while 'using' stereotypes. According to our conception of stereotypes there seems to be no point in trying to convince people, because one has as a 'convincer' the wrong position to achieve any change.

Conclusion

Using positioning theory the concept of stereotypes as used in both socio-psychological research and in everyday life can be criticized and refined. We have argued that stereotypes are not pre-existing mental entities that determine the outcome of social judgements; nor is stereotyping an inevitable outcome of human cognitive functioning. Instead we believe that stereotypes have to be treated as rhetorical devices that people use in order to position themselves and others. If stereotypes are not to be treated as cognitive entities inside human minds that can be 'expressed', then they are best viewed as located in the rules and conventions of the discursive practices of distinct cultural worlds from which they can be appropriated whenever useful in certain conversations. From our point of view change in the way people view one another under categories has nothing to do with either exposure to the 'right' stimuli or with correcting false images. Instead, change of stereotypes can be achieved by changing the discursive conventions by which a self-positioning and the reciprocal positioning of others is achieved on a local basis. But on how this might be achieved by deliberate policy we have no idea. One can chart the history of a transformed discursive convention from its moment of birth in some idiosyncratic use of a discursive device by an individual to its entrenchment as a public conversational mode. At best this appears, as we have argued, as a quasi-Darwinian process over which we have little control.

11

Positioning in the Formation of a 'National' Identity

L. Berman

Introduction

This study explores the power elements of everyday discourse by examining aspects of its application as they appeared in the widely read pages of the local newspaper called *Kedaulatan Rakyat* ('The People's Sovereignty') from the city of Yogyakarta in Central Java. It is from this city, widely recognized as the physical and spiritual centre of the ancient glories of the Javanese empires, that the ethnographic studies on everyday social interactions used here are drawn. But the Javanese standards of indirectness, avoidance of self-indexing, stance-taking and political discussion,[1] can be described in a number of ways, all of which may be equally valid. The Javanese people who live within the royal court city of Yogyakarta speak the standard forms of Javanese and still, on average, adopt the demeanor and style associated with the most complex system of speech levels of any known language. Linguistic etiquette requires speakers to be constantly aware of modulations within one's immediate environment, integrating all fluctuations in social relations into their speech and behavioural practices. This 'order of conduct', or *tata-krama*, is realized through the inherent hierarchies of Javanese social relations and exist in all levels of interaction where the clear indices of respect and honour are manifested through speaker humility and acquiescence. To achieve what the Javanese call *alus* (refined) 'requires constant effort and control to reach a reduction of the spectrum of human feeling and thought' (Anderson, 1990: 50–1).

Acquiescence is often locally considered a strength, attributed to mysticism and conceptions of power aligned to a view of life as the direct link between 'the state of a person's inner self and his capacity to control the environment' (Anderson, 1990: 28). But acquiescence is also considered a 'cultural problem', a weakness and timidity in speaking out, a fear of confronting one's superiors, a lack of ambition and a satisfaction with only the most simple and basic of needs.[2]

This study, then, investigates the role of a local newspaper in the engendering of Javanese 'culture', state philosophy and positions of power. Using one of many examples of how the local press refers to Javanese culture and the values it generates, these public discursive practices will then be explained through theories of positioning, systems of metaphor and the power of the voice of authority. Finally, examples of the discourses of those termed 'outside of the system' will show how that system defines and protects itself.

New order empowerment strategies

Since coming to power in 1966, following an era of massive violence generally referred to as a 'communist coup', President Soeharto's New Order government has embarked upon a programme of drastic social, economic and political change. These changes, called modernization, are based on one major ingredient, stability. Language and its control are powerful and recurring themes within this sociopolitical stage where one very quickly learns what can and what cannot be publicly discussed. Not only are the correct answers posted on every wall, at the crossroads and entrances to every village and community, on door posts and placards in every garden, and emblazoned in greenery on every hillside: these slogans, mottoes and definitions of state philosophies are bordering on the sublime. One may not criticize, disagree with, threaten or object to any of these enshrined words, or the men that speak them. Thus, the emergent differences between public and private discourses cannot be neglected, nor can they be easily distinguished. Words that hint at being 'outside of the system' raise accusations of insanity or subversion.[3] In urban communities where residents live literally on top of each other, required membership in character-shaping organizations instils correct answers to all possible situations. As the Minister for Women's Affairs proudly affirms, through these organizations 'all the government's programs can be settled'.[4] Personal identity, or the individual as a basic unit, is in contradiction to the New Order positioning of all its people as a 'family' and following a family's principles. Notions of individuality, especially in relation to individual rights and possessions, are considered 'Western' and hence out of place in popular Indonesian history. Any legal or social system in accordance with a purely *Indonesian* philosophy must be based on 'sameness and harmony'.[5]

This study will show how New Order discourse is composed of a system of metaphorical concepts that have become institutionalized as the correct answers to defining a Javanese[6] notion of reality. By closely examining what these metaphors entail, as well as what they hide, we can then locate what the authoritarian discourses define as national identity, behaviour and notions of citizens' roles, rights and obligations. The significance of metaphor in the ways in which we conceptualize our experiences has been noted by Lakoff and Johnson (1982), Lakoff (1991) and Schén (1967), whose studies all show how metaphors structure the ways in which we come to understand our reality. Metaphors invoke a coherent network of entailments that highlight some features of our perspectives on reality while they may also de-emphasize or hide other aspects in accordance with our cultural values. These entailments are composed of properties or explanations that actually assist us in the understanding of our experiences by offering a conventional set of terms through which we can both conceptualize and verbally describe our experiences.

Metaphorical utterances, such as those which define the population of workers as a resource, are significant in the ways these images allow us to describe both the group and its activity. As Lakoff and Johnson (1982: 65–6) have shown, the metaphor 'labour is a resource' is culturally grounded in our experiences with material resources. Labour as a resource assists in presenting labour as a purposeful activity which can be quantified, assigned a value and used up progressively as it serves its intended goal. Framing work and workers together as a valuable resource invokes it as a unified instrument which in Western culture is always faced with goals, objectives and purposes that must be achieved. Labour as a resource, however, de-emphasizes the roles of individuals within the labour force as well as how those workers experience the act for themselves.

It is a well-known fact that those in power impose their metaphors on others as a way of gaining an element of control over the ways in which people will conceptualize the idea in question (Lakoff, 1991). The 'labour is a resource' metaphor serves to exemplify the ways in which the Indonesian government justifies positioning its factory workers as a commodity much like any other to be exploited in the name of development. To stimulate overseas investments and industrial growth, wages are kept on national average at 76 per cent of the minimum physical needs for one person per day, with Yogyakarta holding the low end of the average at 50 per cent (Simanjuntak, 1993: 55). Labour, as people or activities, can be devalued on individual terms and collectivized in the name of the state and its promises for a better future. The quantified evidence of the value of labour is flashed nightly on television and printed daily in the press, through which the collective masses are positioned as heroes, and praised for their dedication and sacrifices to the successful development of the state. Conversely, those that vocally object to their low wages can be branded as subversives, that is, 'an obstruction to industry, production, distribution, business'.[7]

The consequences of this system of metaphors can be explained by the concept of positioning, which demonstrates the formative influences of conversation on the structure of individual minds. Positioning recognizes the dynamic forces of interaction as composed of the various positions speakers can take up as generated through the learning and use of certain discursive practices. Positioning, however, can also account for intentional and unintentional power relations in conversations by showing how speakers are not always in control of how they position themselves or are positioned by others. Conformity, or the acceptance of another's discourse, can be attributed to lack of choice. In some of the excerpts presented below, it appears that acceptance of the dominant discourse is intended to position others as powerless.

This study presents three styles of public discourses to illustrate the ways in which the voice of authority attempts to position both itself and others. The analysis is composed by presenting conversations as a series of metaphorical concepts from which we can better view the underlying entailments. Recognition of the entailments highlighted by a metaphor can present how the concept under question is intended to be fitted into everyday experience. Finally, we can observe the aspects of the concept that are hidden by the metaphor in order to locate alternative or underlying perspectives.

Positioning the Masses through Defining Javanese Culture

The article these excerpts come from, 'Sepi ing Pamrih' (*Kedaulatan Rakyat*, 1 August 1993: 1), takes its title from a famous Javanese saying: *rame ing gawe sepi ing pamrih, memayu hayuning donya* (work hard without self-interest to enhance the well-being of the world).[8] What this means in terms of cultural concepts and in relation to the voice of authority is the goal of this section.

The Javanese culture has a long and glorious tradition based upon well-known principles and guidelines. Power elements of social interaction are highly ritualized and widely accepted through local definitions of mystical beliefs and high cultural ideals. These ideals are frequently presented in the centrally controlled media as guidelines for what is defined as good behaviour, although they do occasionally appear as 'cultural problems' and a hindrance to the more open dialogues attributed to modernization. These metaphors have become institutionalized terms which function to satisfy a purpose. They clarify the concept of *Javaneseness* through defining common terms, elaborating their relevance and determining their appropriateness in modern situations.

The institutionalized discourse tells us that the Javanese people are protected from conflict by *tatakrama* (a system of etiquette) which regulates all forms of social interaction. Self-control, politeness, serenity and harmony are synonymous with Javanese adulthood. These terms form the basis of a conventionalized system of metaphors that defines Javanese people and their social behaviours according to these highly valued specific traits. The system of metaphors as presented in the newspaper article defines the concept of developing one's Javaneseness as linked to choice. Upon maturity, each Javanese must select to journey down one of two divergent paths. One is expressed as the good path entailing *nrimo* (acquiescence) and self-sacrifice for the betterment of the community. The bad path, in stark contrast, entails concepts of *pamrih* (profit/greed) and self-indulgences for the betterment of the individual.

Metaphors of Javaneseness imply the selection of a path through which one's Javaneseness can be depicted as a journey along either the right or wrong path. The journey of life is full of dangers, disappointments and choices, all of which can be attended to through the selection of either the right or wrong path. As the article's title informs, the path called *pamrih* is the wrong choice, focusing on the isolation and silence (*sepi*) of self-interest, whereas the other path called *nrimo* is rewarded by the lively, busy, bustling (*rame*) activities of community. 'Pamrih is an evil behaviour of only self-interest without concern for others', the article states. 'Humanity must avoid *pamrih* even though it can lead to a lessening of worry and concern. Freedom from the longing for possessions is the characteristic that shows full self-control and serenity.' The article tells us that 'ethical values demand that good Javanese people surrender their own desires in the noble absence of *pamrih*'. Thus, the path called *pamrih* is no longer one of two possible choices, but rather presented as the unethical, dishonourable counterpart to the noble and righteous path called *nrimo*. The journey of life through the path called *pamrih* is 'evil, self indulgent and without consideration for others'. Pamrih, of course, has certain benefits which make it a desirable choice. It presents its followers with wealth, which entails a 'freedom from worry or concern'. But in Javanese mythology, as it is in local community gossip circles, wealth is almost always ill-gotten with the inevitable side-effect of isolation. The desire for wealth is a self-indulgence that detracts from the serenity of the individual, and inevitably affects the group, whose well-being must be of greater significance than that of its individual parts.

The article then goes on to describe the path called *nrimo*, which it defines as a freedom from the dangers and evil influences of self-indulgence. One achieves this Javanese concept of freedom by practising a higher aesthetic called harmony, the most fundamental requirement of good Javaneseness which functions as a guarantee for group prosperity and stability. According to principles of Javaneseness, 'emotional and open confrontation is not aesthetic, and even dangerous', hence *nrimo* requires one to place the needs of the group over those of oneself. By accepting the righteous path, members are freed from the heavy burdens of passion, greed and desires, seen as the causes of emotion and conflict. 'Nrimo is control and serenity. The ability to *nrimo*, or accept one's fate without protest or rebellion means one can face difficulties

THE GOOD PATH	THE BAD PATH
nrimo = beauty, freedom	*pamrih* = evil, self-indulgence
empowering	disempowering
acquiescence, rational	emotional, open confrontation
surrender, acceptance	desire, greed
aesthetic	dangerous
noble, moral	immoral
serenity, humility	prestige, display
fulfils one's obligations	emphasizes self
liveliness	isolation
prosperity and harmony for all	prosperity and antagonism for self

Figure 11.1   System of entailments associated with the concept of Javaneseness

and disappointments in a rational manner without falling apart, and without useless confrontation. *Nrimo* is the strength to accept the inevitable without being crushed by it. *Nrimo* is a sign of humanity's capacity for serenity and humility in the fulfilment of one's daily obligations, without the *pamrih*-laden desire for prestige or display.' The article concludes with a reminder that all citizens must hold their societal obligations as more important than their own. 'Instead all citizens should donate what ever they are able to the prosperity and harmony of society.'

The metaphor 'Javaneseness is a Journey' can be better understood in terms of the paths the journey may pass through, and the additional metaphors that pertain to the two paths: '*nrimo* is the right path' and '*pamrih* is the bad path' (see figure 11.1). Good and bad notions of Javaneseness are created by presenting a system of entailments that function to institutionalize the group as harmonious and prosperous, and conversely designate the individual as the source of destruction, confrontation and evil desires. Conceptions of the group-orientation are founded by surrender and acquiescence, or high cultural ideals. The peaceful acceptance of one's fates is termed an aesthetic and noble

NRIMO	PAMRIH
weakness	strength
passivity	activity
lacking ambition	ambition
poverty	wealth

Figure 11.2   Hidden entailments of Javaneseness

freedom, whereas those that strive to raise themselves beyond the status quo of the community are presented as desiring profit or prestige. These are the evil and immoral opposites to harmony and stability because they serve to distinguish or separate individuals. These metaphorical definitions of high cultural ideals signify the concept of Javaneseness, its relevance, and its application within the trials and tribulations of the modern world. It is the nature of metaphor, however, to highlight certain features or experiences while they hide others. In a world where wealth and power are finite resources, the notion of *nrimo* can be easily defined and experienced as something quite different from a high cultural ideal. *Nrimo* as freedom from ambitious desires also positions the people as passive acceptors of their poverty and ignorance. The masses can additionally be positioned as willing and silent victims of the greed and cruelty of those in control of the authoritarian voices (see figure 11.2).

The article, none the less, presents one's maturation into Javaneseness as a rite of passage based on selecting either the good or the bad path through life. *Pamrih* and *nrimo* are presented as opposites and the only available alternatives. The polarity of possible choice is introduced by the article itself in its introduction: 'The world is full of conflict. Because of this, there is black, there is white, there is day, there is night.' The proverb, *rame ing gawe sepi ing pamrih*, its interpretation in the article, the system of metaphors and their entailments, all maintain a polarized perspective of life and an individual's access to positions within it. Acquiescence is the key to prosperity and prosperity is weighed in terms of community and national harmony, not material or financial gain. Not acquiescing is conflict and all the evils associated with it. Conflict, as we are clearly told, must be prevented. 'To provide in one's attempts to prevent the rise of conflict, the Javanese community is assisted by *tatakrama* which regulates all forms of direct interaction.' Thus, the Javanese language, with its hierarchical positionings, humility and acquiescence, is the ideal means through which to define the psychological foundation of Javaneseness.

Positioning the Enemy: the Communication of Information

Indonesian news, information of all kinds, and interpretations through any medium are always presented as coming from 'experts', be they high-positioned officials, academic, religious, military or political leaders, or other known spokespersons who are positioned as having a sanctioned voice. These voices of authority function as a metaphor through which information, knowledge and the decision-making roles that coincide with them are positioned as exclusive. These relationships between the voice and the nation are commonly described in terms of metonymy. The voice *is* the nation and thus is imbued with all the rights and privileges of such a position of power. The fact that selected individuals are positioned as empowered to speak allocates public speaking and the presentation of information as confined only to those with the designated authority to do so. The voice of authority is a dominant and privileged voice held by one who speaks for the nation, and hence, able to distance themselves from personally responsible 'I' statements. The impact of such a metaphorical position compounds the unanswerability of public statements, enhancing their detached personification of power and tradition, and its inherent claim to virtue (Lerman, 1983). The voice of authority must be interpreted through its own intrinsic processes of multidimensionality, where indirectness and the unsaid become the tools of absolute power.

Information in Indonesia is carefully controlled through a conception of it as exclusive and powerful. The potency of information classifies it as worthy of designated speakers, mass censorship, a set of laws that prohibit criticism, and a rule of harmony that prevents disagreement through its own set of entailments (see figure 11.1). Strategies of information presentation are a major factor in the positioning of social issues as too important for the people to understand, and too righteous to be questioned. By presenting the metaphor of 'information is a sacred entity', it can easily be made exclusive, controlled and protected. The communication of information and decision-making processes must be performed only by those publicly sanctioned as worthy enough to receive this honour – an honour that can be easily transformed into disgrace by that same authority that sanctioned it in the first place. The metaphor of family-like principles that underlie most New Order actions positions the empowered as benevolent father-figures through such widespread metaphors as 'the nation is a family' and 'the voice of authority is your father'. These paternal figures enforce their own positions through a style of interaction that conversely positions the receptors of information as privileged but thoroughly dependent children. Like all good children, the Javanese people must be grateful, obedient and silent.

The texts presented below are examples of one of the most common strategies through which the voice of authority can maintain that authority. The strategy is simple. Through the invocation of invisible elements and unnamed others the father-figures create an enemy. This enemy, although rarely mentioned, intentionally bears a striking resemblance to the New Order-created image of Communism and all the metaphors and entailments of horrors, murder and instability it carries. Yet, through this non-existent force, the father can present himself as the protector of his helpless children. He can create a real sense of family concerns for the well-being of those in his care. And he can also protect them by withholding information that may prove too shocking. The extent to which these relative positions have become institutionalized through acceptance can mean that the people trust their father-figures implicitly, depending on them for their meagre rewards, and for the modernization, safety and stability their sacrifices for them have preserved.

The information-as-sacred-entity metaphor requires that only the voices of authority speak. Only through the wisdom and insights of authority can the invisible enemy metaphor be recognized for the serious danger it holds for the children. References to these invisible enemies appear frequently in the press, a sure sign of their latent and very real dangers. These enemies are invoked for a variety of reasons as will be specified. Generic dangers are invoked where the Governor of the district of Yogyakarta made the local headlines through his warning to preserve:

the national urgency of caution toward *extreme movements* which have never ceased in their efforts to revive their strength from the destruction they cause. (22 February 1993)

The warning does not name any specific movement, although it states that it is a group that has never ceased activities that have in the past caused destruction. The word *revive* is a hint that the unnamed group holds a tie to the past. The call for vigilance enforces self-policing within community boundaries.[9] It can also affirm the worthiness of trust in the benevolent authority rather than in one's neighbours, who may not be quite what they seem.

Along the same theme, the military leader of the region warned:

Major General Soerjadi: 'The greater Yogyakarta area is becoming a playground for specific forces or groups who use penetrating thought patterns that are not in line with Indonesian philosophies.' (13 January 1993)

This statement is far more threatening than the last because of its specifying that the local area has already been infected by these subversive elements who are attempting to control the minds of the masses, now positioned as ignorant and unable to recognize or protect themselves from these dangers. The inherent threat of contrasting philosophies positions ·the people as unable to distinguish the right from the wrong path and hence they must be protected from such choices.

The latent dangers require full dependence upon the authority, whose benevolence and stability are being threatened. Voluntary concession of choice is required, as is extreme vigilance on the part of all responsible members of society:

> Major General Soerjadi: 'Each and every issue must be treated with vigilance because of the possibilities of their being the work of irresponsible personages who can damage stability and national safety.' (24 December 1992)

Linked to previous notions of right and wrong, taking a wrong path by not aligning oneself to the authority and its model community now becomes more than just irresponsible, but a threat to the prosperity of the nation.

Those that choose the wrong path are irresponsible elements with specific strategies through which they achieve their highly subversive goals. The signs of their treachery are criticizing the government and it's affiliations, and demanding changes in the system. The 'Golkar' mentioned below is the official New Order political party:

> Head of Golkar, Wahono: 'Be cautious toward those that wish to discredit Golkar.' (5 December 1992)

and:

> Try Sutrisno, Vice-President: 'There is a regeneration of Communist strength, which naturally uses methods. Where there are people screaming democracy or openness, that's where he'll enter.' (17 November 1992)

These quotations from the benevolent fathers are presenting a framework within which responsible citizens are to live their lives. The shapeless, nameless enemy, however, is made a doubly potent terror because it can take any shape or name the voice of authority wishes to give it. The polarization of potential positions is further maintained through strengthening the right-and-wrong-path metaphor. One may either agree with, and publicly support the authority, or denounce it. Agreement is, of course, the correct path to prosperity and harmony. Disagreement is conflict, hence, evil and laden with *pamrih*. In the quotation from Try Sutrisno, however, disagreement with the authority is directly linked to Communism and all the fears associated with the 1965–6 era of political transition and violence. The most common result of such metaphorical positionings among the populations of Yogyakarta is widespread silence.

During the 1992 general election campaign, student activists throughout Yogyakarta staged a city-wide, extremely well-coordinated, mass protest by pulling down all flags, banners, posters, and the red and green colours of the two competing political parties, while they left the yellow symbols, posters, flags of the government, i.e., Golkar, intact. This action was staged under cover of darkness and without warning, to mourn the death of democracy during an election whose slogan was 'Festival of Democracy'. This protest, and others, were known as 'Golput', which means 'white group'. White being the colour of mourning in Yogyakarta, the protest also involved raising white flags of mourning all over the city.

The local press initially denied anything had occurred. A day later, Kedaulatan Rakyat stated that the flags and posters had been removed 'from a few major roads' only. Then, the authority's defensive emerged:

> Minister of Information, Rudini: 'Golput in this time of the Festival of Democracy is an absolute evil. Its role is to destroy the unity and oneness of the nation. In fact it is a sin in one's responsibility as a citizen as well as to God. It is a treachery toward those patriots who fought for Indonesian freedom.' (22 May 1992)

Deviating from the true path, as we have seen earlier, is dangerous and self-indulgent. It is also in conflict with the voice of authority which has positioned the people as dependent and silent. Those that vocally supported Golput were arrested. The voices that reject the system learn to do so in silence and under cover of darkness. The Golput act of criticizing the authoritarian interpretation of democracy is a very serious threat to national stability, to everything the state stands for, to freedom, and to God, a further definition of what taking the wrong path entails.

The Minister, however, has named the enemy and its crimes. This is, in fact, unusual from the voice of authority. The Minister soon returns to his proper voice entered on indirectness and unspecified persons and goals:

> Headline: Rudini: 'Be Cautious toward *Third Parties*': 'The people are urged to beware of *groups* or *third parties* who wish to discredit the campaign for *obvious ends*. [regarding the removal of flags and banners:]

I don't understand what their reasons were in this protest which of course can kill democracy.' (24 May 1992)

Here, the Minister maintains the authority's empowering ambiguity, as he also defines disagreement and conflict as undemocratic.

The rising tide of serious social problems is also treated through the voice of authority. Juvenile delinquency has become a problem all over Java, where drug and alcohol abuse, gang violence and school wars were beginning to impinge on public awareness and stability:

Mayor of Jakarta: 'A *third party* must be involved. Clearly violence is not natural in these students. Certainly there is *outside influence* whispering into their ears. (6 December 1992)

In these cases, invisible enemies are invoked as responsible for the conflict, which justifies the deployment of the military to guard all crossroads, schools, transportation depots, markets, etc. The problems are not the responsibility of, or caused by, the righteous system of family principles or the community whose gardening clubs and youth and sport organizations can surely keep the students occupied. If students were linked to one of these organizations, 'their negative energies are [would be] neutralized through moderation'. There must be subversive elements working on these young innocents for the enactment of their evil goals:

Military Director of Social-Political Affairs, Lt. General Harsudiono: 'Local teens are *influenced from outside* of the region.' (12 Dec. 1992)

Locating the dangers as part of the ever-present threat to harmony and national stability lurking *outside* in some unnamed domain, the father-figures present themselves with the authority to order all non-official organizations disbanded. The first to go were political clubs on college campuses which had no connection to the frequent high school street battles that have plagued the island.

When individuals already in privileged possession of the voice of authority are seen as a threat to that authority, invisible enemies are called up to discredit them. Abdulrahman Wahid, or Gus Dur, as the director of the Democratic Forum, had been taking an increasingly bold stand in opposition to the New Order by demanding more democracy and openness for all Indonesians. The authority responded by suddenly banning a meeting the Democratic Forum had scheduled and positioning the organization of intellectuals through the media as not just having taken the wrong path, but as aligned with the invisible enemy. The highly visible military Director of Social and Political Affairs, Lt. Gen. Harsudiono spoke:

> Headline: 'Don't be Deceived by Democratic Forum's Political Maneuvers': 'Harsudiono avows that there are *people or groups* within that forum *affiliated with the past era.*'

As seen earlier, affiliations to the past invoke very specific ghosts that can serve as a major deterrent to the popularity of a prominent figure such as Gus Dur. Strategically, the Communist link opens the article but it is not raised again until the closing line, 13 paragraphs later, 4 columns, and 2 pages, away. Harsudiono was asked by a reporter how he can link the Democratic Forum to the past. The response was:

> 'It's obvious from their statements and processes. I can't classify it, but it can fall outside of *Pancasila*'[10] stresses the Director of Social Political Affairs. (25 April 1992)

The voice of authority does not need to clarify anything. Because of its paternal goodness and knowledge, the people depend upon its judgement and wisdom. Yet, indirectness and vagueness from the privileged voice are not just unarguable, but potent. The evasiveness of defining the boundaries of terms or concepts, such as 'obvious' or 'outside of *Pancasila*', make them a serious threat for readers who can never be sure of exactly what set of rules they are supposed to play by. Safety from the 'obvious' is silence.

The voice of authority maintains its absolute power through invoking sets of metaphors that entail specific positions for itself as having the privileged voice, and others as having no voice. Through the metaphor 'information is a sacred entity', those that are sanctioned to have, interpret and disperse this information are positioned as powerful and wise. Conversely, those who have no voice are precariously positioned as a potential threat to the harmony and stability of the state. The benevolent father-figure, as any responsible parent, takes upon himself the role of protector which conversely positions others as protected, dependent. As with most children, the role of 'protected' addition-ally invokes possibilities of disobedience and longings for independence. (See figure 11.3.) But as we have already seen, the authority does not permit any waywardness in its children.

The metaphors of power discussed above entail a set of correlations that serve to fix relative positions and all the rights and obligations associated with them. Authorities are positioned as in absolute control of power, information, the dispersal of information, and its interpretation. Inversely, the receptors of this information are positioned as dependent and in need of the authority's protection and interpretations. The invoking of the invisible enemy, as well as

VOICE OF AUTHORITY	NO VOICE
power, prestige	disempowered
knowledgeable	ignorant
protector	protected
victim of subversion	concealing the subversive
responsible	irresponsible
innocent	presumed guilty

Figure 11.3   Entailments for the voice of authority

the past, are metaphors for the so-called Communist uprisings of 1965–6. The terror of these massacres is the central – yet unspoken – reference point for much of the New Order discourse. It is the ultimate 'silencer' of the masses.

Positioning the System – *or*, Why Homeless Children are Dangerous

According to positioning theory powerlessness can only be made salient through discourse if that position is taken up. This acceptance entails that individuals learn the discourses that are associated with the position. Just as the powerful must learn how to speak as one so positioned, the disempowered must learn not to question the metaphors imposed upon them. Rejecting the dominant discourses is a rejection of the powerlessness. The rejection of one's position is also termed conflict, and hence a type of subversion within Javanese contexts.   Members of the homeless children's cooperative of Yogyakarta, called GIRLI, only understand their positions in terms of the dominant system as being located firmly outside of it. Since they were never socialized through education or community organizations, they have not learned to fear the discourses of the powerful. Never having learned the metaphors that position them as powerless, these children instead, thoroughly enjoy a freedom of speech that is outlawed by those inside the system. The system has created for itself methods for silencing some, but not all.

In their naive ignorance, these abandoned and runaway children have organized themselves into a family structure united by homelessness, the hardships of the daily struggle for survival, and a mutual need for protection from the dangers of exploitation by others. As a vehicle of their empowerment, these children have created a newsletter specifically for the purpose of uniting and strengthening their own voices. The newsletter, called *Jejal Malioboro*, offers the homeless, beggars, day labourers, prostitutes and all others who live a hand to mouth existence on the streets a forum through which they may voice their experiences, angers, disappointments and successes. The newsletter prints the autobiographies of street children with no censorship and fully respecting the vocabularies of the street child's discourse. The newsletter has been labelled illegal by the authority.

The following excerpt, taken from *Jejal*, offers an example of what happens when two conflicting discourses come into contact. This excerpt describes a street child's interpretation of a recent incident through which an authority-sanctioned organization, the Dharma Wanita,[11] had reneged on a promise. Dharma Wanita is a nation-wide organization where membership is required for all wives of all members of the civil service. But rather than acquiesce in silence, the child publicly questions the legitimacy of such an action. At the heart of the conflict is the KTP,[12] as the official identity cards are called. What is of major significance to this study, however, is the way in which the editor not only allows the child a voice but sanctions its legitimacy in rejecting the representative of authority.

Mas Malio Answers Column: Questions about TV and KTP[13]

Mas Malio, I want to ask about something odd. As a good citizen of Indonesia and as representative of the extended family of GIRLI, we want to ask about our true rights. The situation is this, the district Dharma Wanita had this wish. On July 27, 1993 they were to give a gift to the family of GIRLI in the form of a TV and T shirt. At the start, we were all thankful and thrilled if there would be a TV at the GIRLI house, but what happened, the district darma wanita women said, 'children, the TV won't happen because you all don't have KTP'. We were all shocked, what do you mean just because of the KTP problem the children don't get to have a TV. Mas Malio actually I and all our friends do not want anyone's sympathy or help. But this is just extremely odd, just because of the KTP the children can't enjoy the entertainment of TV at home and besides that those who watch TV are little children below the age of 16. Mas Malio please answer truthfully about the KTP problem and besides we all have a GIRLI card [which is] just the same isn't it. That's enough mas Malio I get a headache thinking about it.

Signed,
YUD. S.

ANSWER:
Yud, after reading your letter Mas Malio also got a headache. To be honest Mas Malio doesn't know the connection between KTP and the gift TV from the Dharma Wanita women. So how can I answer. As far as Mas Malio knows, to watch TV doesn't require an identity card except to watch the 17 and above movies. The excuses I heard from the Dharma Wanita women besides the KTP is that they are afraid that the GIRLI children won't pay the TV subscription. Then what if the children already settled at the house still like to wander until it is difficult to control the TVS where-abouts. So now, instead of thinking too much about the connection between KTP and the TV which actually has no connection, it is better to think about the GIRLI house. House cleaning duties should be carried out so the neighbours are happy to see the clean GIRLI house. Pay the community fees diligently, who knows maybe there's an excess for buying your own TV. Exactly as in your letter the GIRLI children do not expect sympathy. Once again Yud, the incident you spoke about above certainly is impossible. So, mas Malio has no answer. *Seng Mali seng . . . !*[14] (*Jejal Malioboro*, June/July 1993: 20)

This section shows where and why this cooperative of homeless children, ranging in age from 5 to 16, is considered a danger and a threat to the system. The danger lies specifically in the children's ability to reject the voices of authority and see through to the hidden side of their imposed metaphors. In their capacity as representatives of the system/authority, the Dharma Wanita women's group was authorized to make donations to local charitable groups. The gift consisted of a colour TV and T-shirts printed to commemorate and publicize the women's generosity. But the system cannot present its benevolence to those positioned outside of the system *if* they do not aspire to be a part of that system. That aspiration is proven by taking up the discursive practices of disempowerment. GIRLI did not respond appropriately, hence, the system reneged on its promised donations.

In order for a group to be positioned as either inside or outside of the system, the system must be recreated metaphorically as having boundaries. *The voice of authority is a benevolent father* and the *New Order state is a family* lead directly to a view of *the system is an orderly room* with a bounded surface and an in/out orientation. By presenting the system the authority has created as a cozy and orderly space, the system may now be described in terms of spatial fields and familial worthiness. Those who have the benefits of being positioned as inside the system, are awarded all the rights and privileges of admission into such a tidy room. But admission into such a clean and orderly space requires full respect for the wealth and prosperity of those who manage the space. One must *nrimo* in order to preserve the opulence of the space −

INSIDE THE SYSTEM	OUTSIDE THE SYSTEM
KTP = identity, citizenship	NO KTP = no identity or citizenship
obedience to benevolent state	lawlessness
educated	ignorant
mature, adult	child
generous, charitable	receiver of charity
TV, wealth, recreation	No TV, no possessions, no recreation
rules, family structure	no rules or family structure

Figure 11.4   Inside and outside of the system and their entailments

look but do not touch. Being located outside of the system, on the other hand, implies one is rejecting, if not unworthy of, admission into the order-liness and benevolent opulence of the family space. Exile from the system as an orderly room may mean that one will not or cannot abide by the rules through which the room is kept tidy. The system does maintain select groups whose alleged lawlessness demand their never being permitted membership,[15] and there are also those who do not wish to fulfil the stringent obligations. Specific groups, such as the homeless children of GIRLI, may be invited to sit briefly inside the room as an enticement to abide by its rules. Figure 11.4 shows the entailments which frame the Dharma Wanita experience as repre-sentative of the system, while conversely revealing what the system expected from the homeless children it marginalizes.

The question/answer column in the newsletter *Jejal* represents an institu-tional conflict, and how such conflicts are handled by those within the system in comparison to those outside of the system. The incident described defines the boundaries of two metaphorical concepts, and the clash of values that maintain the polarization of its inside/outside positionings. The system, defined metaphorically in terms of a physically bounded, orderly space, is composed of a complex system of rules and regulations. Those outside of the system are conversely positioned as living by no sets of rules and regulations. If the system is composed of rules and order which is the foundation for stability and harmony, those outside the system, with no rules or order, are a threat to the stability of the system by their very lawless existence.

Those inside the system, despite having made the initial error of inviting the children into their pristine space, approach the conflict through deferring responsibility for that error back to the disempowered. As ratified members of the system, they simply invoke the institutional rules of the righteousness of that system and its well-established hierarchical structures of communication. In the position of sanctioned power, the women do not need to explain anything, especially to outsiders. The Dharma Wanita women protect their positions, and assume they have silenced their adversary, through enforcing the rules of KTP, essentially, no KTP equals no identity and all the entailments associated with identity-lessness in a hierarchically oriented society. The children, as outsiders because of their homeless and parentless status, are further branded as outsiders through their lack of KTP. Yet, through their ability to counter and even question the prohibitions of power, they are capable of rejecting the women's discourse as empty. Where the system invokes regulations, those outside of the system invoke humanitarian sentiment. Yet this is one of the sanctioned options.

The children of GIRLI reject their positions as outside of *the* system and all the entailments associated with being so positioned by creating their own system and the far more favourable entailments it permits. This simple act of survival, however, holds serious implications for the symbolic nature of the power structure as it is constructed in Indonesia. It shatters the polarized set of options officially sanctioned by the authority. These children empower themselves through their lack of knowledge of the dominant discourses. Rather than being positioned as passive acceptors of the hierarchical structures surrounding them, they are by chance of ill-fortune exiles from it. The system, in turn, preserves the distance by imposing its rules of order upon them. But the children question these rules as odd, as is a system that insists upon analysing and further victimizing abandoned, homeless children.

The children's discourse illustrates their own conception of a system and its rules for survival. These are in stark contrast to the rules demanded and imposed by the powerful as compared in figure 11.5. As seen in figure 11.5, this band of homeless children have gone as far as creating their own system outside of *the* system, or more accurately a family estranged from *the* family. The exile was imposed upon them, but they accepted it. Furthermore, they were bold enough in their childish ignorance to reject the appropriate discourses of their outsider status, and instead chose the family of GIRLI. They use *merdeka* (freedom) as their slogan, which can function as a symbolic third option to the previous polarity of *nrimo* and *pamrih*. Where the authority expects remorse and silence, Yud states, 'a GIRLI card is just the same, isn't it'. Distance from the system enables the children to see the emptiness of the institutionalized metaphors of power and so they question them. And they challenge them.

INSIDE THE SYSTEM	REJECTING THE SYSTEM
KTP = identity, citizenship	GIRLI card = KTP
rules and family structure	rules and family of GIRLI
obligations to benevolent state	obligations to GIRLI
educated by state	self-taught, street-wise
mature, adult	independent, self-sufficient
generous, charitable	rejecter of charity
TV, wealth, possessions	no need of possessions
acquiescence in the system	freedom

Figure 11.5   Rejecting the system

But as we have already seen, the voices of authority do not like to be questioned nor will they stand for third parties or irresponsible personages, which is what this organization of outsiders can represent. GIRLI is a threat to the safety and harmony of the state. Furthermore, the existence of their newsletter *Jejal* is a blatant rejection of New Order control of information resources. *Jejal* was created by and for the outsiders for the purpose of creating their own discourses of empowerment, widely available to anyone putting pen to paper on the cold and dark shop-front now called 'home'. Yet, only the system has the power to designate voices of authority, an essential factor in the protection of information as a sacred entity. The newsletter is banned, and the editors have been held and interrogated. The future of *Jejal* is bleak, as is the future of GIRLI as a family. Had they taken up the discourses of an outsider group, entailing the lawlessness and humility expected of them, they could easily co-exist with the system. Since this was not the case and the authority being what it is, the discourses of freedom will have to be silenced.

Conclusion

Combining the concept of positioning with Lakoff and Johnson's studies of metaphor has added a deeper element to this demonstration of the power of discursive practices in the creation of a reality. Lakoff and Johnson's studies show how metaphors give structure to the everyday conceptual system of our culture as it is reflected in everyday language. Individuals' 'subjectivity' is generated through the learning and use of discursive practices, and the ways in which we participate in conversations have a formative influence on the structure of our minds. This study has drawn from previous work on metaphors in combination with positioning as a way of exploring the Indonesian discourses of absolute empowerment. More specifically it is an investigation of the role of the voice of authority and the ways in which it maintains its own position of power through the control of informational metaphors and its relational processes of interpretation and decision-making. The construction of these metaphors along with their effectiveness as a discourse of power, seemed to function concurrently with conceptions of positioning. The voice of authority affirms its powerful harmony through positioning others as mere listeners to the conversation and not actual participants. This study has attempted to illustrate how New Order discourse maintains itself as the voice of authority through showing how it invokes a series of interrelated metaphors that serve as expressions of its privileged position. These metaphors define the concept of *nrimo* as highly valued and a required element in the maintenance of the family metaphor. The acceptance of these metaphors as a conceptualization of one's life experiences contributes to the righteous goals of *stability and harmony* as they are defined by the state. Acceptance of the right path is ritually generated through the learning and using of the discourses attributed to these positions, how power relationships within these daily contexts interplay with public presentations of speaker identity. If a people are positioned as receivers of information, rather than having a role in the negotiation of it, they can be prevented from challenging its authority. In essence, they take up the discourses of disempowerment. In contrast to the voice of authority's expressions of exclusive empowerment, a small group of homeless children has rejected these disempowering discourses. Power in Java is finite and exclusive, thus will not be shared with unratified members. Recently the newsletter *Jejal* had been confiscated and pronounced terminated by the Department of Information. The authorities' successes in silencing this tiny voice of dissent, the editors claim, are temporary. Appearances are paramount in modern Java. One of the contributing elements in the FP creation of the mask called harmony, if it is a mask, is the public acceptance of structures of communication that hinder openness, alternative opinions and differences of perceptions. Like the tidy space it both constructs and reflects, conversation in Javanese has a well-established 'tradition' of orderliness whose explicit formulations of the normative order become concretized in actual psychological processes involved in the production of both language and identity. If discourse is the public process through which meanings are achieved, but meaning is tightly controlled by institutionalized voices, to what extent then are the dynamics of human identity, their narratives, creativity, choice and judgement, destroyed?

Notes

1   This is what Geertz (1960) referred to as 'the flatness of affect' and what Errington (1988) calls the 'avoidance or muting of indexically communicative behavior'.

2   'The Javanese are easy to rule . . . Acquiescence is part of their culture and this has been a trenendous resource for the current regime', a foreign diplomat is quoted as stating in Vatikiotis (1989: 42).

3   For example, the following article appeared in the *Jakarta Post* on 1 Feb. 94:

> JAKARTA (UPI) – Indonesia's defense minister said Tuesday the author of a book critical of President Suharto *should be sent to a psychiatric hospital.* Indonesian authorities have banned the book, 'Prime Sin,' which Suharto said aims at discrediting him and his administration. Defense Minister Edi Sudradjat told reporters he considered the author a liar who should be committed to a mental institution . . . the minister said a psychiatrist was being consulted to determine the mental condition of the author Wimandjaya K. Liohote.
>
> Liohote said last week the book was meant as an indictment of Suharto 'in his capacity as president.' The attorney general's office in Jakarta said it banned the book because 'it carries narrow perceptions about statehood and nationhood and could create misunderstanding and confusion among the public.' [my italics]

4   *Kedaulatan Rakyat* published a series on women's organizations, 18 April 1993: 5. See also Wieringa (1992) for information on these groups and their functions.

5   These comments are from a conference held 11 August 1992 at the Philosophy Faculty of the Gadjah Mada University, Yogyakarta, to discuss Indonesia's low ranking in terms of Human Rights abuses. The panel's conclusions were that after only 47 years of independence, Indonesia was still unable to leave behind the influences of feudalism, aristocracy, and the 'family system' still obvious in many districts. Conversely, the UN bases its declarations on 'liberal' philosophy which raises the individual above the government. The panel also asserts that differences in these basic philosophies must be respected. (*Kedaulatan Rakyat*, 12 Aug. 1992: 1)

   Minister of Information Rudini further explains what the 'Family System' means. Aside from its being in 'harmony with the nature of Indonesia', it is a way of settling problems. For example, *coups d'état* and hard play (*main kras*) are eliminated. Regulations are then clearly understood by all members 'so that *individual interpretations are avoided.* This can lead to chaos and quarrels between members.' In *Kedaulatan Rakyat*, 4 April 1993: 2.

6   While the study discusses Indonesian discourses of state, the analysis of texts, reactions and culture in this chapter are limited to that of the Javanese, the largest

of the Indonesian ethnic groups, Yogyakarta, in Central Java, collected during the years 1983–4 and 1991–3.

7 The 'Subversion' law offers a 20-year sentence or death for obstructing development, as was written in *Kedaulatan Rakyat* on 13 Jan. 1993.

8 This is an 'official' translation taken from a book of Javanese proverbs compiled by President Soeharto's family.

9 See Sullivan (1992) for a discussion of village structure, and Havelaar (1991), whose autobiography very boldly describes the fears and insecurities of such neighbourly treacheries.

10 *Pancasila* is the five principles of state philosophy.

11 Dharma Wanita is a nation-wide organization of which membership is required for all wives of all members of the civil service.

12 KTP is the official, state-controlled identity card that must be renewed every three years and carried at all times. This card is stamped with codes to inform if the bearer has a history of political activity. To be entitled to a KTP, one must have a family register card, a fixed address and official registration. Homeless children for the most part have none of these possessions, preventing them from registering for school or living for any length of time in any of the tightly regulated communities. An additional conflict that Yud alludes to is the fact that children under the age of 17 do not need to have a KTP. They still fall under the jurisdiction of their parents. These children, however, have neither KTP nor parents, and thus, fall through yet another crack in the system.

13 Mas Malio is a fictitious name for the column's editor and the founder of GIRLI. Malio is taken from Malioboro, which is the name of the main street of Yogyakarta. This is additionally where most of the local street culture ply their various trades. See Berman (forthcoming) for a description of GIRLI.

The translations as well as sentence structure and punctuation have been kept as faithful as possible to the original texts.

14 *Seng mali seng!* is a street term with no specific semantic meaning other than invoking group membership.

15 See Havelaar (1991) for her description of the life of one so positioned. Her husband was accused and imprisoned without trial for being a Communist supporter, a brand one carries for life.

12

Positioning as Display of Cultural Identity

D. Carbaugh

Introduction

Every social interaction presupposes and creatively invokes culture, intelligible forms of action and identity. Interacting through symbolic forms carries with it claims, tacitly or consciously, about the kind(s) of person one (and other) is, how one is (currently being) related to others, and what feelings are to be associated with the social arrangement. Whether one immediately understands, or agrees with the persons, relations, and feelings being shaped through the symbolic action, once caught up in it, one will find oneself a subject in it, variously (often institutionally) related through it, and feeling from 'good' to 'bad' to neutral about it. In spite of one's intentions to convey such messages, one will find that in effect s/he will have done so (Carbaugh, 1996; Goffman, 1967).

In this chapter, we explore just how the above process works. Through discussing the communication of personhood, I want to develop the idea that through primarily linguistic interaction, participants publicly constitute social standings (not necessarily 'statuses') as moral agents in society, on the assumptions that various forms and meanings of personhood are discursively 'positioned', and that these discursive constructions are historically grounded, culturally distinct, socially negotiated and individually applied (Carbaugh, 1990b). The general argument is that personhood is a transitory, sometimes durable interactional accomplishment that creatively implicates cultural meaning systems.

Explorations of the loci and qualities of agents, as well as the dimensions of agentive interaction and social relations, are especially useful in contexts where social standings are being contested (Carbaugh, 1996). Further, conflicts and confusion between diverse cultural agents, such as some scenes where Russians and Americans interact, show how deeply discourse runs into cultural meaning systems (Carbaugh, 1993; Chick, 1990; Philipsen, 1992; Wieder and Pratt, 1990). To demonstrate some of the cultural foundations of these processes, and the ways in which these interact, I describe and interpret a popular code, a cultural discourse, in which a position is established as 'an American' (the term in quotations being a popularly used geographic and national designator). This makes it easier to identify and compare this cultural shaping relative to Others.

An American Coding of Dignity

As people in America speak and listen in public, at times they create a common position for themselves as 'Americans'. This cultural discourse is partly constructed through assertions that employ key cultural symbols (in quotes) and their associated premises. For example, one hears claims like: The person is 'an individual', with 'a self', that should contest 'social roles, institutions, and society'. Drawing on previous analyses of talk during an American televised 'talk show', instances of that public talk in which these cultural features of personhood come into play can be described and interpreted (Carbaugh, 1988).

Positioning the person as 'an individual': translating social differences into a common humanity

Consider the following social interactions. The first involves responses to a question about whether women should be permitted, or required to engage in combat duty while performing military service. Speakers A and B are audience members. Speaker C is a feminist author. D is the president of the National Organization of Women.

Extract 1 (from Carbaugh, 1988: 22)

1) A: Nobody wants to do it [combat duty] but by the same
2) token I think that a woman ain't made to do some of
3) the things a man can do.
4) Audience: I agree . . .
5) B: Some women are actually
6) C: some women are stronger than
7) men.
8) B: That's true.
9) Audience: [Applause]
10) D: Some individuals are stronger than some individuals.

A second example arose after a discussion in which a few women with working-class, unemployed spouses implicitly blamed 'the feminists' for crowding others, especially unemployed men, out of the job market. E is an audience member who described her situation to F, a panellist and female director of the Democratic National Committee. G is the host of the programme, Phil Donahue.

Extract 2 (Carbaugh, 1988: 23)

11)   E: Three years unemployed. No compensation, no nothin'.
12)   F: That's what's happening throughout this country.
13)   Especially in the industrial heartland. And it's
14)   what's happening to families like yours. It is
15)   happening to men and women. You and I are not opposed
16)   to each other, we are not on different sides. We are
17)   on the same side of individuals who are trying to
18)   make it. . . .
19)   G: If a man and a woman are both out of work and there
20)   is one job opening and they are both equally
21)   qualified, who should get it [the job]?
22)   Audience: The man. [Applause]

These interactions pose and respond to a fundamental question: How shall participants be characterized with regard to present issues? More specifically, through what terms shall agents be described when the topics of military duty and unemployment are discussed?

Note first the two positionings of persons being proposed here. One involves the explication of social difference through gendered positions, making 'men' and 'women' the principal agents in the action. In both extracts, this motivates a second position, an explication of common humanity through an inclusive symbol whereby the principal agent becomes an 'individual'. Note further that by characterizing the issues through a gendered discourse, speakers position themselves as ones who orient to the difference (with regard to the present issue). This often is heard as if one proposes, acknowledges, promotes and so on, the difference, and overlooks the commonality. Likewise, by characterizing the issues with 'individuals', speakers position themselves as ones who orient to commonality, thereby promoting it, and thus overlooking the gendered differences. Therefore, positions are being explicated as the gendered terms of difference ('men' and 'women') are played against another term of commonality ('the individual'). At the same time, other positions are being implicated for the utterer as one who would orient to (uphold, or criticize, or negotiate) the explicated position(s). Thus, the dynamics of positioning occur in two directions. One involves the playing of each explicated position (of difference and commonality) against the other. The second dynamic involves what each such position immediately implicates for the person who is speaking it. Is she or he at this moment ratifying, rejecting, negotiating the – gendered or common humanity – position? In short, the dynamic involves a play between the familiar cultural positions being discussed, and the immediate interactional position being implicated for one who would so position persons.

Note how the play between the explicated and implicated positions occurs within a general vacillating cultural form. That is, the interactional process moves in a 'back-and-forth', spiralling sequence, tacking between the positions of difference and commonality, with each position motivating the other, as speakers with each in turn become positioned by the one, then the other. Through this form, social positions of difference and common identification are being expressed.

If we listen a bit more closely to the content of the gendered positions being mentioned here, we find each is being built on specific premises of difference. For example, in lines 1–3 about combat duty, explicated is a gender-based, biological difference in physical capacity that is used to justify differences in moral rights (as men and women) and institutional duties (as soldiers in the military). Similarly, in Extract 2 regarding unemployment, some characterized the 'unemployed' as 'husbands', leading in line 22 to applause of the familial difference (between men-husbands, and women-wives) as a justification for awarding 'the man' a job (presumably as primary wage earner in the family). This positioning of gender difference (re)creates a sense of 'man' as physically stronger and primary wage earner, and thus implicates for 'woman' a position that is physically weaker and less than, or other than, primary age earner. Further, this positioning process brings rather close to the interactional surface, a domain of family life with 'man's' moral place being measured economically, and 'woman's' being measured relationally (as wife and emotional supporter of the unemployed husband).

This gendered discourse about the military, employment, and family life is speaking about non-present and/or hypothetical persons. In so doing, it casts characters with regard to these issues along gender lines. Yet, as it does, it implicates for the present speakers an identity as one who would so position, that is, as one who would publicly acknowledge, address, and perhaps promote differences of gender. Thus, as speakers invoke a gendered position in their talk, they position themselves (and talk about the issue) within a culturally based and historically grounded system of personas, social relations and institutions. As the discourse is being spoken, others are being invited to speak and hear the issues in this way, each gender being distinctive (e.g., men are men and women are women), based upon differing capacities (e.g., physically), and with differing responsibilities (e.g., militarily and familially). Structuring discourse this way thus implicates one's self (and others) as ones who in some way come into contact with, 'live' (or should live, or should contest living) at least on some occasions this difference, as a basic condition of social life. Spoken as such, distinctive positions for 'man' and 'woman' are being created, and are thus made basic determinants of social positions, relations (e.g., soldier, wife and husband), and institutions (e.g., armed services, family).

Yet, this discourse of difference, like many others concerning race, class and so on, amplifies the sounds of social stratification (along gender lines) and divisiveness (e.g., disagreements over the nature, value and application of the gendered difference). Through the vacillating form, this precipitates challenges to this kind of discourse itself, and its speakers, and generates counterproposals that explicate yet another type of position. For example, through the comment on lines 5–7, one belief of difference was challenged as the audience member and the feminist author co-constructed the premise: 'some women are actually . . . stronger than men'. This saying invites a characterization of persons in terms other than social difference. Similarly, the gendered answer (line 22) to Donahue's question (lines 19–21) while applauded or ratified by many, was not unanimously endorsed. The discourse of difference thus stratified participants not only through the vision of social life it created (i.e. by drawing distinctions between men and women), but also because the immediate social reaction to this discourse was itself somewhat divisive (see e.g. lines 4, 8). Thus, as discourse explicates gender differences, it implicates differences of opinion about that difference, and thus precipitates a site of contest, not necessarily between men and women, but between the different evaluations, from ratifications to rejections, of the value and use of gendered discourse. Created in the face(s) of this difference is a felt need for and expression of a position of commonality.

After the challenge on lines 5–8, the president of the National Organization of Women (NOW) said: 'Some individuals are stronger than some individuals.' Similarly, on lines 16–18, the female director of the Democratic National Committee (DNC) said: 'We are on the same side of individuals who are trying to make it.' In both of these examples, the language shifts from a gendered positioning to another that does not deny nor does it elaborate gender, but re-positions the debate onto a different agentive plane, to a more inclusive cultural space, a common denominator of persons, where all are deemed 'individuals'. The language the director of the DNC uses is particularly interesting in this regard, because it artfully builds such a space (see lines 12–18). She prepares the position carefully through inclusive and centralizing geographic terms ('this country' and 'the industrial heartland'), familial images ('families like yours'), conjunctive phrasing ('men and women'), explicit negations of difference ('not opposed to each other', 'not on different sides'), pronominal shifting (from 'you and I' to 'we'), with the eventual 'we' as 'individuals' (line 16) functioning as a potently inclusive anaphoric reference that entitles all of the above, previously quoted phrases.

The explicating of persons as 'we-individuals' thus carries a possible arbitral tone through the assertion of an alleged (and perhaps unquestionable here?) universalizing cultural premise of common humanity: Each person, and every people (men and women, blacks and whites, rich and poor, and so on) are all at base deemed 'individuals'. This potent symbol and premise is part of a political code because it derives prominently from the US Constitution. Part of its cultural force is as an 'equivocal affirmative' in that its common use at once affirms, or asserts, what is both radically distinctive to each person (as a uniquely particular 'self') and what is universal to all persons (as an organismic embodiment of humankind). In an 'individual' breath, dual beliefs in a distinctive humanness of each and a common humanity for all are affirmed (Carbaugh, 1988: 21–39ff). These beliefs are elaborated through statements such as (with the words in quotations being potent cultural terms): 'We-individuals' as citizens in 'this country' are 'not opposed to each other' but 'on the same side'. Such statements implicate cultural beliefs about being a person and its associated political institutions (e.g., the United States Constitution, and the Bill of Rights), and thus powerfully foreground, if equivocally, commonalities in uniquely personal capacities and duties (as 'individual' citizens). The movement between positions is thus not a mere shift of phrase, but the marking of a cultural transition from social identities and institutions of difference to another, a cultural persona of a common humanity, a potent political agent.

In the extracts presented here, some tensions are possibly discussable, but significantly not taken up. We cannot claim to know exactly of what the phrase, 'our side' or 'those trying to make it' consists (because this was not explicated). While the cultural and political beliefs just cited provide one possible account of 'our side' (i.e., we-individuals), there are possible others, for example, of women against the patriarchy. In fact, using the principle of the vacillating form, we can expect the sequence to turn yet again back upon itself, as the mentioning of 'our side' precipitates yet an 'other side'. That such a position is not taken up attests both to the robustness of the cultural position described above, and the difficulty of formulating a position 'other' than 'individuals who are trying to make it'. But if we were to speculate about possible 'other (third?) sides' on this occasion, those brought close to the interactional surface by these speakers are perhaps 'Republicans' (for the director of the DNC) or 'men' (for the president of NOW), neither being pursued here. Perhaps such a vacillating form, so positioned, occasionally plays itself out.

Note a related consequence of the above vacillating cultural form. Because of its solidified positioning of an 'only one' (self) or an 'everyone' (we-individuals), discourse of social-group difference is difficult to elaborate and sustain. Explications of identities that build images of difference based upon gender or ethnicity or class or social groupings, rather than those based upon commonality (or an everyone-or-only-one kind of talk), seem eventually to succumb to 'inclusive' language. In this case, especially domestic discourses of difference from unemployed family members get quickly talked over, and supplanted by another which is more inclusive and politically based. American public discourse, political language, consumerism, and some parts of television, being in a sense numbers driven – here's a little something for everyone – easily assumes an inclusive political position as a common denominator, and mutes, or quickly refracts some of the more particular group-based and serious discourses of difference. Such a vacillating tendency between positions of commonality and difference seems somewhat general and almost inevitable, although its nature and use needs to be understood, so that voices worthy of being elaborated, be they of difference or commonality, can indeed be heard.

The 'individual' has a 'self': from relational constraints to personal independence

The one cultural premise stated above, that each person is uniquely particular, is elaborated with cultural terms of 'self' and its closely associated terms, as one who has 'rights', and makes 'choices'. Use of these terms and their meanings positions participants as uniquely independent sites of personal reflectiveness. What is deemed worthy of elaborate expression, from the vantage point of this system, is the highly particular, idiosyncratically distinct world of the one (Carbaugh, 1988: 41–86ff).

Consider the following story told by a nun about the effects of an 'anger clinic' that she attended.

Extract 3 (Carbaugh, 1988: 69–70)

23)   Nun: Before that [the clinic] I was a people pleaser. I
24)   Grew up being a people pleaser. I'm fourth in the family
25)   and that made a lot of difference. The only way I could
26)   get along is really by pleasing my parents all the time.
27)   I learned I don't have to please anybody else, I can
28)   please myself. And once I became really convinced I can
29)   please myself, I don't have to do what you're telling
30)   me, then I became free and I was able to tell them,
31)   'hey, I don't want to do that!'

[. . .]
32)   Donahue: Thanks a lot sister . . .
33)   Audience: [Applause]

In lines 23–6, the nun is narrating a phase of life in which she is positioned solely within a relationship in which her primary task was to work for others, as both a 'people pleaser' and 'fourth in the family'. So positioned, duties to others overshadowed senses of her self. In lines 27–9, she re-positions her story through 'self', relocating her as one who now is not solely a constrained relation ('people pleaser'), but a 'self' who is 'free' from such constraint, and further she is able to say so (line 31).

Stories such as this one again show a vacillating form of positioning, yet here the movement is not from positions of difference to commonality, as above (although there are similarities), but from an explicit, constraining relatedness to an extricable, uniquely independent site of reflectiveness and expressiveness. Her story tells us why she went to an anger clinic: to learn to extricate her being from obligatory constraints and thus to discover her self. Forms such as this one, not without a deep structural link to the Odyssey, demonstrate a voyage in which there is positional movement from one caught up in an historical system of constraining relations, to the charting of new territory in which one's uniqueness and independence is discovered.

Of what does this renewed position consist? Consider the following meta-phorical utterances (each in fact was made, but not within the following sequence).

Extract 4 (Carbaugh, 1988: 79)

34)   I filled myself up with drugs.
35)   To be angry with a stranger or someone who only knows
36)   you a little bit is to reveal a piece of yourself
37)   that you don't want that other person to see.
38)   Now that I have a part-time job, I feel much more secure
39)   within myself.
40)   The problem is that we never really learn who we are
41)   before we give ourselves away to somebody in marriage.

As is demonstrated here, the resources of 'self' are material (the body, its parts, and what they contain, e.g., 'drugs'), symbolic (e.g., information 'revealed', feelings of 'security'), or both material and symbolic (e.g., something 'given' to another 'in marriage'). From this position, all such resources (including one's physical capacities, thoughts, feelings, consciousness) are conceived as within a contained body, with a necessary and deeper awareness of these resources becoming a motive for the journey of 'self' (Carbaugh, 1988: 77–84).

Given a discursive form like this one, in which the relationally constrained person (social deixis) and the independent self (personal deixis) are played against one another, the task of 'self' becomes the shaping of a position, a site of extricable one-ness, in which personal uniqueness of resources and freedom from past constraints can become realized and expressed.

The 'self' vilifies 'social roles' (institutions, history): Renouncing role restraints

As 'self' becomes positioned in discourse, it runs rather uneasily into other positions that are institutionally constrained and/or historically grounded. These positions are identified variously as 'social roles', the 'society', 'history', or 'this country'. Specific examples include 'husband' or 'wife' or any such term that implicates duties to another, or 'worker' and 'soldier' or any such term that implicates institutional ('stereotypical') constraints on one's actions. The nun's comments above are partly constructed in this way with the roles of 'child' and 'people pleaser' explicating the constraints on action that hampered 'self' (not to mention being a 'nun'). Extracts one and two likewise show how the duties or expectations of constraining positions, such as 'man'/'woman', are played against another, the freer 'individual'. Positioning in this way consists in an agonistic form of discourse in which a site of enslavement is identified, such as 'social role', or 'society', and is subsequently vilified and renounced, because such positions constrain 'self'. This motivates a re-positioning of person onto the preferred, freer plane of self. The form thus again plays the culturally solidified positions of constraint and difference against its more liberating senses of 'self' (Carbaugh, 1988: 87–107ff; 1988/1989).

Consider the following utterance, made by a woman during a discussion of gender roles:

Extract 5 (Carbaugh, 1988: 100)

42)   While we're talking about men and women, if people would
43)   just concentrate on themselves, and their goals, and
44)   being individuals. Society says that you have to earn
45)   money to be of any value. I feel that that's very
46)   ingrained in men right now. That is what women are
47)   fighting. I feel that I am fighting that right now
48)   myself.

The form of this utterance is agonistic, or polemical; it plays two positions for persons, one against the other, while preferring the one over the other. In particular, the playing of the position goes this way: the terms, 'men' and 'women' (42, 46), and 'society' (44) identify historically grounded, socially differentiated, institutionally bounded notions of being; so positioned, one's place is said to be duty-ridden, predicating actions here as a 'have to' (44); it is deemed a cultural rut, enslaving or 'ingrained' (46); and because such positions are duty-ridden and enslaving, they must be fought (47). The preferred position from which and for which the fighting is done requires and prefers 'concentration' on 'self' (43, 48), and 'being individuals' (44).

In folk terms of the preferred position of the person, 'if we could just be ourselves, and stop trying to be something else, we all would be better off'. Put in terms of folk forms for action that are associated with the position, 'if we could just sit down and talk it out, we all [each of us] would be better off'. Such positions and forms of action seek to shed one restraining position, the common sense of which includes institutional and historically based identities (e.g., men, women, the unemployed, Blacks), in favour of a freer other, the 'self'. Or, so they say in some American scenes.[1]

Coding Dignity over Honour

The above symbols, forms and premises of positioning can be summarized as a coding of personhood. Treating this discursive position as a deeply coded one is an effort to cast more generally the beliefs and values immanent in this kind of discursive action. Following prior work about similar discursive activities, I call the code a code of dignity (Berger, Berger and Kellner, 1974; see especially Philipsen, 1992).

When a coding of dignity is occurring through terms like 'individual' and 'self', a model for the person is being presupposed and implicated, preferred and promoted. One cluster of values relates to indigenous conceptions of the person, and thus I refer to them as an ontological dimension of the code. These support the cultural notion of personhood described above and figure prominently as values when personhood is coded as such: The *intrinsic* worth of each person, the ability to recognize and support individuals as holding some socially redeemable value, even if this is difficult at first to notice; *self-consciousness*, or self-awareness, or personal reflectiveness, the ability to ascertain who one is and is not, what one can and cannot do, to know one's necessities, abilities, capacities and limits, independent of, as well as within, one's typical roles; *uniqueness*, to know how one's necessities, abilities, and capacities differ from others; *sincerity*, or authenticity, or honesty, to be forthcoming and expressive about one's self, to coalesce one's outer actions with one's inner thoughts and feelings.

The above clustering of values of person are associated with and overlap another. This other clustering of values adds a pragmatic dimension to the code, and thus refers to valued means of sociation, or preferred ways of relating person, so conceived, with others. The basic social principle is: *Equality*, to ensure persons have inalienable rights to being and acting, and (equal) opportunities to make choices, and to conduct evaluations, if necessary, on the basis of standardized criteria (applied to each equally). Favoured actions include: *Cooperative negotiation*, saying who one is and what one strives toward, to ably hear who another is and what they strive toward, and to conduct action with both in view; *validation of personal differences*, acknowledging through cooperative conduct the unique qualities of each person; *flexibility* being willing to change one's sense of oneself, others, one's relationship with others, one's habits of action, and so on (e.g., 'to grow'), as a result of cooperative conduct.

In the above extracts, all of these values for persons, sociation and pragmatic action are appealed to. Note however the exigencies for this coding of the person. What precipitates the coding of dignity are discourses in which different, often stratified positions and domains are being explicated or implicated (e.g., gender and family, or the military; race and education). These alternate social positions bring into discourse a coding based not upon personal uniqueness, but upon institutional and historical precedence, a positioning of honour. Philipsen (1992) has elaborated the code of honour, with its attendant emphasis on political connections, historical precedence, magnanimity, loyalty, piety. From the vantage point of a code of dignity, the positions of honour are often heard as relationally constrained or stereotypically obliged. Such a hearing presses the code of dignity into service. This is nicely exemplified above as women discussed through a version of the honour code, 'unemployed' men and the 'man's' need of a job to support the family, but were responded to in another code that emphasized equal standings while muting the gendered and familial divisions of labour. Thus the vacillating forms in use here suggest deeply different systems of values about what person, relations and pragmatic action is (and should be). Displayed therefore is not just differences in the positioning of the immediate persons, but deeper differences between ways of culturally coding social interaction, persons and life itself.

How the Code of Dignity hides its cultural features and forms

There is an irony built into the above discourse of dignity. It consists of a general dynamic: the common meanings made when coding conversation this way are highly individualized and liberating, while the forms and moral status of those very meanings are largely collectivized and constraining. Put differently, discursively coding the person in terms of dignity amplifies meanings of individual and self, while muting the common cultural premises and forms that make those very meanings possible (Carbaugh, 1988, 28–33, 57–9, 84–6, 109–12ff; 1988/1989).

For each feature – each symbol, form and premise – of the code of dignity discussed above, we can formulate a statement that must be practically necessary for the discursive action to take the shape it does. For each, the meaning the form promotes (i.e., individualized persons and actions) silences the form of those meanings (i.e., collectivized persons and actions). Consider the following summary of the ways the coding of dignity works:

1   The cultural construction of individuality.
2   The collective celebration of the unique self.
3   The communal rejection of group-based roles and identities.

For the first two, the common meanings of, for example, individual boundedness and uniqueness hide the connecting forms of action (the cultural and collective) that are required for their promotion and realization. Similarly, in the third, the overt meanings of, for example, obligation or conformity to a group or audience, are renounced, just as the group conforms in being ones who so obediently renounce. In this way, each feature of the code both grants through its cultural contents, yet takes away through its cultural forms, the conditions of its making. Bateson of course reminded us that being agents-in-society is inherently double-binding, and here we have demonstrated in discursive practices just how this is so.

One possible danger of this coding to which I now turn – there are others – is its unreflective application, especially in intercultural contexts. It is sometimes naively used to assert or to replicate its own presumably universalizing sense: that is that all people are at base individuals, or constructable as such. This is especially troublesome in multicultural contexts such as some courtrooms and classrooms, where the coding of dignity confronts deeply different others, whose codes for being operate quite differently.

Coding dignity in cross-cultural perspective: Personhood and politeness

Larry Wieder and Steven Pratt (1990) have discussed a psychology classroom in America's heartland that was convened on the topic of race and ethnic relations. The professor of the class had asked the students to get together in groups to discuss their own cultural heritages. For students tutored in the code of dignity, this presented no problem. One's unique background could be put into a disclosive form of action, thus positioning that person as an able discussant. For others, especially for some native (Osage) people, this was not permissible. To position as a native first of all required a relational assessment of the situation, leading to the culturally salient condition of being with tribal members previously unknown to them. If Osage wanted to display the native identity under this condition, they must orient to the cultural rule of modesty: do not sound more knowledgeable than other group members, especially when discussing matters of the tribe's heritage. Under this condition, the most knowledgeable natives produced appropriately vacuous comments, ostensibly about their cultural heritage, saying things like, 'I don't know, what do you think?' Ironically, such statements explicated (but implicated much more deeply) to present natives true membership as a native, while those natives voluble on the topic explicated, in effect, non-membership as a native (although at the same time aligning them with the position being presupposed and valued by their professor). The complexity in the situation runs deep, as those natives highly disclosive on the topic displayed, in the special sense introduced above, some position of dignity, while simultaneously dishonouring another, of their tribe.

Many other cultural positions and their other-than-dignity workings could be described, ranging from the positioning of persons as sites of trans-individual consciousness as is the case in the Russian 'dusa' or soul (Wierzbicka, 1989; Carbaugh, 1993), as dispersable particles and substances as is the case among some Hindi speakers (Marriott, 1976), as well as other positions that are astrally projectable, among many others (see the reviews in Carbaugh, 1988: 15–19, 112–19; Shweder and Bourne, 1984). Each such cultural agent, so acted and conceived, provides a radically alternate conception of persons, social relations, emotions and actions. Such dynamics run deeply into many discourses and cultural worlds, even into aspects of Western worlds where parasocial positions are at work (Caughey, 1984). Further, there are undoubtedly other general ways of culturally coding positions than the ones of dignity and honour discussed above.

Of special interest with regard to intercultural dynamics are differences in what constitutes 'positive face' among various peoples, especially the nature and value of likeness or difference among such 'faces'. Ronald and Suzanne Scollon (1981), building on politeness theory (Brown and Levinson, 1978), have described how Athabaskans prefer positioning with cultural others on the basis of deference (thus asserting and assuming difference), while Anglos position with cultural others on the basis of solidarity (thus asserting and assuming similarity). They note how assertions of solidarity hold a kind of logical and often cultural power over others, as when the code of dignity presumes a common humanity for all (e.g., as basically individuals who can and should speak their mind). Coding persons and actions this way can lead easily to supplanting others' faces, those for whom real differences are presumed and preferred (see also Chick, 1990). The extent to which oral and literate discourse positions persons with culturally distinctive faces, and the extent to which the coding of dignity supplants others, perhaps even in academic theories (see Barnlund, 1979), face-to-face interaction (Liberman, 1990), and upon mediated occasions (Carbaugh, 1993) needs to be understood. Each such discursive activity activates cultural positions, and how this is so warrants our serious attention (see Brown and Levinson, 1987: 13–15). We can and must better understand the cultural pragmatics that are at play, for such dynamics, especially in the New Europe, increasingly animate the stages of our multicultural world.

Reflective Positioning of an Academic and Cultural Sort

Throughout the above discussion the concepts of personhood and cultural agent have been used rather interchangeably, avoiding commitment to either one. The purpose has been to begin by granting equal status to a diverse range of cultural positions, from those humanly embodied (a more familiar sense of personhood) to others that are not necessarily embodied in human organisms (other cultural agents). Examples of the latter include sacred crocodiles among the Tallensi that are considered to be persons because they 'combine the human spiritual aspects with a living body' (La Fontaine, 1985: 127), the witch's 'fairies' mentioned earlier that are not necessarily embodied at all (Mahoney, 1993), or still others for whom a human body is insufficient for granting the status of 'person', although still presumably holding some social position (La Fontaine, 1985: 131). Some of these notions risk sounding rather fanciful or farcical because they challenge deeply held positionings of 'person' in which the human body contains the site of conscious activity. This is a strong and pervasive belief about persons and cultural agents, but it is no less cultural in its form and meaning because of that.

For purposes of reflecting upon one's own cultural ways, and for better theorizing, it would behove us to distinguish the qualities of claims we are attributing to a discursive position, and whether these consist 1) in a socially explicated, implicated and ratified being (a person, or agent-in-society), 2) in a phenomenal site of consciousness, awareness or reflectiveness (a self), and/ or 3) in an organismic entity (an individual member of humankind or some other species). The distinctions are important because they help disentangle the array of cross-cultural data being accumulated about personhood and discursive practices, such as those mentioned above. The questions here of course are not whether, for example, a disembodied consciousness is 'real', but whether and to what degree this kind of agent is coded, explicated, elaborated and ratified (or renounced) in a discursive scene or system (see Carbaugh, 1996). Furthermore, the distinctions help cut into the sources of some public disputes that are very lively, at least in some corners. For example, many environmental discourses revolve precisely around the cultural status granted certain agents such as owls, plants, valleys, animals, and so on. Current US Vice-President Al Gore has been criticized for granting 'butterflies' the same status as 'people'. The issue, so presented, draws attention to the 'butterfly' as a cultural agent-in-society, and suggests asking whether, and to what degree, this agent resembles other agents (especially 'people') in terms of its social standing. If a 'California valley' is a 'legal person', as a famous court case declared, then what about 'owls', 'butterflies', and so on. Environmental debates are notable sites for alternate positionings of persons, places, animals, plants, and so on, and warrant our careful study. With regard to other court cases, the abortion debate rests heavily upon the question of what a 'constitutional person' is. What status, if any, does (and should) a 'result of pregnancy' have as a cultural agent? From the vantage point of legal discourse, as well as moral, domestic, political and religious discourses? What various positions of agents and persons are being created in this debate? Of what does each consist? Similarly, what of surrogate parenting? What standing does a woman donor of an egg have, regarding the result of the egg's use? Is she more like a 'man' who donates sperm, or a 'woman' who gives birth? Or is there another position needed? If a 'child' is a fully fledged constitutional 'person', able to exercise a legal proceeding (e.g., divorce from its parents), what effect does this have on other institutions of social interaction such as the family, school or law enforcement agencies? On another front, some feminist discourse rests firmly on the explication and assertion that female consciousness or feminine consciousness is inherently trans-individual, thus positioning a kind of cultural agent (but not necessarily a biological type?) as distinct from a traditional male or masculine one (Gilligan, 1982; Tannen, 1990; but see Goodwin, 1990; West and Zimmerman, 1991). These practical issues and cultural matters would repay careful scrutiny through cultural pragmatic studies of personhood and positioning.

Like the concept of personhood, the concept of positioning adopted here needs further development (see especially Levinson, 1989). From the vantage point of cultural pragmatics, I attempted to draw attention to these aspects of the positioning of persons: 1) To the cultural premises, symbols, forms and meanings of positioning, and their sometimes unreflective use, especially in intercultural encounters that involve an American coding of dignity. 2) To discursive activity, especially to situated social interactions, as the site of person – social and cultural – positions, treating discourse *as if* prior to positions, and not the other way around. (I shall return to this shortly.) 3) To the forms of interaction through which positioning gets done. Particularly noteworthy was the way one positioning of the person occurs as a response to another. This suggests a perhaps general cyclical or spiralling form of positioning that inheres within a relationally based, vacillating process. Some resulting questions are: What is the nature and function of this position, so discursively produced? Yet further, to what prior position, or role, or social, or cultural agent is this one responding? if knowingly responding to another at all? What does the play between or among these positions produce? 4) Positioning thus consists in a *system* of terms (pronouns, nouns, conjunctions, etc.), forms, and their meanings, including a consideration of oppositional positions (and their terms, forms and meanings). Considering one term (e.g., a pronoun, or a noun), therefore, is deemed insufficient for locating the cultural positioning of persons in conversation. 5) Some positions suggest a code, or a deep structuring of beliefs and values that is immanent in various forms, terms and meanings of persons and actions.

Different types of analyses are suggested with the vocabulary introduced earlier (Carbaugh, 1996), specifically a move-by-move account of explications, implications (avowed and addressed), elaborations, ratifications, rejections, and so on. Thus, what I present here is only one working-through of the general possibilities, with a special focus on agentive qualities, codes and vacillating forms. Others are of course invited to develop these and other features of the framework, and the discursive activities that amplify (or mute) them. Of particular interest is a system for interpreting implications, with messages about persons, relations, institutions, emotions and discourse itself (Carbaugh, 1988/1989) being already of some value in, for example, discursive studies of self (Harré, 1991), with other such studies being recommended (Varenne, 1990). Other investigators have used the system to describe students' statements about their forms of communicative action (Baxter and Goldsmith, 1990), to explore relations between oral and literate forms in a classroom (Gnatek, 1992), to examine various forms of actions in a new age community (Mahoney, 1993), to comparatively assess discourses of two cultural communities (Philipsen, 1992), and to further explore the discursive bases some Americans use to build a renunciative voice (Scollon, 1991).

Cultural pragmatic studies of positioning take discourse as if primary, then ask of it, what positioning of persons is getting done here? Or, put differently, cultural pragmatic studies hypothesize that social and cultural kinds of positioning is getting done in discourse, then collect a corpus to discover if this is indeed the case, and if so, how so, with what consequences? One begins, then, not by assuming a typology of persons, relations, or actions as something prior to discursive action, but by assuming that activities of positioning indeed take place in discourse, and then investigating the nature of that activity in that discourse through a conceptual framework. What positions are getting discoursed here? What are their social locations, qualities, processes of ratification (or refusal)? What social relations are being constructed in these activities? The framework suggests ways to pose such problems and a vocabulary with which to address them. Beginning with discourse and questions about it helps construct a communication theory, and a communicative explanation of positioning. One therefore does not begin with blank grids of content to fill, but with parameters of positioning along which to look and listen (see Zeitlyn, 1993). Investigating this way enables one to describe a particular shaping of discursive activity, and eventually to posit a system of culturally potent terms and forms of expression that accounts for persons being conceived, and conducted as such. The resulting argument is, that the discursive activity, as a culturally shaped form of communication, provides one account for persons and agents, on some occasion, being what they are.

It is only appropriate that an essay on positioning conclude with a bit of authorial self-explication. The author, as one writing, cannot escape positioning address. One cannot, nor could anyone, address all of its implications. Yet there are two features of the authored position developed here that are particularly worthy of mention in ending. Each is a voice of criticism discussed in some detail elsewhere (Carbaugh, 1990). One has to do with the status of this chapter as an 'academic discourse', as it uses and criticizes theory. In particular, it adapts and develops a (for example, communication) theory that explores sociocultural notions of the person. A main objective of this theoretical position is to integrate a cultural dimension into interactional studies of positioning, and to offer a conceptualization of identity, traits, personality and the like, as well as more macro concerns – culture, race, ethnicity – in terms of communicative practices, symbols and forms. By exploring these concerns in this way, we can better grasp how the moment-to-moment living through everyday practices constructs positions for ourselves, for others, and develops social relations among us. We can also further adopt and advocate the approach for the study of all social and even physical matters, such as in studies of time (e.g., Brockmeier, 1992) and space (e.g., Carbaugh, 1996). Part of our efforts, then, are being constructed from an academic position with the development of academic concerns, theories and methods in mind. We should also draw attention to our discourse, here, as an exercise in cultural criticism. In this spirit, we deem it essential that popular cultural discourse include a reflective ability, an ability to see itself as a cultural artefact, an ability that we are trying here and elsewhere to develop. Our tactic has been to select typical everyday discursive practices, and describe some of what they interactively produce by way of positioning people through a vacillating form. By holding this discourse up for reflection, we try to loosen its grip on us by discussing some implicit ironies and paradoxes in its use. Thus, this essay is caught in a grand kind of vacillating movement including a movement not only between gendered and collective positions, but also between others more theoretical *and* cultural. Our main proposal in positioning our discourse in these ways, in the more academic and cultural matters, is to conceive of positioning more as transitory interactional accomplishment that creatively implicates, (re)produces and possibly develops cultural meaning systems (which are themselves thus cross-culturally variable). Our main butt has been treatments of identity that rely more exclusively on immutable psychological or biological endowments (with the expressive sense of these becoming, from the vantage point of our proposals, the result of potent discursive heritages). Persons, social interactions and relations, from individuals to nations, then, are not everywhere positioned the same, nor are they anywhere positioned the same in all social contexts. Our cultural practices, and our theories too, should recognize as much, position themselves accordingly, and help move us along as well.[2]

Notes

1   That 'self' is no less an historical and institutional practice tends to escape the common cultural sense. Further, that each individual's self-concept is in its way subject to constant symbolic explication, elaboration and ratification/rejection also escapes the common cultural sense. This is the result of cultural conceptions of persons based more upon biology and psychology, and less upon social and cultural communicative processes. Some of the ironies and dynamics of this belief are taken up in this chapter and elsewhere (Carbaugh, 1988).

2   The perspective and concerns discussed here are further applied and developed in Carbaugh (1996).

13

Positioning in Intergroup Relations

Sui-Lan Tan and F. M. Moghaddam

Introduction

> Ross Perot, in his first campaign speech to a largely black audience, offended many in the room yesterday when he referred to them as 'you people' . . . Perot's first reference to 'you people' came as he was talking about the souring economy, warning that 'it's going to be a long, hot summer.' He continued: 'Now I don't have to tell you who gets hurt first when this sort of thing happens, do I? You people do. Your people do. I know that. You know that.' One young listener in the room shouted, 'Your people . . . our people.' Another person demanded, 'Correct it.' Perot seemed to have heard the voices, but not the words. (John W. Mashek, the *Boston Globe*, 12 July 1992)

The concept of 'positioning' was originally introduced to analyse *interpersonal* encounters from a discursive viewpoint (Hollway, 1984), and further explored with particular attention to the development of a social psychology of selfhood. In a previous discussion, we argued that positioning is also of central importance in *intrapersonal* experiences, and used the concept of reflexive positioning to elaborate on this idea (Tan and Moghaddam, 1995). In the present discussion, we demonstrate that positioning theory can be usefully extended in the other direction to the level of *intergroup* analysis. After all, positioning does not solely involve the discursive production of 'selves' as individuals, but also 'selves' as members, representatives and mediators of groups.

In the incident reported by the *Boston Globe* above, for example, the phrase 'you people' was met with heated controversy when uttered by Ross Perot (a white American who was running for President in 1992) to African American delegates of the National Association for the Advancement for Colored People. To the minority group, the phrase pointed to a 'you'–'us' distinction. Someone responded 'Your people . . . our people', urging the speaker to adopt a 'we' position that included 'African Americans' within the larger group of 'Americans'. In light of the history of race relations in America, 'you people' was heard by the minority group as a 'condescending', 'patronizing' and 'alienating' remark. A listener demanded that his group be repositioned when he said, 'Correct it.' Perot and many others, however, were baffled that a group would take offence at a seemingly neutral reference.

Accounts of the event quickly reached the public through the media and friends. In telling the story these third parties positioned all groups involved, as well as their own groups and those of their listeners. For example, the *Boston Globe*'s reporter constructed a particular storyline in choosing how to report the event, and especially by adding inferences such as 'Perot seemed to have heard the voices, but not the words.' During the next few days, discussions about the event arose between friends, at meetings, and on talk shows, as people provided their own and other persons' glosses on the event ('In my opinion . . .', 'But I heard someone else say that . . .'). New storylines were collaboratively produced, again positioning all prior groups involved, as well as the tellers' and hearers' groups.

The focus of this chapter will be on positioning at this – the *intergroup* – level. First, we shall summarize some important limitations in current research and theories of intergroup relations. Second, we shall explore intergroup positioning and show how positioning theory helps focus attention on these previously neglected aspects of intergroup relations. Finally, we shall use positioning theory to examine what is probably the most well-known study in the history of intergroup research – the classic so-called 'Robbers Cave Experiment' conducted by Sherif, Harvey, White, Hood and Sherif (1961).

Limitations of Intergroup Research and Theories

Despite the impressive growth of psychological literature on intergroup relations since the 1970s (Abrams and Hogg, 1990; Austin and Worchel, 1979; Billig, 1976; Brown, 1988; Hogg and Abrams, 1988; Moscovici, 1985; Tajfel, 1978, 1982; Worchel and Austin, 1986), there are several important limitations evident in both the research methodology and the major theories of intergroup relations. These limitations include a lack of attention to three key issues: 1) the dynamic nature of intergroup relations, 2) the histories of the groups, and 3) the differential power relations between groups (Taylor and Moghaddam, 1994, ch. 10).

Lack of attention to the dynamic nature of intergroup relations

Underlying the laboratory method is a causal model of human behaviour. Consequently, the entire exercise is intended to establish a relationship between assumed causes (independent variable) and their assumed effects (dependent variable). The explicit goal of such experimental procedures is to test the reaction of participants within the confines of predetermined independent and dependent variables. Thus, the encounter in the experimental laboratory has been static, in the sense that a stage has been set, a script prepared for everyone except the participant, and the 'research question' has been to see how the participant will fill in the gap left in the script (see Moghaddam and Harré, 1992). Typically, there is little or no room for the participant to alter any aspects of the situation, or the script being followed by other people (i.e., the experimenters and their collaborators).

The major psychological theories also tend to support more static rather than dynamic conceptions of intergroup relations (Taylor and Moghaddam, 1994). By far the most important psychological theory of intergroup relations since the mid-1970s has been social identity theory (Tajfel and Turner, 1979, 1986). Social identity theory assumes that individuals are motivated to achieve a positive and distinct social identity, defined as 'that part of an individual's self concept which derives from his knowledge of his membership in a social group (or groups) together with the value and emotional significance attached to that membership' (Tajfel, 1978: 63). It is assumed that individuals make a number of decisions about how to best maintain or improve their social identities. These decisions depend on various factors identified by the theory as influential, most importantly the perceived adequacy of their social identity, the availability of cognitive alternatives to the present system, and the perceived legitimacy and stability of the present system. Depending on these factors, the theory predicts a number of strategies will be adopted. The detailed predictions of the theory have been discussed elsewhere (Abrams and Hogg, 1990; Taylor and Moghaddam, 1994), but we focus here on its lack of attention to the dynamic process of intergroup behaviour.

An important goal of social identity theory is to move beyond the reductionism and individualism of mainstream psychology, and to develop a more *social* account of intergroup relations. However, the actual methodology associated with the theory has led to development in a very different direction. Social identity theory evolved out of the experimental procedures of the minimal group paradigm, and has remained restricted by these procedures. The focus of the minimal group paradigm is the fleeting judgements of individual persons, arbitrarily placed in temporary groups. Little has been done to build on the implications of this research for the social construction of identities, and the dynamic process whereby group identities are negotiated.

This neglect is surprising, because there are several places in social identity theory where Tajfel and his associates took the initial step toward developing a more dynamic perspective. For example, in the very definition of social identity, the idea is raised that individuals can belong to many different groups and, by implication, have many different social identities. Second, the minimal group experiment itself represents an instance of category construction, with an implication that the meaning of categories can be negotiated and can change over time and across contexts.

This is clearly demonstrated in a study by Moghaddam and Stringer (1986), which extended the basic minimal group paradigm by establishing categorization on, what were from the perspective of the participants, first a trivial and second an important criterion. The participants in this study where British schoolboys, following the tradition set by the early Tajfel studies. In one condition, following the standard minimal group paradigm procedures, the boys were placed in groups 'X' and 'Y' on the basis of a trivial criterion, a dot-estimation task. In a second condition, a matched sample of boys were placed in groups 'X' and 'Y' on the basis of an important criterion (the school house system, which served as a basis for competition in daily life for the boys). Results showed that irrespective of the importance of the criteria in the world outside the laboratory, when a 'trivial' and then an 'important' criterion was used as the only basis for categorization, the group members showed the same level of intergroup bias. In other words, in the context of the study, a basis for categorization that serves as the *only* cue to a participant as to how they should behave, can have the same level of influence. This suggests the power of context for establishing the meaning of group membership.

Lack of attention to the histories of groups

Although the seminal studies of Sherif (1966) were conducted in the field, and despite the concern of researchers with 'real world' issues such as discrimination and affirmative action (Blanchard and Crosby, 1989; Hewstone and Brown, 1986; Zanna and Olson, 1993), the vast majority of studies have been conducted using standard experimental laboratory procedures. Much of the research in the United States has followed a gaming tradition, using procedures such as the prisoner's dilemma game (see Taylor and Moghaddam, 1994, ch. 3), or Deutsch's (1973) trucking game. The European research has, for the most part, elaborated on Tajfel's minimal group paradigm (Taylor and Moghaddam, 1994, ch. 4), or used some variation of Moscovici's (1985) minority influence paradigm, which evolved from Asch's (1956) studies on majority influence.

Irrespective of the particular paradigm employed, experimental laboratory studies on intergroup relations have usually involved the following procedures. First, strangers have been brought together to interact briefly and then to part without any expectation of meeting one another again. The 'groups' these participants 'belong to' are as temporary as the experimental situation itself, and are completely manufactured by the researchers. In the vast majority of cases, these strangers have been middle-class college students, majoring in psychology. As a result, very little experimental psychological research has focused on relationships involving people who have *long-term* relationships as members of different groups with *long and complex histories*. The major theories of intergroup relations have also not directly addressed the histories of the respective groups, nor the history of the relations between the groups. This is particularly true of equity theory, relative deprivation theory and realistic conflict theory. Elite theory and the Five-Stage Model are two of the major theories of intergroup relations that most directly incorporate a developmental perspective (Taylor and Moghaddam, 1994, ch. 10).

Elite theory proposes that all societies are composed of elite and non-elite groups, and that elites always rule. However, history is a 'graveyard of the aristocracy' because each elite digs its own grave by refusing to allow free circulation of talented individuals. The 'development' conceived by elite theory involves the stages of individual attempts at upward mobility by talented non-elite members, the eventual closing of upward mobility channels to talented non-elite, the mobilization of the non-elite by talented non-elite members, a revolution and the downfall of the old elite, the coming to power of a new elite, and the repetition of the entire cycle with the new elite repeating the mistakes of the old. The Five-Stage Model is a modern version of classic elite theory, with the added proposition that there are distinct historical stages to the cycle of elite rise and decline. Each stage is associated with a particular belief system that helps to maintain the status quo. For example the present American system is associated with a belief in individual merit and effort – anything is possible, all you have to do is 'go for it'! However, elite theory is neglected by contemporary psychologists, and the Five-Stage Model is a new theory that has stimulated relatively little research as yet.

Lack of attention to differential power relations between groups

One of the most important aspects of intergroup relations concerns power inequalities between groups. Some groups have more power to influence the societal storylines adopted by various groups, through the mass media, the educational system, religious institutions, and other mechanisms of socialization. A number of attempts have been made to incorporate the dimension of power as a variable in laboratory studies on intergroup relations (e.g., Ng, 1980, 1982; Sachdev and Bourhis, 1991), but these suffer from some important limitations. Typically, experimentally created groups are very temporary and fail to capture the dynamics of power relations over the long term. More specifically, focus needs to be placed on the evolution, negotiation and adoption of the particular storylines that explain and legitimize these power inequalities.

Social identity theory (Tajfel and Turner, 1986) does incorporate groups with unequal power, as do a number of other theories to differing degrees (Taylor and Moghaddam, 1994). However, none of these major theories focuses directly on the dynamic process through which dominant and subordinate groups negotiate and achieve their positions, and come to accept certain power inequalities as legitimate.

Positioning at the Intergroup Level

Positioning involves the process of the ongoing construction of the self through talk, particularly through 'the discursive construction of personal stories that make a person's actions intelligible and relatively determinate as social acts and within which the members of the conversation have specific locations'. We argue here that these 'personal stories' we tell include not only fragments of autobiographical storylines, but also *group* storylines, *group* myths, *group* histories, etc. of the groups of which speakers are members and the outgroups with which they interact. More specifically, a person's 'history as a subjective being' must include his or her story, not just as a relatively unique and isolated individual, but as a member of a constellation of groups.

The term 'intergroup positioning' will be taken here to refer to (i) the process by which individual persons or groups of persons position themselves and other individuals on the basis of group membership(s) (e.g., when a person hurls a racial slur at a member of another race); and (ii) the process whereby persons or groups position their own or other groups (e.g., in cases of international conflict, where each nation positions itself and other nations involved in the conflict).

Intergroup positioning is fundamentally achieved through the use of linguistic devices such as 'we', 'they', 'us', 'them', 'I' (as a member of a certain group), 'you' (as a member of a certain group), and specific group names. Group affiliation and disaffiliation are also achieved largely through linguistic devices, such as '*I am* a true-blue patriotic American', '*We* Irish are a resilient people', or '*Most* lawyers seem to be interested in high-profile cases, *but I* . . .' When persons distance themselves from their groups (e.g., '*I am not like* most wealthy folk . . .'), they inevitably position their group even if they do not characterize it in explicit terms: 'Not like most wealthy folk' entails a particular position for 'most wealthy folk'.

The stories people tell about groups vary widely according to such things as the sort of occasion in which the encounter is taking place, past relations between the groups in contact, the particular issues and events that are likely to be discussed, the types of moral evaluations that become salient, and so on, thereby making different positions available for speakers to take up or challenge. By the use of rhetorical devices, one may, for example, position one's own group in stories as 'superior', 'heroic', 'trustworthy' and 'progressive', and other groups as 'belligerent', 'untrustworthy' and 'disadvantaged.'

Rights, Duties and Obligations Associated with Different Positions: Mediators and Representatives

Positions in discourse are associated with particular rights, duties and obligations for speakers and hearers, as interlocutors operate within certain moral orders of speaking. Perhaps the most fundamental of these rights is the 'right to speak' and the 'right to hear'. In many situations, only a few claim the right and/or are socially ascribed the right to speak and be heard. A person who has the 'right to speak on such an occasion' has already been positioned in a particular way. There are numerous types of speaking rights afforded by different discursive positions – such as the right to speak out of turn, the right to question, the right to declare that someone else's utterance be 'stricken from the record', etc. In other cases, speakers (e.g., a hostile courtroom witness on the stand) may have a 'duty or obligation to speak', even if they do not particularly wish to speak. Similarly, there are many cases in which only a select number is given the 'right to hear', for instance in a board meeting. There are many kinds of rights as hearers – such as the right to hear but not repeat, or the right to hear only portions of what is said. Again, the person (e.g., a jury member) may also have a 'duty or obligation to hear', even if he or she does not wish to hear.

We can identify two important roles in intergroup positioning according to the particular rights, duties and obligations associated with them as speakers: representatives and mediators. These two terms are left necessarily imprecise in our account, as we take them to be highly unique roles which are progressively and dynamically achieved (and therefore defined and redefined) through ongoing discourse.

Group representatives are persons whose group memberships are made more explicit by the speaker's claim ('As the attorney for the Smith family, I . . .'), by the acknowledgement of others ('She is here on behalf of the Jones Corporation . . .'), or by the situation or context (e.g., finding oneself to be the only minority in the room as the topic of racial discrimination emerges in a discussion). In such instances, a person is exercising the claimed and/or socially ascribed right and duty to 'speak on behalf of'. In such instances, and particularly when one's status as having 'the right to speak on behalf of' is formally recognized, a person's utterances are likely to be taken as a group commitment rather than as an individual undertaking. The illocutionary effect of what is said extends to the whole group on whose behalf the representative speaks. The group represented, however, may engage in second order positioning, by refuting the way that they have been positioned by their representatives and claiming that they have been 'misrepresented'.

There are many different types of mediators used extensively in intergroup positioning — such as counsellors, judges, arbiters, reviewers and the media. Mediators of groups in conflict often explicitly or formally position themselves as 'impartial' and 'disinterested'. It is important to note, however, that to make a claim to a neutral and objective position is still to adopt a position. Indeed, the mediator, when successfully positioned by other groups as 'trustworthy', 'fair', 'impartial', etc., often has the most power in terms of rights, duties and obligations among speakers. In the interest of 'facilitating', 'arbitrating', 'peace-making', the mediator is often granted more freedoms and rights to control the conversation. The mediating party may initiate interaction, direct the flow of conversation, present the views and terms of agreement of each of the groups of conflict to other groups, decide when to conclude the negotiation, and so on.

Perhaps most importantly, the mediator plays an influential role in offering new storylines for the groups in conflict. In many cases, the mediator's role is focused not so much on fulfilling each side's original wishes and removing each side's initial fears about the other group or groups, but on repositioning the groups' relative positions to one another so that their readings on each other's motives, plans, future actions, etc. are more positive (see for example Gibbs, 1974). Each group holds old and prevailing storylines (which may span many centuries) about its own group, the opposing group and their past relations. Sometimes, each group's beliefs about the ingroup and outgroup will be 'mirror images' of the other groups (Bronfenbrenner, 1961; White, 1977; Plous, 1985). Each group, for example, might see itself as 'heroic', 'peace-seeking' and 'accommodating', and the outgroups as 'evil', 'belligerent' and 'inflexible.' Each group sees the other group from certain relative positions, and interprets the other group's words and actions with regard to these particular vantage points.

The mediating party adds another dimension to the positioning arena, in that it will typically also aim to position itself positively and favourably, and in that it views the positions of the two groups in conflict from a third and new vantage point (e.g., see Burton, 1969; Kelman and Cohen, 1979). By providing alternate storylines of its own to each group, new storylines are collaboratively negotiated by all parties. When 'frozen' narratives begin to unfreeze, possibilities for novel approaches to old problems may be discovered.

A key issue in the context of intergroup relations is the question: who has the power to influence mediators? By definition, power majorities enjoy most influence. For example, in the context of international intergroup negotiations involving the United Nations, a small number of countries and Russia (Commonwealth of Independent of States) have veto power in many resolutions. Indeed, as the source of about a quarter of the total United Nations budget and as the host nation, the United States exerts the greatest influence on issues such as who will act as mediator, and how the mediator might behave in negotiating international disputes.

Positioning Theory as Applied to Research and Theories in Intergroup Relations

In the first section, we listed three aspects of intergroup relations which we believe have been largely neglected in the empirical and theoretical literature on intergroup relations. Specifically, these were: (i) dynamic aspects of intergroup relations, and the role groups and group members play in actively negotiating and achieving group positions, (ii) the histories of groups and their relations with each other, and (iii) the differential power relations among groups. In this section, we will discuss how positioning theory addresses some of these neglected areas in the psychological literature on intergroup relations.

The dynamic aspects of intergroup relations, and the role groups and group members play in actively negotiating and achieving group positions

Positioning theory, with its metaphor of an unfolding conversation in which groups stand in various discursive relations to one other, is receptive to the inherently dynamic character of intergroup relations. The focus is on intergroup relations as *process*, rather than product. For instance, terms such as 'group status', 'group image' and 'group stereotypes', emphasized in traditional views on intergroup relations, might imply fixed states rather than ever-changing conditions, and do not point to how these might have originally been achieved. From the perspective of positioning theory, it might be argued, for example, that the traditional method of researching group stereotypes allows only 'snapshots' of intergroup positions. This traditional method typically involves presenting research participants with lists of descriptors (e.g., lazy, industrious, smart, trustworthy, etc.) on which they are asked to rate ingroups and outgroups (Judd and Park, 1993). Missing from the traditional research on group stereotypes is the investigation of the dynamic processes through which groups come to be positioned as 'trustworthy', 'lazy' or 'industrious', and so on.

By applying positioning theory to intergroup relations, social phenomena such as 'intergroup relations', 'group conflicts' and 'group stereotypes' can be more clearly understood in terms of a discursively constructed world. 'Intergroup relations' can be taken to refer to the relative positions of groups, which emerge out of jointly constructed storylines in which the groups play parts. 'Group conflicts' may arise when storylines adopted by different groups are incompatible or in direct opposition with each other. In terms of positioning theory, a group does not have a fixed attribute such as '*a* group image' or '*a* group stereotype' associated with it, but the group plays ongoing parts in many and diverse storylines (including its own), so that its positions constantly emerge, shift and change as the narratives unfold. In Davies and Harré's (1990: 46) words: 'conceptual schemes are static repertories located primarily in the mind of each individual thinker or researcher almost as a personal possession, whereas discourse is a multi-faceted public process through which meanings are progressively and dynamically achieved'.

Important to the concept of positioning is the idea that positions are actively negotiated and achieved, rather than ascribed and passively received. Discursive positions themselves are not pre-existing 'locations' that are merely 'occupied' in discursive practices, but are immanent and collaboratively made available and realized by speakers *in the act of conversing itself*. There is always room for the unexpected and the innovative. In these and other important ways, the concept of 'position' differs from the more static and prescriptive notion of 'role' (e.g., Goffman, 1959).

The histories of groups and their relations with each other

Positioning theory as applied to intergroup relations directly incorporates the respective histories of the groups and the history of their past relations, as group storylines play an important role in the mutually determining triad of speech-acts, positions and storylines. Further, the theory emphasizes that 'group histories' and 'histories of intergroup relations' are not fixed, objective narratives, but are collaboratively produced and ever-changing storylines, seen from particular positions.

The differential power relations among groups

While there has been little research or theorizing on the dynamics of relations between groups of unequal power, positioning theory draws attention to the differential rights, duties and obligations afforded to speakers occupying particular positions. Indeed, the main interest in the positioning process lies in the fact that these rights, duties and obligations are usually unequally distributed among speakers.

The primary objective in positioning practices is to try to reposition one's own and other groups in such ways as to achieve and legitimize the particular positions which will allow one to be most effective and powerful as a speaker. Because people vary greatly in terms of their personally achieved and socially ascribed resources to position themselves and others, and because positions are always emerging and shifting, there is a constant 'battle' of sorts for advantageous positions.

Why is it, then, that disadvantaged group members often perceive their lower status as legitimate, or at least do not take effective action to achieve greater equality? Psychological theories have tried to address this issue by reference to the psychological or subjective basis of perceived justice. Equity theory and relative deprivation theory have particularly given attention to this issue. However, these major theories have not given attention to the means by which one or another view of the world is legitimized. Positioning theory directs our attention to the role of the story construction (particularly by the media) in legitimizing power relations.

Example: A Brief Analysis of the Robbers Cave Experiment Using Positioning Theory

The best way to demonstrate the usefulness of positioning theory may be to show how it can be used to reinterpret and enrich an understanding of a classic study. We will use as our example what is probably the most well-known psychological study in the history of intergroup research: an experiment on intergroup conflict and cooperation conducted by Sherif, Harvey, White, Hood and Sherif (1961). Because an in-depth analysis of the study lies beyond the scope of this discussion, we will focus on only a few incidents that occurred during the three stages of the study.

The study – commonly known as the 'Robbers Cave Experiment' – was conducted at a campsite in the Sans Bois Mountains of Oklahoma, surrounded by Robbers Cave State Park. Twenty-four boys of about 12 years of age were chosen to participate in the study after careful and lengthy screening. The boys were all normal, well-adjusted individuals with no marked differences in terms of sociocultural background or physical characteristics. The setting was that of a typical summer camp, and the boys were not aware that they were being observed or that the main sequence of events was experimentally produced.

Stage 1: Ingroup structure and functioning

In Stage 1, two experimental ingroups were formed as the boys were separated into groups which were designed to be as similar as possible in terms of the number and composition of their members. Various group activities provided all members of each group with opportunities to participate and excel in performance as individual members. The two groups, who later named themselves the 'Rattlers' and the 'Eagles', did not have contact with each other at this stage. At this point, therefore, positioning took place at the *intra*-group level (e.g., during the formation of ingroup structure and functioning). We include a brief discussion of it here because of its implications for intergroup relations in the second and third stages of the experiment.

One critical incident (recounted by Sherif (1966:77)) occurred during a cook-out in the woods, when a boy took a knife to cut a watermelon for his group, but was stopped by the protest of some of the members. Another boy, who was highly regarded by the group, took the knife and cut the watermelon and said, 'You guys who yell the loudest get yours last.'

Clearly, the second boy was positioning himself as one claiming the right not only to cut the watermelon but to choose his own criterion by which the pieces were to be distributed. In positioning himself as one with the 'initiative', 'power' and 'courage' (etc.) to be the group 'leader' of the activity, he was inevitably positioning the other group members as 'followers' who would be 'loyal' and 'respectful' and agree with his demands. As every position exists only as the reciprocal of the other, this was a critical moment in the negotiation of the positions of all the boys. At this point, each group member was free to refuse or modify the way that he had been positioned. If a member had refused to take up the position that he had been invited to take, engaging in second order positioning, further renegotiation of all positions (particularly of the boys vying for leadership) would have been necessary.

When the members of the group did not challenge the boy's claims to be the leader of the activity, they allowed him a privileged position (at least for that moment) which would further afford the boy special rights, duties and obligations as a speaker that other members would not have. We might expect, for example, that if this particular boy were to say 'Stop!' his words would have greater illocutionary force (i.e., to halt all action) than if a lower-ranking member were to utter the same words.

Attempts to position oneself as a person with leadership qualities were not always so successful. During the cook-out, a member of the Eagles built a fire and then argued with the other members on their method of roasting marshmallows. Another boy put an end to the argument by saying, 'You're not the boss' (Sherif et al., 1961).

During this stage, ingroup solidarity was established. The groups chose group names, group songs, and established their own methods for accomplishing their duties. Members who did not participate or help received reprimands, ridicule, penalties, or were ignored by the others. When the groups were informed on the third day before the end of Stage 1 that there was another group at camp, one Rattler said, 'They better not be in our swimming hole.' The Rattlers immediately wished to challenge the Eagles, and the Eagles referred to the Rattlers by a derogatory name. Even before encountering each other or gathering much information about each other, each group had already positioned itself in particular ways *vis-à-vis* its own members, with regard to 'who we are', 'what we are like', 'what we do not tolerate', 'what is ours', and had convinced themselves that 'we are the best'. This was contrasted with the other group, who were positioned as outsiders and intruders, and inferior to 'us'.

Stage 2: Negative attitudes towards the outgroup

In the second stage, the two experimentally formed groups were brought together in situations in which they were in direct competition with each other. These involved conditions which brought about some frustration in relation to each other.

One spontaneous (i.e., not experimentally planned) incident in particular, which took place on the very first day of an intergroup tournament, ignited a chain of events which led to intense intergroup conflict. After being defeated in a game, the Eagles burned the Rattler's banner which they had left behind on the ballfield backstop. Mason, the leader of the Eagles, grabbed the banner. Following unsuccessful attempts to tear it up, Mason and two other Eagles burned the banner and hung the scorched remains on the backstop. Mason said, 'You can tell those guys *I* did it if they say anything. I'll fight them' (Sherif et al., 1961: 104). Here we see the Eagle's attempt to destroy something that belonged to the entire group (i.e., that was 'theirs') and which served as a symbol for the opposing group's identity, thus denigrating the whole opposing group by their actions. Mason also maintains his position as a 'fearless', 'responsible', 'powerful' group leader and as their representative by taking responsibility for his group's actions, and threatening the 'enemy' group. In so doing, he was claiming that he indeed had the right or obligation to lead and represent the entire group, and when group members did not challenge his claims, they accepted the position of loyal followers.

The following day, when a member of the Rattlers asked the Eagles who had burned their flag, a representative of the Eagles replied that *they* all had. The Rattler's initial question was essentially a request for the storyline. When the Eagle replied that they had all burned the Rattlers' flag, the boy offered a storyline in which an action was undertaken by the group as a whole, not a solitary few. Thus, a group storyline had been established which pitted the two groups in positions of conflict. One of the Rattlers began to physically attack one of the Eagles to begin a fight, showing that the Rattlers had accepted this group claim of responsibility.

During the series of competitive contests, the two groups refused to have anything to do with each other. The Rattlers bragged among themselves, telling each other they were 'brave', 'winners', 'not quitters', 'tough', and 'good sports'. The Eagles bragged that they were 'good sports' who 'did their best' and 'didn't curse' (Sherif et al., 1961: 125). Even during a quiet afternoon away from each other while engaging in pleasant activities, the Rattlers referred to the Eagles as 'sissies', 'cowards', 'little babies', while the Eagles referred to the Rattlers as 'a bunch of cussers', 'poor losers' and 'bums' (p. 112). Each group glorified the character of their own *entire* group and attacked the character of *all* the boys in the outgroup, so that positioning was not taking place at the individual level of 'a few of us' and 'a few of them' or 'some of us' and 'some of them', but on the *group* level of 'us' (all of us) and 'them' (all of them).

In another overt act of positioning, a member of the Rattler team said, 'You're not Eagles, you're pigeons!' As the Eagles had chosen their own group name, we can assume that it embodied the particular qualities that the group considered to be important, and the way in which the group hoped to position itself and be positioned by others. In poking fun at the Eagles' group name, the member of the Rattlers directly refused to position the Eagles in the way they had been urged to position them, and at the same time taunted and positioned themselves in a negative way.

During this time, intergroup conflict heightened solidarity, cooperativeness and morale within groups. Competition with another group ('them' and 'theirs') heightened awareness of 'us' and 'ours', and 'who we are' compared to 'who they are.' Each group fashioned its own banner, made claims on its own territory, speaking of posting 'Keep Off' signs in the ball field, and selecting and naming their favourite retreats. In the dining-hall, where they were in casual contact with each other, group members shoved those on the opposing team and shouted 'Ladies first!' at the winner as they headed for the food line. When a Rattler bumped an Eagle, he was told by his fellow Eagles to quickly brush 'the dirt' off his clothes.

Stage 3: Reducing conflict

In Stage 3, superordinate goals were introduced with the aim of studying the reduction of intergroup tension. Superordinate goals are 'goals of high appeal value for both groups, which cannot be ignored by the groups in question,

but whose attainment is beyond the resources and efforts of any group alone'
(Sherif et al., 1961: 202). By introducing superordinate goals, camp counsellors acted as mediators. However, since the boys were not aware that the
situations in which superordinate goals were presented had been planned and
since the camp counsellors did not often intervene directly, the mediating
party's role was a relatively 'invisible' one.

As part of the plan to introduce superordinate goals to the groups, the boys
were taken 60 miles away from the campsite to Cedar Lake, which represented a 'neutral' and novel setting for part of Stage 3. After a morning spent
swimming at Cedar Lake, the boys were eager to have their picnic lunch. A
staff member announced to everyone that he would drive an old truck down
the road to fetch some food. Both groups watched as he climbed into the
truck, and (according to plan) 'unsuccessfully' tried to start it. Soon, members
of both groups began to make suggestions. 'Let's push it', several Rattlers
suggested. When it became clear that the truck was too heavy to push,
another Rattler said, 'Twenty of us can.' 'Twenty of us can pull it for sure',
said the leader of the Rattlers. A member of the Eagles group assisted in tying
a rope to the bumper. One of the Rattlers suggested that the Eagles pull one
rope and the Rattlers pull the other. By the second attempt to pull the truck,
the groups were intermixed on both ropes. Some members of the groups
began chanting, 'Heave, heave.'

Finally, the truck started, and all the boys cheered triumphantly. A member
of the Rattlers said, 'We won the tug-of-war against the truck!' and a member
of the Eagles said, 'Yeah! We won the tug-of-war against the truck' (Sherif
et al., 1961: 171). Members of both groups cheered and agreed. Here we
see that both groups had repositioned themselves in alignment toward a
superordinate goal. In the foregoing exchange they produced a shared
storyline in which they had both experienced a frustrating situation together,
worked together towards a difficult goal, and had all emerged victorious. In
this way, the two groups had become 'we' and 'us', blurring the boundary line
between the Rattlers and the Eagles that had once been so sharply drawn.

This repositioning occurred gradually, as the groups began to cooperate
with each other toward the same ends. One of the first indications that the
groups were aligning with each other may have been the phrase 'twenty of
us . . .' As there were only eleven or twelve boys in each group, it is clear that
'twenty of us' must have included what had been considered to be 'us' and
'them'. The boundary between the two groups was shifting. This was clear
from the fact that members of both groups intermingled as they attempted to
pull the truck. After their triumph, both groups positioned themselves under
the pronominal 'we', positioning the entire larger group as 'winners' who
were 'smart', 'capable', 'persistent', 'strong', etc.

During this stage, and particularly by the termination of the study, conflict and hostility between the groups gradually subsided. The two groups began to interact in more friendly ways, intermingle with each other, and deal politely and fairly with each other (for example, in turn-taking during games and activities). The groups no longer called each other by derogatory names, and they sometimes complimented each other on a job well done. In one incident, for example, a Rattler whom the Eagles had particularly disliked was referred to as 'a good egg'.

Clearly, Sherif and his colleagues have shown that positions and relations between positions, while sometimes somewhat persistent, do not have to remain 'frozen'. Storylines which were once incompatible ('we would win if they weren't such stinkers and cheaters' and 'they are just sore losers who cuss all the time') can be replaced by new ones in which, for example, the groups triumph together to achieve a common goal ('we won the tug-of-war against the truck'). Group positions which once stood in opposing relation ('us' versus 'them', 'insiders' versus 'outsiders', 'good sports' versus 'cheaters') can be realigned in complementary and amicable positions ('we' must overcome great odds together, 'we' are victors).

Conclusion

We have argued that positioning theory can enrich psychological research on intergroup relations, and enables scholars to focus more on the dynamic aspects of intergroup behaviour. The major issues in intergroup behaviour, such as justice, discrimination and collective rights and obligations, are all in one way or another based on the power of storylines. Similarly, the stability or change brought about in minority–majority relations depends on certain storylines being accepted or rejected.

The grand theories of intergroup relations, such as those of Karl Marx and Vilfredo Pareto, ultimately concern the processes through which power minorities assimilate and are influenced by the storylines manufactured to maintain the status quo or further enhance the positions of power majorities. The Marxist term 'class consciousness', for example, refers to a process whereby a power minority fails to perceive itself as a distinct group with interests that conflict with those of the power majority. In other words, the power minority experiencing class consciousness adopts the storylines that endorse intergroup relations as they are and not as they might be according to alternative ideals. In this sense, then, intergroup positioning is at the heart of the grand theories of intergroup relations.

And what of revolutionaries themselves? What of those calling for radical change in class or gender or ethnic or other types of intergroup relations? Ultimately, revolutionaries are inviting us to accept new storylines and new positions to engender social changes in the status quo of intergroup relations.

14

Epilogue: Further Opportunities

R. Harré and L. van Langenhove

Reflection on what has been achieved in the work reported in the foregoing chapters and what might yet be done with the concept of positioning suggests several developments that are prefigured but not fully anticipated in the work to date.

Positioning and Related Concepts

There seems to be considerable room for further exploration of connections with and contrasts to other concepts that work in similar ways to 'position'. By 'working in similar ways' we mean comprising clusters of attributions which, if met, engender moral standings. Thus there are certain personal and social requirements that have to be met for anyone to take up the role of 'judge'. Once these are met they confer certain rights and duties on the role holder, that constrain and enjoin action in a quite demanding way, while leaving certain areas to individual discretion. Requirements on someone to achieve a Goffman-type 'footing' are less formally expressible but they do involve personal and social attributes. For example, to have a footing in a conversation one must be seen as a proper conversant by the others, and one must have some claim, for example, to expertise that entitles one to speak. Rights, duties and obligations are not so clearly formulable as in the case of the judge but moment by moment and case by case could be spelled out in some detail. They may need to be established in the very conversation to which they offer entitlement as one with a footing in the interaction. One must be able to say the right sort of thing about the game of rugby to have a footing in discussion of the Five Nations competition. Technical gaffes are particularly fatal to footings of this sort.

Turning to the methodology of positioning theory we need to ask whether such sibling concepts as 'role' and 'footing' can be used in analyses of real interactions in ways complementary to the use of 'position', or whether they simply occupy parts of the same territory. Role and position are related, we suggest, as determinable and determinable. That is, 'a role' is to 'a position' as 'colour' is to 'red'. Another role is related to some other positions as 'shape' is to 'square', etc. Adopting or being assigned a role fixes only a range of positions, positions compatible with that role. Footing and position are sometimes complementary, and it seems to us that when they are, both may have their uses in an analysis. Certainly to have a footing in a conversation or some other social interaction is at the same time to have a position, but the exploitation of that position may require the display or attribution of personal characteristics that were not relevant to the gaining of a footing. For instance, a little knowledge of rugby gets you a footing in a discussion of the Five Nations, but one may still be positioned as naive as the conversation unfolds. Women rugby enthusiasts, who do not generally play rugby, may have to do further work to establish a worthy position even after they have found a footing.

Internal Structure of Positions with Respect to their Relational Character

Each level of 'positions' needs development, in respect of the cluster of attributes that define a position for an entity of the relevant sort, for example be it a person, a collective or a notional person in intrapersonal conversation with itself, and so on. This development raises all sorts of difficult problems. But before we undertake studies of the internal structure of particular positions we need to try to extricate or propose some principles by which we do seem to move from a set of attributes, ascribed or displayed by someone in a certain episode, to the moral constraints or opportunities provided by a position. To investigate real cases requires attention to matters that are not usually part of the agenda of social psychology, such as the inner workings of a religious tradition. In Much and Harré (1994) there is a detailed comparative study of the different ways that two well-known religious traditions draw out moral principles from specific psychologies. The structure of these discourses is very complex indeed. Fourth-century Christianity developed a set of moral principles, general prescriptions of right conduct, from a psychology based on the idea of two antithetical personal 'forces', both of which must find a place in a realistic way of living. One of the classical schools of Bhuddist thought drawing on a different psychology, one in which the very idea of antithesis is rejected in favour of a step-by-step transcendence of seeming contradictions, brings out a different morality, in which the struggle between opposites of the

Christian tradition is not found. Instead there are prescriptions for techniques of reconciliation.

What sorts of attributes do we ascribe to persons? A rough division can be made between the occurrent attributes that a person displays continuously, most of which will be physical, and the dispositional, including skills and powers, which are displayed only on demand, so to speak. Then there are some which are in a sense continuous, but appear only with the display of a disposition or skill, namely matters of temperament and personality – sunny, gloomy, etc. In general in positioning others we do not take account of their views of their own attributes, but when someone challenges an imposed or ascribed position, they may well do so for the reason that the grounding personal attributes are not what they know themselves to be. Positioned as helpless and in need of care, someone may snap back that they are not as helpless as it seems. This sort of moment is particularly likely, it seems, when issues of honour and respect are up front. The ground of their resistance is of course what they think they know or believe about themselves. It may be that someone positions themselves in relation to the positioning of others on the ground of what they know or believe about themselves. All this needs close study with concrete examples.

We are even less certain what sorts of attributes come to the fore when examples of intra personal positioning are looked at very closely and in wide variety of cases. But that surely is one dimension along which much interesting work could be done. What attributes do I ascribe to that interlocutor which is in one way myself? There are studies of such phenomena as akrasia (weakness of will) which seem to bear directly on this question. Self-address has been presented in literary genres, above all in the drama of the sixteenth century and the novels of the modern era. Jane Austen's character Emma interrogates and castigates herself at certain moments of self-understanding, brought on by the disastrous results of her meddling in the romantic attachments of others. Or there is the format that Dostoevsky gives to this phenomenon when the Inspector becomes the alter ego of Roskolnikov's self-examination. Of course there is real self-address, and that is where, guided perhaps by the insights of the literary tradition, we will hope to go.

The fine structure of the internal relations of the components of a position cluster will differ on which psychological, physical, characterological, autobiographical or personality characteristics are taken as salient for the episode in question. What are the principles by which some attributes, say characterological ones, give rise to moral standings? How does unreliability give rise to distrust? How do matters of physical skill and efficacy sustain duties and obligations? A novel typology of different kinds of attributes will be needed in respect of their tendency to give rise to the moral aspects of positions. For example, there are standing attributes, such as cognitive skills, and ephemeral attributes such as state of health, that are relevant to moment by moment positioning. But there are all sorts of intermediate cases, indeed cases in which the very act of positioning makes salient and indeed may actually bring forth attributes which verify or undercut the positions adopted or ascribed. More complex still are cases in which the attributes are conditional, be they Rylean dispositions, for instance 'knowing how' and 'knowing that', and other more complex skills, some of which are problematic combinations of the cognitive and the motor, for example nicely judging a backhand passing shot. Many of these seemingly motor and cognitive attributes, be they conditional or not, can be tied up with personality. Complexes of attributes such as these suggest will make fascinating topics for research, in so far as they do or do not sustain the moral aspects of positioning.

Duties are generic and derive from powers and capacities. Obligations are to other people, and are entered into. In so far as a position engenders an obligation it will be because in occupying that position a person has explicitly or implicitly given an undertaking to someone as to what they might or will do for them. By taking on the position of nurse a person acquires the obligation to look after the person positioned as patient. Rights are also generic, at the same level as duties, and derive from vulnerabilities. There is a problem here. Is it useful to include among positions, 'positioned as a human being'? So some vulnerabilities will not engender the rights that form part of a position cluster. How far towards the particular do we have to go? Some positioning theorists would begin the application of the positioning concept at the level of gender. 'Positioned as a woman . . .' It might be justified by pointing out that a level is appropriate for the use of the positioning idea when at that level the positioning could be challenged. For example, someone might challenge a gender attribution as a position relative either to a superordinate position – for example 'person' – or a more specific or subordinate position – say, 'chauffeur'. In each case the rejection of the type as defining the relevant position cluster has obvious effects on how vulnerabilities can support claims to rights.

With respect to position relevant attributes of collectives there are yet more variants of characterological and dispositional attributions to play around with. We do position culturally distinct others as 'untrustworthy', 'formalistic', 'romantic' and so on. This is the field of stereotype research which we see as directly relevant to much intergroup positioning, a field which could be developed in much more detail than we have attempted in this book. But there is also the idea of the attributes of a collective *per se*, not as seen through the attributes of stereotypical members. Here we enter a realm of sociology and anthropology, even history, where the problems are at least as much philosophical as they are scientific. What is it to ascribe attributes to nations or social classes, and what is it to position them in respect to what they might or might not be legitimated to do, and the storylines they are licensed to live out? Topics like the doctrine of Manifest Destiny, on the more mundane level, or the Monroe Doctrine, are the sorts of cases where we do see something like positioning, and where the familiar issues of acceptance or rejection of positions can be seen to be taking place on a national scale. Here too there are obvious but subtle links between what attributes a nation is ascribed or what it takes to itself that are tied in with the moral standings that define moment by moment positions from which nations act. But can this be sustained? We can hardly avoid taking some account of the philosophical problems of the ontological status of collectives and their alleged attributes and moral qualities.

There are, we believe, all sorts of dimensions along which positioning theory might develop and issues that it will help to illuminate. Wherever and whenever people get together and do or say things that make sense only in the uptake of others (and sometimes that other may be myself in another guise) there surely the phenomenon of positioning is to be found.

References

Abrams, D. and Hogg, M. A. (eds) (1990). *Social Identity Theory: Contrastive and Critical Advances*. London: Harvester Wheatsheaf.

Anderson, B. (1990). *Language and Power: Exploring Political Cultures in Indonesia*. Ithaca: Cornell University Press.

Anderson, J. A. and Rosenfeld, E. (1988). *Neuropsychology: Foundations of Research*. Cambridge, Mass.: MIT Press.

Asch, S. E. (1956). 'Studies of Independence and Conformity: A Minority of One Against a Unanimous Majority'. *Psychological Monographs*, 70 (9, whole no. 416).

Austin, J. L. (1961). *How to Do Things with Words*. Oxford: Clarendon Press.

Austin, W. G. and Worchel, S. (eds). (1979). *The Social Psychology of Intergroup Relations*. Monterey, Calif.: Brooks/Cole.

Bakhtin, M. (1973). *Problems of Dostoyevsky's Poetics*, trans. R. W. Rotself. Ann Arbor, Mich.: Ardis. (Original work published 1929.)

Bakhtin, M. (1981). *The Dialogic Imagination: Four Essays*. Austin, Tex.: University of Texas Press.

Bakhtin, M. (1986). *Speech Genres and Other Late Essays*. Austin, Tex.: University of Texas Press.

Barnlund, D. (1979). 'Communication: the Context of Change'. In D. Mortensen (ed.), *Basic Readings in Communication Theory*. New York: Harper and Row.

Baxter, L. and Goldsmith, D. (1990). 'Cultural Terms for Communication Events Among Some American High School Adolescents'. *Western Journal of Speech Communication*, 54, 377–94.

Berger, P., Berger, B. and Kellner, H. (1974). *The Homeless Mind*. New York: Vintage.

Berger, P. and Luckman, T. (1971). *The Social Construction of Reality*. Harmondsworth: Penguin.

Berkowitz, L. (1988). 'Introduction'. In L. Berkowitz (ed.), *Advances in Experimental Social Psychology*. New York: Academic Press.

Berkowitz, L. (1988). *Advances in Experimental Social Psychology*. New York: Academic Press.

Berman, L. (1996). (MS). 'Women in Development: the Status and Roles of Women in Java'. Paper Presented at the CIEE Seminar at IKIP Malang.
Berman, L. (Forthcoming). 'The Family of GIRLI: the Homeless Children of Yogyakarta'. In *Inside Indonesia*.
Best, E. (1922). *Spiritual and Mental Concepts of the Maori*. Wellington, NZ: Dominion Museum.
Bijker, W. E., Hughes, T. P. and Pinch, T. J. (1987). *The Social Construction of Technological Systems. New Directions in the Sociology and History of Technology*. Cambridge: MIT Press.
Billig, M. (1976). *Social Psychology and Intergroup Relations*. London: Academic Press.
Billig, M. (1987). *Arguing and Thinking*. Cambridge: Cambridge University Press.
Blanchard, F. A. and Crosby, F. J. (1989). *Affirmative Action in Perspective*. New York: Springer-Verlag.
Bleathman, C. and Morton, I. (1988). 'Validation Therapies with the Demented Elderly'. *Journal of Advanced Nursing*, 13, 511–14.
Bloor, D. (1976). *Knowledge and Social Imagery*. London: Routledge & Kegan Paul.
Bowen, M. (1990). 'Family Therapy'. In *Family Therapy in Practice*. Northdale: Jason Aronson, Inc.
Breakwell, G. M. (1992). *Social Psychology of Identity and the Self Concept*. London: Surrey University Press.
Brockmeier, J. (1992). 'Anthropomorphic Operators of Time: Chronology, Activity, Language and Space'. Paper presented at the 8th Triennial Conference of the International Society for the Study of Time, Cerisy-la-Salle, France.
Bromley, D. (1977). *Personality Description in Ordinary Language*. London: John Wiley & Sons.
Bronfenbrenner, U. (1961). 'The Mirror Image in Soviet–American Relations: A Social Psychologist's Report'. *Journal of Social Issues*, 17, 45–9.
Brown, P. and Levinson, S. (1978). 'Universals of Language Usage: Politeness Phenomena'. In E. Goody (ed.), *Questions and Politeness*. London and New York: Cambridge University Press.
Brown, P. and Levinson, S. (1987). *Politeness*. London and New York: Cambridge University Press.
Brown, R. J. (1988). *Group Processes: Dynamics Within and Between Groups*. Oxford: Blackwell.
Brownstein, R. (1984). *Becoming a Heroine: Reading about Women in Novels*. Harmondsworth: Penguin.
Bruner, J. (1990). *Acts of Meaning*. Boston: Harvard University Press.
Bruner, J. (1993). 'The Autobiographical Process'. In R. Folkenflik (ed.), *The Culture of Autobiography: Constructions of Self-representation*. Stanford: Stanford University Press.
Buber, M. (1966). *The Way of Response*. New York: Shocken Books.
Burton, J. W. (1969). *Conflict and Communication: the Use of Controlled Communication in International Relations*. London: Macmillan.
Candaele, A. (1992). Constructieve Technology Assessment van Informatietechnologie. Een verkenning en integratieve invulling op inhoudelijk en methodologisch vlak.

Brussels: unpublished BA thesis, Dept of Communication Science, Vrije Universiteit Brussel.

Cantor, N., Markus, H., Niedenthal, P. and Nurius, P. (1986). 'On Motivation and the Self Concept'. In R. M. Sorrentino and E. T. Higgins (eds), *Handbook of Motivation and Cognition*. New York: Guilford Press.

Caplow, T. and McGee, R. (1961). *The Academic Marketplace*. New York: Basic Books.

Carbaugh, D. (1988). *Talking American: Cultural Discourses on Donahue*. Norwood, NJ: Ablex.

Carbaugh, D. (1988/1989). 'Deep Agony: 'Self' vs. 'Society' in Donahue Discourse'. *Research on Language and Social Interaction*, 22, 179–212.

Carbaugh, D. (1990a). 'The Critical Voice in Ethnography of Communication Research'. *Research of Language and Social Interaction*, 23, 262–82.

Carbaugh, D. (ed.) (1990b). *Cultural Communication and Intercultural Contact*. Hillsdale, NJ: Lawrence Erlbaum.

Carbaugh, D. (1993). "Soul' and 'Self': Soviet and American Cultures in Conversation'. *Quarterly Journal of Speech*, 79, 182–200.

Carbaugh, D. (1996). *Situating Selves: the Communication of Social Identities in American Scenes*. Albany, NY: State University of New York Press.

Caughey, J. L. (1984). *Imaginary Social Worlds: a Cultural Approach*. Lincoln: University of Nebraska Press.

Chick, J. K. (1990). 'The Interactional Accomplishment of Discrimination in South Africa'. In Carbaugh (1990b).

Coenen, R., et al. (1991). 'Parlamentarische TA-Einrichtungen und ihre gegenwertige Themen'. TA-Monitoring Bericht I. TAB-Arbeitsbericht 5/91. Karlsruhe: AFAS.

Cohen, A. and Eisdoréer, C. (1986). *Alzheimer's Disease: the Loss of Self*. New York: Norton.

Coppierters, F. (1981). *Social Psychology and Improvised Theatre*. University of Antwerp doctoral dissertation.

Coulter, J. (1981). *The Social Construction of Mind*. London: Macmillan.

Crapanzano, V. (1988). 'On Self Characterization'. *Working Papers and Proceedings of the Center for Psychosocial Studies*, 24.

Daey Ouwens, C., et al. (1987). *Constructief Technologisch Aspecten Onderzoek*. Den Haag: NOTA (V4).

Davies, B. (1982). *Life in the Classroom and Playground: The Accounts of Primary School Children*. London: Routledge.

Davies, B. (1989). *Frogs and Snails and Feminist Tales: Preschool Children and Gender*. Sydney: Allen and Unwin.

Davies, B. and Harré, R. (1990). 'Positioning: the Discursive Production of Selves'. *Journal for the Theory of Social Behaviour*, 20 (1), 43–63. [Reprinted with modifications as ch. 3 in the present volume.]

Dawkins, R. (1989). *The Selfish Gene*. Oxford: Oxford University Press.

De Mey, M. (1982). *The Cognitive Paradigm*. Dordrecht: Reidel.

Deutsch, M. (1973). *The Resolution of Conflict*. New Haven: Yale University Press.

De Waele, J. P. and Harré, R. (1979). 'Autobiography as a Psychological Method'. In G. P. Ginsberg (ed.), *Emerging Strategies in Social Psychological Research*. Chichester: Wiley.

Dierkes, M. and Hoffmann, U. (1992). *New Technologies at the Outset: Social Forces in the Shaping of Technological Innovations*. Frankfurt/New York: Campus Verlag.

Elbaz, R. (1988). *The Changing Nature of the Self: A Critical Study of the Autobiographic Discourse*. London: Croom Helm.

Emerson, R. W. (1836 [1971]). *Nature*. Hartford: Transcendental Books.

Erchak, G. M. (1992). *The Anthropology of Self and Behavior*. New Brunswick, NJ: Rutgers University Press.

Erikson, E. (1950). *Childhood and Society*. New York: Norton.

Errington, J. (1988). *Structure and Code in Javanese*. Philadelphia: University of Pennsylvania Press.

Feuerstein, R. and Hoffman, M. B. (1985). 'Intergenerational Conflict of Rights: Cultural Imposition and Self-realization'. *Journal of the School of Education*, 58, 44–63.

Feuerstein, R., Rand, Y. and Hoffman, M. B. (1979). *The Dynamic Assessment of Retarded Performers: the Learning Potential Assessment Device, Theory, Instruments, and Techniques*. Baltimore: University Park Press.

Feuerstein, R., Rand, Y., Hoffman, M., and Miller, R. *Instrumental Enrichment: An Intervention Program for Cognitive Modifiability*. Baltimore: University Park Press, 1980.

Finnegan, R. (1988). *Literacy and Orality Studies in the Technology of Communication*. Oxford: Blackwell.

Frazer, L. (1990). 'Feminist Talk and Talking about Feminism'. *Oxford Review of Education*, 15 (2).

Freeman, M. (1991). 'Convergence of Sociology and Psychology in the Work of Reuven Feuerstein: Toward a Semantic for Expressing the Inseparability of the Individual and Society'. In R. Feuerstein, P. S. Klein and A. J. Tannenbaum (eds), *Mediated Learning Experience (MLE): Theoretical and Learning Implications*. London: Freund Publishing House.

Fuentes, C. (1964). *El Muerto de Artemio Paz*. Translated as *The Death of Artemio Paz* by S. Hilem. New York: Farrar, Straus and Giroux.

Garfinkel. H. (1967). *Studies in Ethnomethodology*. Englewood Cliffs, NJ: Prentice-Hall.

Geertz, C. (1960). *The Religion of Java*. New York: the Free Press.

Geertz, C. (1973). *The Interpretation of Cultures*. New York: Basic Books.

Geertz, C. (1984). 'From the Native's Point of View'. In R. A. Shweder and R. A. Levine (eds), *Culture Theory: Essays on Mind, Self and Emotion*. Cambridge, Mass.: Cambridge University Press.

Gergen, K. (1977). 'The Social Construction of Self-knowledge'. In T. Mischel (ed.), *The Self: Psychological and Philosophical Issues*. Oxford: Blackwell.

Gergen, K. (1985). 'The Social Constructionist Movement in Modern Psychology'. *American Psychologist*, 40, 266–75.

Gergen, K. and Gergen, M. (1988). 'Narrative and Self as Relationship'. In L. Berkowitz (ed.), *Advances in Experimental Social Psychology*. New York: Academic Press.

Gibbs, G. I. (ed.) (1974). *Handbook of Games and Simulation Exercises*. Beverly Hills, Calif.: Sage.

Giere, G. N. (1989). 'The Units of Analysis in Science Studies'. In S. Fuller, M. De Mey, T. Shinn and S. Woolgar (eds), *The Cognitive Turn: Sociological and Psychological Perspectives on Science*. Dordrecht: Kluwer Academic Publishers.

Gilbert, G. N. and Mulkay, M. (1982). 'Social Construction of Belief'. *Social Studies of Science*, 12, 383–408.

Gilligan, C. (1982). *In A Different Voice*. Cambridge, Mass.: Harvard University Press.

Ginsburg, G. P. (ed.) (1979). *Emerging Strategies in Social Psychological Research*. Chichester: Wiley.

Gnatek, T. (1992). *Terms for Talk in Peer-group Teaching of Literacy*. Unpublished doctoral dissertation, University of Massachusetts, Amherst.

Goffman, E. (1959 [1969]). *The Presentation of Self in Everyday Life*. New York: Doubleday.

Goffman, E. (1967). *Interaction Ritual*. New York: Anchor.

Goffman, E. (1968). *Stigma*. Englewood Cliffs, NJ: Prentice-Hall.

Goffman, E. (1974). *Frame Analysis*. Cambridge, Mass.: Harvard University Press.

Goffman, E. (1981). *Forms of Talk*. Philadelphia: University of Pennsylvania Press.

Goodwin, M. (1990). *He-said, She-said: Talk as Social Organization among Black Children*. Bloomington: Indiana University Press.

Greenwald, A. G. (1980). 'The Totalitarian Ego: Fabrication and Revision of Personal History', *American Psychologist*, 35, 603–18.

Greenwood, J. D. (1991). *Relations and Representations: An Introduction to the Philosophy of Social Psychological Science*. London: Routledge.

Greenwood, J. D. (1994). *Realism, Identity, and Emotion*. Thousand Oaks: Sage.

Guba, E. and Lincoln, Y. (1989). *Fourth Generation Evaluation*. London: Sage.

Harré, R. (1975). 'Images of the World and Societal Icons'. In K. D. Knorr, H. Strasser and H. G. Zilian (eds), *Determinants and Controls of Scientific Development*. Dordrecht: Reidel.

Harré, R. (1981). 'Psychological Variety'. In P. Heelas and A. Lock (eds), *Indigenous Psychologies: the Anthropology of the Self*. London: Academic Press.

Harré, R. (1983). 'Identity Projects'. In G. Breakwell (ed.), *Threatened Identities*. London: John Wiley & Sons.

Harré, R. (1983). *Personal Being*. Oxford: Blackwell.

Harré, R. (1986). 'Social Sources of Mental Content and Order'. In J. Margolis, P. Manicas, Harré and P. F. Secord (eds), *Psychology: Designing the Discipline*. Oxford: Blackwell.

Harré, R. (1987). *Varieties of Realism*. Oxford: Blackwell.

Harré, R. (1990). 'Some Narrative Conventions of Scientific Discourse'. In C. Nash (ed.), *Narrative in Culture*. London: Routledge.

Harré, R. (1991). 'The Discursive Production of Selves'. *Theory and Psychology*, 1, 51–63.

Harré, R. (1992). 'What's Real in Psychology: A Plea for Persons'. *Theory and Psychology*, 2(2), 153–8.

Harré, R. (1993). Positioning in Scientific Discourse. In: R. Harré (ed.), *Reason and Rhetoric: Anglo-Ukranian Studies in the Rationality of Scientific Discourse*. Lewiston: the Edwin Mellen Press.

Harré, R. and Gillett, G. (1994). *The Discursive Mind*. Thousand Oaks: Sage.

Harré, R. and Secord, P. F. (1972). *The Explanation of Social Behaviour*. Oxford: Blackwell.

Harré, R. and Secord, P. F. (eds) (1972), *Psychology: Designing the Discipline*. Oxford: Blackwell.

Harré, R. and van Langenhove, L. (1992). 'Varieties of Positioning'. *Journal for the Theory of Social Behaviour*, 20, 393–407.

Harris, R. (1980). *The Language Makers*. Ithaca: Cornell University Press.

Haug, F. (1987). *Female Sexualisation*. London: Verso.

Havelaar, R. (1991). *Quarterings: A Story of a Marriage in Indonesia During the Eighties*. Monash Papers on Southeast Asia No. 24. Clayton: Monash University.

Henriques, J., et al. (1984). *Changing the Subject: Psychology, Social Regulation and Subjectivity*. London: Methuen.

Hermans, H. J. M. (1987). 'Self as Organized System of Valuations: Toward a Dialogue with the Person'. *Journal of Counseling Psychology*, 34, 10–19.

Hermans, H. J. M. (1989). 'The Meaning of Life as an Organized Process'. *Psychotherapy*, 26, 11–22.

Hermans, H. J. M. and Kempen, H. J. G. (1993). *The Dialogical Self: Meaning as Movement*. San Francisco: Academic Press.

Hermans, H. J. M., Kempen, H. J. G. and Van Loon, R. J. P. (1992). 'The Dialogical Self: Beyond Individualism and Rationalism'. *American Psychologist*, 47, 23–33.

Hewstone, M. and Brown, R. (eds) (1986). *Contact and Conflict in Intergroup Encounters*. New York: Blackwell.

Hogg, M. A. and Abrams, D. (1988). *Social Identifications: A Social Psychology of Intergroup Relations and Group Processes*. London: Routledge.

Hollway, W. (1984). 'Gender Difference and the Production of Subjectivity'. In J. Henriques, W. Hollway, C. Urwin, L. Venn and V. Walkerdine (eds), *Changing the Subject: Psychology, Social Regulation and Subjectivity*. London: Methuen

Howie, D. (1992). 'Assessing and Enhancing Decision-making and Self-advocacy Skills: Report to the New Zealand Foundation of Research, Science and Technology'. Auckland: University of Auckland Department of Education.

Howie, D. and Cuming, J. (1986). *Self Advocacy by Mentally Retarded Persons: A New Zealand Study*. Otago: New Zealand Institute of Mental Retardation.

Howie, D., Cuming, J. and Raynes, N. (1984). 'Development of Tools to Facilitate Participation by Moderately Retarded Persons in Residential Evaluation Procedures'. *British Journal of Mental Subnormality*, 30, 92–8.

James, W. (1890). *The Principles of Psychology*. New York: Holt.

Johnson, F. (1985). 'The Western Concept of Self'. In A. J. Marsella, G. Devos and F. L. K. Hsu (eds), *Culture and Self: Asian and Western Perspectives*. New York: Tavistock.

Jones, E. E. and Pittman, T. (1982). 'Toward a General Theory of Strategic Self-

Presentation'. In J. Suls (ed.), *Psychological Perspectives on the Self*. Hillsdale, NJ: Lawrence Erlbaum and Associates.

Judd, C. M. and Park, B. (1993). 'Definition and Assessment of Accuracy in Social Stereotypes'. *Psychological Review*, 100, 109–28.

Katz, R. (1988). *Managing Professionals in Innovative Organizations*. Cambridge: Cambridge University Press.

Kelman, H. C. and Cohen, S. P. (1979). 'Reduction of International Conflict: An Interactional Approach'. In W. G. Austin and S. Worchel (eds), *The Social Psychology of Intergroup Relations*. Monterey, Calif.: Brooks/Cole.

Kitwood, T. and Bredin, K. (1992). 'Towards a Theory of Dementia. Care: Personhood and Well-being'. *Ageing and Society*, 12 (3).

Knorr-Cetina, K. D. (1981). *The Manufacture of Knowledge. An Essay on the Constructivist and Contextual Nature of Science*. Oxford: Pergamon Press.

Kuhn, T. S. (1962). *The Structure of Scientific Revolutions*. Chicago: University of Chicago Press.

La Fontaine, J. (1985). 'Person and Individual: Some Anthropological Reflections'. In M. Carrithers, S. Collins and S. Lukes (eds), *The Category of the Person*. New York: Columbia University Press.

Lakatos, I. (1978). *The Methodology of Scientific Research Programmes*, eds J. Worral and G. Currie. Cambridge: Cambridge University Press.

Lakoff, G. (1991). 'Metaphor and War: the Metaphor System Used to Justify War in the Gulf'. *Vietnam Generation, Inc.*, 3 (3), 32–9.

Lakoff, G. and Johnson, F. (1982). *Metaphors We Live By*. Chicago: University of Chicago Press.

Lalonde, R. N. and Gardner, R. C. (1989). 'An Intergroup Perspective on Stereotype Organisation and Processing'. *British Journal of Social Psychology*, 28, 289–303.

Latour, B. (1987). *Science in Action*. Milton Keynes: Open University Press.

Latour, B. and Woolgar, S. (1979). *Laboratory Life*. Los Angeles: Sage.

Lerman, C. (1983). 'Dominant Discourse: the Institutional Voice and Control of Topic'. In H. Davis and P. Walton (eds), *Language, Image, Media*. New York: St. Martin's Press.

Levinson, D. J. (1978). *The Seasons of a Man's Life*. New York: A. A. Knopf.

Levinson, S. (1989). 'Putting Linguistics on a Proper Footing: Explorations in Goffman's Concepts of Participation'. In P. Drew and A. Wootton (eds), *Goffman*. Cambridge: Polity Press.

Liberman, K. (1990). 'Intercultural Communication in Central Australia'. In Carbaugh (1990b).

Lippman, W. (1922). *Public Opinion*. New York: Harcourt, Brace and Co.

Logan, R. D. (1987). 'Historical Change in Prevailing Sense of Self'. In K. Yardley and T. Honess (eds), *Self and Identity: Psychosocial Perspectives*. Chichester: Wiley.

Luria, A. R. (1976). *Cognitive Development: its Cultural and Social Foundations*. Boston: Harvard University Press.

Lyons, J. (1977). *Semantics*, vol. 2. Cambridge: Cambridge University Press.

Mahoney, J. (1993). *Which is Witch?: Identity Construction in a Salem, Massachusetts Community*. Unpublished Master's thesis, University of Massachusetts, Amherst.

Maloney, J. D. (1982). 'How Companies Assess Technology'. *Technological Forecasting and Social Change*, 22, 321–9.

Manicas, P. (1987). *A History and Philosophy of the Social Sciences*. Oxford: Blackwell.

Markus, H., Herzog, A. R., Holmberg, D. E. and Dielman, L. (1992). *Constructing the Self Across the Lifespan*. Unpublished manuscript, University of Michigan, Ann Arbor, Mich.

Markus, H. and Kitayama, S. (1991). 'Culture and the Self: Implications for Cognition, Emotion, and Motivation'. *Psychological Review*, 98, 224–53.

Markus, H. and Nurius, P. (1986). 'Possible Selves'. *American Psychologist*, 41, 954–69.

Markus, H. and Nurius, P. (1987). 'Possible Selves: the Interface Between Motivation and the Self-concept'. In K. Yardley and T. Honess (eds), *Self and Identity: Psychological Perspectives*. New York: Wiley.

Markus, H. and Wurf, E. (1987). 'The Dynamic Self-concept: A Social Psychological Perspective'. *Annual Review of Psychology*, 38, 299–337.

Marriott, M. (1976). 'Hindu Transactions: Diversity Without Dualism'. In B. Kapferer (ed.), *Transaction and Meaning*. Philadelphia: Institute for the Study of Human Issues.

Mashek, J. W. (1992). 'Perot Alienates NAACP Audience with 'You People' Remark'. the *Boston Globe*, 12 July, pp. 12, 1.

Mbiti, J. S. (1966). *Akamba Stories*. Oxford: Clarendon Press.

Mead, G. H. (1934). *Mind, Self and Society*. Chicago: University of Chicago Press.

Miller, J. G. (In press). 'Cultural Psychology: Bridging Disciplinary Boundaries in Understanding the Cultural Grounding of Self'. In P. K. Bock (ed.), *Handbook of Psychological Anthropology*. Westport, Conn.: Greenwood.

Moghaddam, F. M. (1987). 'Psychology in the Three Worlds: As Reflected by the Crisis in Social Psychology and the Move Towards Indigenous Third World Psychology'. *American Psychologist*, 43, 912–20.

Moghaddam, F. M. (1994). 'Managing Cultural Diversity: North-American Experiences and Suggestions for the German Unification Process'. *International Journal of Psychology*, 28, 727–41.

Moghaddam, F. M. and Harré, R. (1992). 'Rethinking the Laboratory Experiment'. *American Behavioral Scientist*, 36, 22–38.

Moghaddam, F. M. and Stringer, P. (1986). ' "Trivial" ' and "Important" Criteria for Social Categorization in the Minimal Group Paradigm'. *Journal of Social Psychology*, 126, 345–54.

Moghaddam, F. M., Taylor, D. M. and Wright, S. C. (1993). *Social Psychology in Cultural Perspective*. New York: Freeman.

Moscovici, S. (1983). 'The Phenomenon of Social Representations'. In Farr, R. M. and Moscovici, S. (eds), *Social Representations*. Cambridge: Cambridge University Press.

Moscovici, S. (1985). 'Social Influence and Conformity'. In G. Lindzey and E. Aronson (eds), *The Handbook of Social Psychology*, 3rd edn, vol. 2. New York: Random House.

Much, N. C. and Harré, R. (1994). 'How Psychologies 'Secrete' Moralities'. *New Ideas in Psychology*, 12, 291–321.

Muhlhausler, P. and Harré, R. (1990). *Pronouns and People*. Oxford: Blackwell.

Munsch, R. (1980). *The Paperbag Princess*. Toronto: Annick Press.

Nash, W. (1990). *The Writing Scholar: Studies in Academic Discourse*. London: Sage.

Ng, S. H. (1980). *The Social Psychology of Power*. New York: Academic Press.

Ng, S. H. (1982). 'Power and Intergroup Discrimination'. In H. J. Tajfel (ed.), *Social Identity and Intergroup Relations*. Cambridge: Cambridge University Press.

Ong, W. J. (1982). *Orality and Literacy: the Technologizing of the Word*. London: Ballinger Publishing Company.

Pearce, W. B. (1989). *Communication and the Human Condition*. Carbondale, Ill.: Southern Illinois University Press.

Pearce, W. B. and Cronen, V. (1981). *Communication, Action and Meaning*. New York: Praeger.

Philipsen, G. (1992). *Speaking Culturally*. New York: State University Press.

Pinch, T. J. and Bijker, W. E. (1984). 'The Social Construction of Facts and Artefacts; or How the Sociology of Science and the Sociology of Technology Might Benefit from Each Other'. *Social Studies of Science*, 14, 399–441.

Plous, S. (1985). 'Perceptual Illusions and Military Realities: A Social-psychological Analysis of the Nuclear Arms Race'. *Journal of Conflict Resolution*, 29, 363–89.

Postman, N. (1985). *Amusing Ourselves to Death: Public Discourse in the Age of Show Business*. Harmondsworth: Penguin Books.

Potter, J. and Wetherall, M. (1988). *Social Psychology and Discourse*. London: Routledge.

Propp, V. (1968). *Morphology of the Folk Tale*. Austin: University of Texas Press.

Richardson, L. (1990). *Writing Strategies: Reaching Diverse Audiences*. London: Sage.

Rip, A. (1991). 'Mutual Positioning and Expectations'. Personal communication.

Robinson, D. N. (1976). 'What Sort of Persons are Hemispheres? Another Look at the 'Split Brain' Man'. *British Journal for the Philosophy of Science*, 27, 73–8.

Robinson, D. N. (1982). 'Cerebral Plurality and the Unity of the Self'. *American Psychologist*, 37, 904–10.

Rosaldo, M. Z. (1984). 'Toward an Anthropology of Self and Feeling'. In R. A. Shweder and R. A. Levine (eds), *Culture Theory: Essays on Mind, Self and Emotion*. Cambridge: Cambridge University Press.

Ross, M. and Conway, M. (1986). 'Remembering One's Own Past: the Construction of Personal Histories'. In R. M. Sorrentino and E. T. Higgins (eds). *Handbook of Motivation and Cognition*. Chichester: Wiley.

Sabat, S. R. and Harré, R. (1995). 'The Construction and Deconstruction of Self in Alzheimer's Disease'. *Ageing and Society*, 12, 443–61. [Reprinted with modifications as ch. 7 in the present volume.]

Sabini, J. and Silver, M. (1982). *Moralities of Everyday Life*. Oxford: Oxford University Press.

Sachdev, I. and Bourhis, R. Y. (1984). 'Minimal Majorities and Minorities'. *European Journal of Social Psychology*, 14, 35–52.

Sampson, E. E. (1977). 'Psychology and the American Ideal'. *Journal of Personality and Social Psychology*, 35, 767–82.

Sampson, E. E. (1981). 'Cognitive Psychology as Ideology'. *American Psychologist*, 36, 730–43.

Sarbin, T. R. (1986). *Narrative Psychology: the Storied Nature of Human Conduct*. New York: Praeger.

Sapir, E. (1929). 'The Status of Linguistics as a Science'. *Language*, 5, 207–14.

Schön, D. A. (1967). *The Invention and Evolution of Ideas*. London: Tavistock.

Schutz, A. (1966). 'Equality and the Meaning Structure of the Social World'. In A. Broderson (ed.), *Collected Papers of Alfred Shutz, II: Studies in Social Theory*. The Hague: Martinus Nijhoff.

Scollon, R. (1992). *The Shifting Discourse of American Individualism from the Authoritarian to the Infochild*. Haines, Ark.: Unpublished manuscript.

Scollon, R. and Scollon, S. (1981). *Narrative, Literacy, and Face in Interethnic Communication*. Norwood, NJ: Ablex.

Searle, J. R. (1979). *Expression and Meaning*. Cambridge: Cambridge University Press.

Secord, P. F. and Backman, C. W. (1964). *Social Psychology*. New York: McGraw-Hill.

Sherif, M. (1966). *Group Conflict and Cooperation: Their Social Psychology*. London: Routledge & Kegan Paul.

Sherif, M., Harvey, O. J., White, B. J., Hood, W. R. and Sherif, C. (1961). *Intergroup Conflict and Cooperation: the Robbers Cave Experiment*. Norman: University of Oklahoma Book Exchange.

Shotter, J. (1973). 'Acquired Powers: the Transformation of Natural into Personal Powers'. *Journal for the Theory of Social Behaviour*, 3 (2), 141–56.

Shotter, J. (1983). *Social Accountability and Selfhood*. Oxford: Blackwell.

Shotter, J. and Newson, J. (1974). 'How Babies Communicate'. *New Society*, 29, 34–7.

Shutz, A. (1962). *Complete Works*, vol. 1. The Hague: Nijholt.

Shweder, R. (1992). *Thinking Through Cultures*. Chicago: University of Chicago Press.

Shweder, R. and Bourne, E. (1984). 'Does the Concept of the Person Vary Cross-culturally?'. In R. Shweder and R. Levine (eds), *Culture Theory: Essays on Mind, Self and Emotion*. Cambridge: Cambridge University Press.

Silverman K. (1983). *The Subject of Semiotics*. New York: Oxford University Press.

Simanjuntak, P. (1993). 'Manpower Problems and Government Policies'. In C. Manning and J. Hapono (eds), *Indonesian Assessment 1993*. Oxford: Oxford University Press.

Smith, J. (1981). 'Self and Experience in Maori Culture'. In P. Heelas and J. Lock (eds), *Indigenous Psychologies*. London: Academic Press.

Smith, P. (1988). *Discerning the Subject*. Minneapolis: University of Minnesota Press.

Smits, R. and Leyten, J. (1991). *Technology Assessment: Waakhond of Speurhond? Naar een integraal Technologiebeleid*. Zeist: Kerkebosch BV.

Spence, D. (1981). *Narrative Truth and Historical Truth: Meaning and Interpretation in Psychoanalysis*. New York: Norton.

Stengers, I. (1990). *La Raison Dans Les Sciences: Fiction et Mobilisation*. Paris: Gallimard.

Stewart, R. A., Powell, G. E. and Chennwind, S. J. (1979). *Person Perception and Stereotyping*. Westmead: Saxon House.

Strawson, P. F. (1956). *Individuals*. London: Methuen.

Sullivan, J. (1992). *Local Government and Community in Java – An Urban Case Study*. Southeast Asian Social Science Monograph. Singapore: Oxford University Press.

Tajfel, H. J. (1978). 'Social Categorization, Social Identity and Social Comparison'. In H. J. Tajfel (ed.), *Differentiation between Social Groups: Studies in the Social Psychology of Intergroup Relations*. London and New York: Academic Press.

Tajfel, H. J. (1981). *Human Groups and Social Categories*. Cambridge: Cambridge University Press.

Tajfel, H. J. (1982). *Social Identity and Intergroup Relations*. Cambridge: Cambridge University Press.

Tajfel, H. J. and Turner, J. C. (1979). 'An Integrative Theory of Intergroup Conflict'. In W. G. Austin and S. Worchel (eds), *The Social Psychology of Intergroup Relations*. Monterey, Calif.: Brooks/Cole.

Tajfel, H. J. and Turner, J. C. (1986). 'The Social Identity Theory of Intergroup Relations'. In S. Worchel and G. Austin (eds), *Psychology of Intergroup Relations*. Chicago: Nelson-Hall.

Tan, S. L. and Moghaddam, F. M. (1995). 'Reflexive Positioning and Culture'. *Journal for the Theory of Social Behaviour*, 25, 387–400. [Reprinted with modifications as ch. 13 in the present volume.]

Tannen, D. (1990). *You Just Don't Understand Me*. New York: Morrow.

Taylor, D. M. and Moghaddam, F. M. (1994). *Theories of Intergroup Relations: International Social Psychological Perspectives*. New York: Praeger.

Thoreau, H. (1950). *Walden and Other Writings*. New York: Modern Library.

Todorov, T. (1981). *Mikhail Bakhtin: the Dialogic Principle*. Minneapolis: University of Minnesota Press.

Toulmin, S. (1972). *Human Understanding*. Princeton: Princeton University Press.

Triandis, H. C. (1989). 'The Self and Social Behavior in Cultural Contexts'. *Psychological Review*, 96, 506–20.

Triandis, H. C., Leung, K., Villareal, M. J. and Clack, F. (1985). 'Allocentric versus Idiocentric Tendencies: Convergent and Discriminant Validation'. *Journal of Research in Personality*, 19, 395–415.

Urban, G. (1989). 'The "I" of Discourse'. In B. Lee and G. Urban (eds), *Semiotics, Self and Society*. New York: Mouton de Gruyter.

Vallacher, R. R. and Wegner, D. M. (1985). *A Theory of Action Identification*. Hillsdale, NJ: Erlbaum.

Vallacher, R. R. and Wegner, D. M. (1989). 'Levels of Personal Agency: Individual Variation in Action Identification'. *Journal of Personality and Social Psychology*, 57 (4), 660–71.

Van Boxel, J. (1992). 'The Relevance of Technology Dynamics for the Practice of Constructive Technology Assessment'. Unpublished paper. MERIT, P.O. Box 616, 6200 MD Maastricht, Netherlands.

Van Dijk, T. A. (1980). *Macrostructures: An Interdisciplinary Study of Global Structures in Discourse, Interaction and Cognition*. Hillsdale, NJ: Lawrence Erlbaum.

van Langenhove, L. (1989). *Juryrechtspraak en Psychologie* [Juror Sentencing and Psychology]. Antwerp: Kluwer-Gouda Quint.

van Langenhove, L. (1995). 'The Historical and Ontological Basis of Experimental Psychology and its Alternatives'. In J. Smith, R. Harré and L. Van Langenhove (eds), *Rethinking Psychology. Vol. 1: Conceptual Foundations*. London: Sage.

van Langenhove, L. and Harré, R. (1995). 'Positioning and Autobiography: Telling Your Life'. In N. Coupland and J. Nussbaum (eds), *Discourse and Life-span Development*. London: Sage. [Reprinted with modifications as ch. 5 in the present volume.]

Varenne, H. (1990). 'Review of D. Carbaugh's *Talking American*'. *Language in Society*, 19, 434–6.

Vatikiotis, M. (1989). 'The Open Question'. *Far Eastern Economic Review*, 16 November 1989: 42–4.

Vygotsky, L. S. (1962). *Thought and Language*, eds and trans. E. Hanfmann and G. Vakar. Cambridge, Mass.: MIT Press. (Original work published 1934.)

Vygotsky, L. S. (1978). *Mind in Society: the Development of Higher Psychological Processes*. Cambridge: Harvard University Press.

Wade, D. A. (1986). 'Social Categorisation: Implications for Creation and Reduction of Intergroup Bias'. In L. Berkowitz (ed.), *Advances in Experimental Social Psychology* vol. 19. New York: Academic Press.

Wales, K. (1980). 'Exophora Reexamined: the Uses of the Personal Pronoun We in Present-day English'. *UEA Papers in Linguistics*, 12, 21–44.

Watkins, M. (1986). *Invisible Guests: the Development of Imaginal Dialogues*. Hillsdale, NJ: Erlbaum.

Weedon, C. (1987). *Feminist Practice and Poststructuralist Theory*. Oxford: Blackwell.

Wells, A. J. (1992). 'Variation in Self-esteem in Daily Life: Methodological and Developmental Issues'. In R. R. Lipka and T. M. Brinthaupt (eds), *Self-perspectives Across the Lifespan*. New York: State University of New York Press.

West, C. and Zimmerman, D. (1991). 'Doing Gender'. In J. Lorber and S. Farrell (eds), *The Social Construction of Gender*. London: Sage.

Whewell, W. (1967). *The History of the Inductive Sciences*. London: Cass.

White, R. K. (1977). 'Misperception in the Arab–Israeli Conflict'. *Journal of Social Issues*, 33, 190–221.

Wieder, L. and Pratt, S. (1990). 'On Being a Recognizable Indian Among Indians'. In Carbaugh (1990b).

Wieringa, S. (1992). 'Ibu Or the Beast: Gender Interests in Two Indonesian Women's Organizations'. *Feminist Review*, 4 (1), Summer, 98–113.

Wierzbicka, A. (1989). 'Soul and Mind: Linguistic Evidence for Ethnopsychology and Cultural History'. *American Anthropologist*, 91, 41–58.

Williams, B. A. O. (1973). *Problems of the Self*. Cambridge: Cambridge University Press.

Wittgenstein, L. (1953). *Philosophical Investigations*. Oxford: Blackwell.

Wolf, D. P. (1990). 'Being of Several Minds: Voices and Versions of the Self in Early Childhood'. In I. D. Cicchetti and M. Beeghly (eds), *The Self in Transition: Infancy to Childhood*. Chicago: University of Chicago Press.

Wood, L. and Ryan, E. B. (1991). 'Talk to Elders: Social Structures, Attitudes and Forms of Address'. *Ageing and Society*, 11, 167–87.

Woolgar, S. (1989). 'Representation, Cognition and Self: What Hope for an Integration of Psychology and Sociology'. In S. Fuller, M. De Mey, T. Shinn and S. Woolgar (eds), *The Cognitive Turn: Sociological and Psychological Perspectives on Science*. Dordrecht: Kluwer Academic Publishers.

Worchel, S. and Austin, W. G. (eds) (1986). *Psychology of Intergroup Relations*. Chicago: Nelson-Hall.

Zanna, M. P. and Olson, J. (eds) (1993). 'The Psychology of Prejudice'. *The Ontario Symposium* (vol. 7). Hillsdale, NJ: Erlbaum.

Zeitlyn, D. (1993). 'Reconstructing Kinship, Or the Pragmatics of Kin Talk'. *Man*, 28, 199–224.

Ziman, J. (1990). 'Academic Science as a System of Markets'. London: Science Policy Support Group. In S. Fuller, M. De Mey, T. Shinn and S. Woolgar (eds), *The Cognitive Turn: Sociological and Psychological Perspectives on Science*. Dordrecht: Kluwer Academic Publishers.

Zipes, J. (1986). *Don't Bet on the Prince*. Aldershot: Gower.

Index

Only authors substantially cited in the text are recorded in the index.

Lightning Source UK Ltd.
Milton Keynes UK
UKHW011844280120
357766UK00002B/141